A Lasting Gift of Heritage

A History of the North Carolina Society
for the Preservation of Antiquities
1939-1974

A JOINT PUBLICATION OF

PRESERVATION NORTH CAROLINA

AND

DIVISION OF ARCHIVES AND HISTORY

NORTH CAROLINA DEPARTMENT
OF CULTURAL RESOURCES

A Lasting Gift of Heritage

A History of the North Carolina Society for the Preservation of Antiquities 1939-1974

David Louis Sterrett Brook

RALEIGH
DIVISION OF ARCHIVES AND HISTORY
NORTH CAROLINA DEPARTMENT OF CULTURAL RESOURCES

This publication was generously underwritten by
the Cannon Foundation, Inc., and the Kellenberger Historical Foundation.

*I dedicate this book to my wife, Mary Ashley Wilson Brook,
and to our children, Mary Grayson Brook and James Sterrett Brook,
whose North Carolina roots go back nearly three centuries.*

*I also dedicate this book to the founders and members
of the North Carolina Society for the Preservation of Antiquities.*

Contents

Illustrations

Foreword

As a congressional district vice-president of the North Carolina Society for the Preservation of Antiquities and later as president of the Historic Preservation Society of North Carolina, I was privileged to observe and ultimately know some of the outstanding women who led the society in the Cannon years, 1944-1956. As a beginner in historic preservation in the early 1950s, I found the annual meetings of "Antiquities" during Culture Week to be quite a show. Ruth Coltrane Cannon presided with a white-gloved "iron fist." Gertrude Carraway was there to promote Tryon Palace. Maude Latham and her daughter, May Kellenberger, were there to give of themselves and their financial resources to rebuild the palace. Cora Smith, Elizabeth Cotten, Faye Gardner, Inglis Fletcher, Katherine Pendleton Arrington, and "Buffie" Ives all added color and their strongly held opinions to the discussions at hand. But despite the furs and orchids, these women laid the foundation of the modern historic preservation movement in North Carolina.

Gertrude Carraway was successful with Tryon Palace. After I had known her many years, she confessed to me that the way the General Assembly was persuaded to support the reconstruction of Tryon Palace was through the Sir Walter Cabinet (spouses of state legislators), who practiced "pillow talk" to sway the vote in favor of the reconstruction. That was a revealing lesson in practical politics! And Lura Tally, who represented the "new generation" during the Cannon era, served as president and went on to the General Assembly, where she served with distinction, especially in regard to cultural issues. Virginia Zenke closed out the Antiquities Society with grace and vision and became the first president of the Preservation Society, predecessor of Preservation North Carolina (PNC). She remains a committed preservationist.

When the reader finishes David Brook's excellent story of the Antiquities Society, it will be clear that the leaders of that organization foresaw the very successful revolving fund program of PNC, which to date has saved more than 275 historic structures in sixty counties throughout the state. Those leaders also attempted to initiate what is now known as the Stewardship Program, under which PNC has assumed ownership of several historic properties and is operating them for public visitation; examples include Coolmore plantation in Edgecombe County, the Bellamy Mansion in Wilmington, and the Banker's House in Shelby. Certainly, the early leaders saw the need for advocacy with the General Assembly and the public, and that effort continues to this day through the individual efforts of PNC members, the "newsletter," and the annual statewide historic preservation conference. The Cannon Cup established by Ruth Coltrane Cannon has come to be the highest annual award given to an individual Tar Heel for historic preservation work. The Gertrude Carraway Awards, implemented under the leadership of Jack Tyler, recognize individual historic-site success stories. Other awards, such as the Stedman Grant, underwritten by Marion Stedman Covington, have been established.

A Lasting Gift of Heritage continues a history of preservation publication in North Carolina that began with the 1939 production of *Old Homes and Gardens of North Carolina* under the direction of Ruth Coltrane Cannon. In 1989 PNC published *North Carolina Architecture*, by Catherine Bishir, with photographs by Tim Buchman, to celebrate the fiftieth anniversary of the founding of the Antiquities Society. And today other books have been or will be issued to spread the word about historic preservation in the state.

It has been an exciting experience to be a volunteer in historic preservation in North Carolina. To understand and appreciate the movement and its roots, we now have *A Lasting Gift of Heritage* , a readable and enjoyable history of the North Carolina Society for the Preservation of Antiquities, 1939-1974. In this book David Brook has carefully laid a foundation of scholarship that I hope will soon lead to a writing of the history of Preservation North Carolina from 1974 to the present.

Banks C. Talley Jr.

Raleigh

Acknowledgments

This book grew out of research I conducted in pursuit of a master's degree in history at North Carolina State University. My acknowledgments, therefore, fall within two categories: those who assisted and guided me in that pursuit and those who helped me transform my thesis into this book. Gail W. O'Brien, chair of my thesis committee, was chief among those who offered me encouragement and support with the thesis. Dr. O'Brien gave me kind and patient guidance that saw me through the project. Her course on the social history of the New South fired my enthusiasm for researching the history of historic preservation. Dr. William S. Price Jr., former director of the North Carolina Division of Archives and History, was the first to encourage me to seek a graduate degree in history and generously gave me the administrative support I needed to succeed. A key mentor and friend was Robert E. Stipe of the School of Design at North Carolina State University and a member of my thesis committee. He willingly shared his insights and wisdom, as well as his personal archives generated over the years through his leadership in the preservation movement in North Carolina and the nation.

David J. Olson, state archivist, was very helpful in assuring that the records of the Antiquities Society were easily available to me during my research. He served on my committee and gave me a thorough grounding in the theory and practice of archival research. Dr. Joseph Caddell likewise served on my committee, and his course on modern American history stood me in good stead in researching and writing my thesis. Dr. James A. Mulholland, who instructed me in historical writing, gave me valuable comments on the draft of my first chapters. I feel beholden to all of my professors in the Department of History at North Carolina State University for collectively giving me the excitement of intellectual challenge and the fundamental satisfaction of scholarship. Special appreciation is due Deborah Hurlbert Begley of the history department office who, from the very first, cheerfully and capably helped me through the intricacies of graduate school bureaucracy. Dr. Lee A. Craig of the Department of Economics, North Carolina State University, generously shared with me a very useful time series for the consumer price index (CPI) for the United States from 1789 through 1990. Glenda Peace of Raleigh gave me valuable editorial suggestions.

In addition to William S. Price Jr. and David J. Olson, I thank fellow staff members of the North Carolina Division of Archives and History for providing encouragement, information, and assistance with my thesis. Among them are Catherine W. Bishir, Dr. Jerry C. Cashion, Dr. Boyd D. Cathey, Dr. Jerry L. Cross, Elizabeth Di Orio Dowd, Paul Fomberg, A. L. Honeycutt Jr., Dr. Richard F. Knapp, Mark A. Mathis, Charles E. Morris, Dee Nelms, Rose Ogden, Michael T. Southern, Jim L. Sumner, F. Mitchener Wilds, Kay Williams, and the Archives and Records Section Search Room staff, including Debbie Blake, William H. Brown, Earl Ijames, and Ronald Vestal. Especially valuable were the assistance and memories of A. L. Honeycutt Jr., an employee of the division since 1958. I called upon Al many times for his recollections. Michael Southern was very generous with his time in helping me to develop my computer capabilities, as were Mark Mathis and Dee Nelms.

Also of assistance were the following former staff members of the Department and later Division of Archives and History: Sara Bell, John D. Ellington, Dr. H. G. Jones, Joye E. Jordan, Paul Kiel, Russell Koonts, Trinnie McMillan, Ruby Newton, Mattie Erma Edwards Parker, William S. Powell, E. Frank Stephenson Jr., William Samuel Tarlton, and Frances Harmon Whitley. Dr. Jones was particularly helpful in granting two interviews, sending me valuable information, and shepherding me through the North Carolina Collection of the University of North Carolina Library. I also owe special thanks to William L. Murphy, formerly of the staff of Preservation North Carolina (PNC), for giving me full access to the Antiquities Society meeting minutes in possession of the foundation and allowing me to copy them.

I am indebted to many people in North Carolina and out of state who aided me with my thesis either by giving me information, filling out my questionnaire, or permitting me to interview them. These people, who are otherwise not mentioned above, include: Joseph B. Cheshire Jr., Edward Clement, T. Harry Gatton, James A. Gray, Thomas A. Gray, Joanne Gwaltney, John E. Hunter Jr., Matt Ransom Johnston, William J. Moore, Virginia Camp Smith, James A. Stenhouse Jr., Dr. Banks C. Talley Jr., Lura Self Tally, John Edward Tyler II, R. Beverly R. Webb, Sarah D. Williamson, and Virginia Ford Zenke.

Dr. Price was the first person to recognize the potential value of my thesis as a book and advocate that it be published in that form. The thesis never would have been transformed into this book, however, had it not been for J. Myrick Howard, executive director of PNC, who brought the project to the attention of the Cannon Foundation and the Kellenberger Historical Foundation, both of which responded generously with grants to support publication costs. Dr. Jeffrey J. Crow, director of the Division of Archives and History, North Carolina Department of Cultural Resources, was also key in pledging the editorial and sales assistance of his agency. Joe A. Mobley, administrator of the division's Historical Publications Section, and his staff rendered invaluable editorial and administrative support. Special thanks are due for the thoughtful and effective editing of Robert M. Topkins, head of the General Publications Branch of the Historical Publications Section, and for the meticulous proofreading of Lisa D. Bailey of that section.

Dr. Jerry C. Cashion, chief of the Research Branch of the Division of Archives and History, and his staff members—Dr. Wilson Angley, Dr. Jerry L. Cross, and Michael Hill—were of invaluable assistance in helping me with factual verifications and enabling me to address a number of detailed editorial matters ranging from the proper spelling of a High Point street name to additional information on the federal Public Works Reserve Project of the early 1940s. Dr. Cashion was especially helpful in identifying misspelled names, which were endemic in the various original rosters replicated in the appendixes. Likewise, historian Michael Southern of the State Historic Preservation Office helped me with factual verifications and research questions; he also supplied me with newly uncovered information on the "true" age and history of several of the historic houses that had excited the interest of the Antiquities Society. Michael's most valuable service, however, was his magnificent assistance to Nan Farley and me in untangling myriads of issues and questions that arose during the preparation of appendix E, which addresses the current status of North Carolina buildings and sites mentioned in the text. Additional staff members of the Division of Archives and History who provided information or assistance during the publication stage of the project were

Jeffrey Adolphsen, Elaine Beck, Debra Kraybill Bevin, Catherine W. Bishir, Debbie Blake, Claudia Roberts Brown, William H. Brown, Chandrea Burch, Linda Carnes-McNaughton, Kimberly Anderson Cumber, Linda Jordan Eure, Bill Garrett, Robert L. Harrelson, A. L. Honeycutt Jr., Valerie Jones Howell, Earl Ijames, Dean Knight, Phillippe Lafargue, Beth Lawrence, Stanley Little, Linda McRae, Barbara Mann, Stephen E. Massengill, Rose Ogden, Nancy E. Richards, Tim E. Simmons, Robin Stancil, Reid Thomas, Nancy S. Turner, Sondra Ward, Alan Westmoreland, F. Mitchener Wilds, Kay Williams, and Edith Woodcock. Linda Jordan Eure, Earl Ijames, Dean Knight, and Stephen E. Massengill were especially helpful in locating photographs. Bill Garrett cheerfully undertook the photographic replication of a wide variety and large number of documents and photographs for use in this book.

Banks C. Talley Jr. of the staff of PNC rendered splendid service as book-project liaison between that organization and the division. Dr. Talley also provided assistance in my search for illustrations. PNC volunteer Nan Farley served as my chief assistant in the search for photographs and also developed the appendix that provides information on the current status of the buildings mentioned in the text; she also offered valuable editorial suggestions. PNC staff member John Murphy, along with Nan Farley, prepared the index. PNC staff members Charlene Askew, Michelle Michael, and Anna Norfleet Tilghman rendered cheerful assistance whenever requested. Elizabeth Stanton Kolstelny, director of museum operations, Association for the Preservation of Virginia Antiquities, provided me with a valuable history of that organization and a photograph of Margaret Wilmer, its president from 1935 through 1946.

I also received helpful pertinent information and assistance from John Acker, executive director of Preservation Greensboro, Inc.; Shirley Ballou, coordinator for the Latimer House Museum of the Lower Cape Fear Historical Society; Louise Benner, Vicki L. Berger, and Sandra Webbere of the North Carolina Museum of History; Kathryn Bridges and Steve Gainey of the Cabarrus County Library; Dan Cameron; Bettie Colson of the Chowan College staff; Dr. John D. Costlow; Janet Cunningham, executive director of the Moore County Historical Association; T. Harry Gatton; Mariam Cannon Hayes; Mrs. Marshall De Lancey (Margaret) Haywood Jr.; Betty Rose Heath; Steven Herman, chair of the Statesville Historic District Commission; Katherine Hodges; Jimmie R. Hutchens, chair of the Historic Richmond Hill Law School Commission; Lynn Moody Igoe; Robert Johnson, director of community development and appearance, city of Statesville; Archibald Henderson Kelly; Frances J. Moody; William J. Moore, director of the Greensboro Historical Museum; Mrs. Fred W. (Emma Neal) Morrison; Bruce Naegelem, publicity/events coordinator for the Beaufort Historical Association; William S. Powell; Janet K. Seapker, director, and Pat Voorhees of the Cape Fear Museum; Virginia Camp Smith; E. Frank Stephenson Jr.; Mrs. John Douglas (Mary) Taylor; James Walker, executive director of the Iredell Arts Council and treasurer of the Vance Memorial Fund; James Webb; and Virginia Ford Zenke.

I gratefully acknowledge the assistance of the late James Gunn, biographer of Minnette Chapman Duffy. Thanks also go to Mrs. Duffy's daughters Mary Ann Bell, Minnette Bickel, and Sophia Sue Taylor. Virginia A. Stevens, Leej Copperfield, and Dr. Rorin M. Platt were generous in their moral support and encouragement to me. I am also grateful to Robert E. Stipe for advising me on the arcane topic of computer-generated photographic restorations. Special thanks go to the following members of the United Daughters of the Confederacy who helped me with information on the Vance House in Statesville: Ellen R. Bissell, North Carolina Division president; Charlotte R. Carrere, registrar of the Captain Samuel A. Ashe Chapter, No. 2572; and Elizabeth McElwee King, president of the Statesville Chapter, No. 276.

Other people outside the Division of Archives and History not previously credited for assisting in my search for photographs include: Blair R. Beasley; Prof. Robert P. Burns of the School of Design, North Carolina State University; Ann Clifford of the Society for the Preservation of New England Antiquities; Jerry W. Cotten of the North Carolina Collection, University of North Carolina Library; Cathy Grosfils of Colonial Williamsburg; Lillian Moore Hawfield; Mariam Cannon Hayes; Paul Kiel of the Special Collections Department, North Carolina State University Libraries; Janie Morris of the Special Collections Library, Duke University; Karen Van Epps Peters of the Mount Vernon Ladies Association; staff of the Southern Historical Collection, University of North Carolina Library; E. Frank Stephenson Jr.; Lura Self Tally; W. Samuel Tarleton; Maurice Toler of the Special Collections Department, North Carolina State University Libraries; Cathleen D. Turner, executive director of the Alliance for Historic Hillsborough, who spent the better part of a day guiding me through the records of the Historic Hillsborough Commission and the Hillsborough Historical Society (both of which organizations have my thanks for allowing me to examine their records and photographs); John E. Tyler II; Susan Whitehead; and Frances Harmon Whitley.

Finally, I thank my wife, Mary Ashley Wilson Brook, for her suggestions, encouragement, and patience during the preparation of this book.

David Louis Sterrett Brook
Raleigh, August 1997

Introduction

The Historic Preservation Foundation of North Carolina, founded in 1939 as the North Carolina Society for the Preservation of Antiquities (SPA), was rechartered and renamed the Historic Preservation Society of North Carolina in February 1974. In 1984 the Preservation Society merged with the Historic Preservation Fund of North Carolina (founded in 1975) to form the present Historic Preservation Foundation.

In 1958 McDaniel Lewis, the second president (1942-1944) of the society, attempted without success to prod Archibald Henderson, one of the SPA's 1939 incorporators, to write a history of the society's formation. Failing in that effort, Lewis wrote his own brief account—no more than one and one-half pages. In 1964 another of the original incorporators and founders, Christopher Crittenden, director of the Department of Archives and History, suggested that a history of the SPA be written in observance of its twenty-fifth anniversary. No action was taken at that time, but in 1971 the society hired writer Lee Wilder to prepare a history. Wilder apparently undertook preliminary research but, for reasons that are unclear, never completed the work.

The purpose of this study is to narrate the heretofore unwritten history of the old Antiquities Society. It is a subject over which no other scholar has labored, and it will provide a reference where none currently exists. The study seeks to determine why and how the SPA was founded, to identify and describe the society's founders and leaders, and to identify and describe the organization's goals and programs. Eventually the history of the organization after 1974 must be written as well.

Another motivation for this project was the realization that a number of the leaders of the SPA were still alive and available for interviews. When I began my research, seven of the twelve presidents of the SPA were living; now there are four, all of whom I was able to contact. Perhaps most frustrating to me was learning that the society's first secretary-treasurer, Janie Fetner Gosney of Raleigh, lived until 1986, just seven years before I began my research. Gosney had functioned as the society's de facto executive director and during the society's first years was part of a leadership triumvirate with Col. Joseph Hyde Pratt, the SPA's first president, and Christopher Crittenden.

An Overview

The founding of the North Carolina Society for the Preservation of Antiquities reflected a growing tendency for Americans to find their history in their architecture and not just in written documents. In the early twentieth century the great English historian R. G. Collingwood wrote that "the past simply is wholly unknowable; it is the past as residually preserved in the present that is alone knowable." Much of that residue is contained in the human-made or built environment, including buildings, structures, sites, and objects. As in the case of documentary materials, that environment reflects the past thoughts, adaptations, and experiences of humanity, and their destruction forever eliminates a portion of the historical record.

Those resources face their own peculiar array of threats, since most of them are used primarily for nonhistorical purposes—for houses, offices, stores, farms, factories, and recreation. They are commodities on the real estate market, and most are in private ownership, beyond the reach of governmental protection.

The view that historic properties should be preserved because they provide evidence of history and because they remind Americans of history in the course of their everyday lives was adopted as national policy in the National Historic Preservation Act of 1966. In the act's preamble Congress declared that "the spirit and direction of the Nation are founded and reflected in its historic past [and] that the historical and cultural foundations of the Nation should be preserved as a living part of our community life and development in order to give a sense of orientation to the American people."

The past as a guide (and gift) to the future is a theme frequently echoed by modern preservation scholars. Brown Morton III of Mary Washington College wrote in *The American Mosaic*: "we are beginning to understand that historic preservation has more to do with the future than the past." Preservation is also a process of intelligently trying to decide what should be saved for the future and of trying to save it once the decision is made. James Marston Fitch of Columbia University stated the concept of preservation more precisely as the "curatorial management of the built world." A general view that historic preservation is an integral part of the environmental movement has arisen in modern times. Conservation of historic resources saves natural resources otherwise expended for energy and materials in new construction.

There is, of course, much disagreement on the criteria for the selection of resources and the means of preservation—the "whys" and "hows." The great "keep history in historic preservation" debate of recent years is a "why" argument. Do we save properties because of purely national-level historical importance, or do we also save because of state and local importance? Do we save for economic, social, and environmental purposes? The "hows" are debated in terms of zoning powers, tax credits, and other public policies used to accomplish preservation objectives.

As the history of the preservation movement has unfolded, radical changes have occurred in preservation philosophy and methodology. In the movement's first stirrings in the nineteenth century it was pietistic, limited to properties of transcendent national importance, and confined to the private sector. Historic preservation was equated with house museums and battlefields. In the early twentieth century the same commemorative spirit spurred preservation efforts on the state and local level.

In the last generation, however, the movement has shifted rapidly to an understanding that our social, economic, and cultural life are affected by our built environment—an environment that is important not only because it is evidence of our history but also because it is a resource by which we can achieve many other desirable ends. The history of the SPA is part and parcel of those broad trends.

Acronyms Used in this Book

APVA: Association for the Preservation of Virginia Antiquities
CWA: Civil Works Administration
DAR: Daughters of the American Revolution
HUD: U.S. Department of Housing and Urban Development
NPS: National Park Service
PNC: Preservation North Carolina
SPA: North Carolina Society for the Preservation of Antiquities
SPNEA: Society for the Preservation of New England Antiquities
UDC: United Daughters of the Confederacy
WABPS: Woman's Association for the Betterment of Public School Houses
WPA: Works Progress Administration

Chapter 1:
Antecedents

Origins of the National Historic Preservation Movement

Historic preservation, though visibly blossoming as a force for change in America in the mid-twentieth century, has roots in the early nineteenth century. With the winning of independence came some popular appreciation for the need to save individual historic properties associated with the Founding Fathers and great events of the American Revolution. In 1813 citizens of Philadelphia petitioned the Pennsylvania legislature to save Independence Hall from destruction, arguing that the hall was "hallowed . . . by many strong and impressive recollections." Thanks to their efforts the hall narrowly missed demolition three years later.

As the nineteenth century unfolded, house museums became popular, forming what James Marston Fitch called the "basic module of historic preservation" and the "nursery for the entire movement." Individual properties associated with the lives of great American heros such as George Washington were saved from demolition, almost always by private individuals in the face of governmental indifference. It was only after building a national organization of women that Ann Pamela Cunningham, a crippled spinster from South Carolina, was able to save Mount Vernon in 1858 from continued deterioration and possible demolition for a hotel site. Assisting her were socially prominent women such as Miss Mary Morris Hamilton of New York, granddaughter of Alexander Hamilton, and Letitia Morehead Walker (1823-1908), daughter of North Carolina governor John Motley Morehead. Described as a tower of strength, and dean of the Mount Vernon regents, Walker worked to preserve Mount Vernon until her death.

Cunningham's achievement set the pattern of private preservation efforts and inspired others to save Jefferson's Monticello and Stratford Hall, birthplace of Robert E. Lee. Other groups dealt with properties of lesser importance throughout the United States, often with limited success. As part of the post-Mount Vernon surge of interest in preservation, the Association for the Preservation of Virginia Antiquities (APVA) was formed as the first statewide private preservation group in the nation.

Letitia Morehead Walker of Greensboro served as vice-regent from North Carolina of the Mount Vernon Ladies Association of the Union from 1858 to her death in 1908. In this ca. 1873 photograph, Walker is standing second from the left. Ann Pamela Cunningham, regent, is seated and looking at the bust of Washington. Photograph courtesy Mount Vernon Ladies Association.

Established in 1889, the APVA was the precursor to all statewide and regional groups that appeared in the twentieth century. Although its membership was not limited to women, its founders and the great majority of members were female. The APVA concentrated on the preservation of single sites important to American and Virginia history; examples included Jamestown Island and the John Marshall House in Richmond. It also conducted its work through chapters that were responsible for the maintenance and interpretation of historic properties. In the 1930s the APVA found itself weighed down by the management of many house museums and accused of being a moribund social organization.

The restoration of Williamsburg, Virginia, in the 1920s and 1930s materially spurred the patriotic and educational appeal of American historic house museums. The restoration was the brainchild of Rev. William A. R. Goodwin, former rector of Williamsburg's Bruton Church and, beginning in 1923, head of the religion department of the College of William and Mary. Goodwin's dream was to set aside a place in which Americans could experience their preindustrial past. Such an endeavor ran against the tide of the 1920s, in which prosperity and the loss of idealism after World War I led to a national feeling that the study of the past was irrelevant.

Meeting John D. Rockefeller Jr. at a Phi Beta Kappa dinner in New York in 1924, Dr. Goodwin eventually persuaded the philanthropist to visit Williamsburg and to underwrite much of its restoration. Departing from the usual practice of house museums, Goodwin set the restoration on a course of representing more than an elite view of history. Envisioning a multifaceted educational experience for the public, Goodwin worked to present Williamsburg as an early settlement and to highlight the lives of people from all areas of the social spectrum. On his part, Rockefeller was drawn to the project by the beauty and charm of the old city.

Out of the thorough documentary research, archaeological investigations, and restoration and reconstruction of Williamsburg that stressed authenticity came standards and technology that were to put the practice of historic preservation on a professional basis for the first time. Ironically, of all the allied professions, historians proved to be the most reluctant pioneers in the new movement. In 1932 the Williamsburg directors failed in an attempt to enlist the aid of historians in developing an interpretive program. Charles Hosmer Jr., noted historian of the American preservation movement, attributed the failure to a lack of interest by historians in popular education and observed that the historians who disappointed the Williamsburg staff "were not ready to view old buildings seriously as documents; their concept of interpretation was to publish pamphlets and monographs."

Williamsburg gave further impetus to the American preservation movement by becoming a national clearinghouse for preservation information. As it developed through the 1930s it also served as an example for the federal government, which was motivated to undertake public works projects that employed historians, archaeologists, and design professionals. The Williamsburg staff pushed for national preservation legislation that culminated in the Historic Sites Act of 1935. The act declared historic preservation to be a national policy and authorized the secretary of the interior to survey, acquire, and restore properties of national significance.

The Williamsburg example inspired other preservation efforts in the 1930s and 1940s; examples include Deerfield and Old Sturbridge Village in Massachusetts, Henry Ford's Greenfield Village in Michigan, and, in North Carolina, Old Salem in Winston-Salem and Tryon Palace in New Bern. In some historic communities and outdoor museums, authentic buildings in original locations were emphasized, as in the case of Deerfield and Old Salem. In others, such as Greenfield Village and Old Sturbridge Village, buildings were moved in from other locations or reconstructed.

Ironically, the growth of museum house and outdoor museum activity was aided by the automobile, which is destructive of sites but which also increased tourism at a time when Americans were beginning to enjoy more spare time and greater earning capacity. National Park visitation rose from 240,000 visitors in 1914 to 2,315,000 in 1926 as affordable cars began to be mass-produced and America's roads began to be paved and modernized.

The Society for the Preservation of New England Antiquities (SPNEA), founded in 1910 by William Sumner Appleton, was the forerunner of a new type of preservation organization. The SPNEA stressed architectural as well as historical importance. It also championed adaptive use, with the realization that there was a limit to the number of house museums that could be maintained. By the eve of World War II, however, most private sector preservation organizations were still dedicated to saving single-site museum houses.

North Carolina's Early Preservation Efforts

In the nineteenth century the state of North Carolina appropriated funds for historic monuments, centennials, and Confederate cemeteries. In 1896 a private nonprofit group, the Roanoke Colony Memorial Association, purchased the site of Fort Raleigh, seat of the first English settlement in America, but in the early twentieth century there was no organized statewide preservation organization to undertake a systematic effort such as existed in Virginia.

In 1907 the General Assembly charged the North Carolina Historical Commission (founded in 1903) with the "preservation of battlefields, houses, and other places celebrated in the history of the state." In the same year, the state government commenced efforts to preserve North Carolina military sites with a legislative appropriation for the preservation of Guilford and Moores Creek Battlegrounds, and in 1909 for Alamance Battleground. The total expenditures for the three sites was nearly $103,000, equivalent to $1.5 million in 1990. In 1908, with the help of the legislature, a local chapter of the United Daughters of the Confederacy (UDC) acquired the 1813 Lincolnton Academy for a museum and county library. Likewise, in 1919 the Daughters of the American Revolution (DAR) received a legislative appropriation for the

In 1918 Edenton residents rallied to save the 1758 Cupola House in probably the first organized community-wide effort in North Carolina to preserve a historic structure. Photograph (1905) courtesy North Carolina Division of Archives and History, Raleigh. (All other photographs courtesy the Division of Archives and History unless otherwise indicated.)

In the late 1930s the National Society of Colonial Dames of America in the State of North Carolina commenced restoration of the ca. 1770 Burgwin-Wright House of Wilmington for use as its state headquarters. This photograph of the house dates from the early twentieth century.

restoration of the Constitution House in Halifax. Thus, the precedent was set for the state's role as an enabler of private sector preservation efforts.

In the closing months of World War I Edenton's Cupola House Library and Museum Association purchased the 1758 Cupola House, but not before Tillie Bond, the financially strapped owner of the property, sold the priceless interior of the first floor to the Brooklyn Museum. The association's acquisition of the Cupola House was probably the first community-wide effort in North Carolina to preserve a historic structure.

For the next few decades, house museum organizations and women's patriotic groups carried out most of North Carolina's preservation activities. Local preservation work gained momentum in the 1920s and 1930s. In 1920 the local chapter of the DAR purchased and moved the small frame Constitution House in Halifax for restoration the following year. According to tradition, North Carolina's first constitution was written in the house. In 1927 the Wake County Committee of the North Carolina Society of Colonial Dames of America in the State of North Carolina purchased and initially restored the Joel Lane House, which dated from 1775. Lane's plantation became the site of Raleigh, the state capital.

In 1926 the North Carolina Daughters of the American Revolution attempted unsuccessfully to purchase the remaining wing of Tryon Palace, the old colonial capitol in New Bern. And in 1929 Mrs. William N. Reynolds of Winston-Salem, former state DAR regent, donated, as a restoration fund for the palace, the proceeds from a successful historical pageant in New Bern directed by Minnette Chapman Duffy (Mrs. Richard Nixon Duffy). Unfortunately, the fund languished from lack of public response.

The John Wright Stanly House in New Bern was restored in 1935 with Works Progress Administration (WPA) labor for use as a public library. George Washington spent two nights in the house during his southern tour of 1791. At the urging of Minnette Chapman Duffy and Gertrude Sprague Carraway (1897-1993), also of New Bern, a portion of the funds raised in 1929 for the future restoration of Tryon Palace was used for the Stanly House project. In 1937 the National Society of Colonial Dames of America in the State of North Carolina purchased the ca. 1770 Burgwin-Wright House of Wilmington for use as its state headquarters. As of 1939 it was being restored under the direction of restoration architect Erling H. Pederson, whose previous work included Stratford Hall in Virginia. By the same year, the Kinston Woman's Club had acquired for restoration the Peebles House (presently known as Harmony Hall), then erroneously believed to have been owned at one time by Richard Caswell, North Carolina's first governor. The earliest section of the Peebles House, thought to be the oldest house in Kinston, dates from the time of the American Revolution.

Not surprisingly, military sites continued to excite interest. In 1923 the state accepted the donation of the homesite and three and one-half acres of land at the Bennett Place, where in April 1865 Gen. Joseph E. Johnston surrendered the last major army of the Confederacy. The North Carolina General Assembly also created the Bennett Place Memorial Commission with Mr. R. O. Everett of Durham as chairman. By February 1941 the state still owned three and one-half acres, and Durham County owned twenty-six and one-half acres of the site. In the mid-1930s Erla (Mrs. Robert R.) Stone of Wilmington vigorously campaigned to defeat plans by the U.S. War Department to sell Fort Johnston, at the mouth of the Cape Fear River, to private interests.

Antiquities Society records also reveal that by World War II the UDC had developed one acre at Fort Fisher and had erected a monument there. In addition, a local chapter of the DAR had purchased the Iredell County site of Fort Dobbs, an outpost of the French and Indian War, and established a committee for its restoration. In the 1930s the Civilian Conservation Corps was enlisted to restore Fort Macon, a Civil War bastion near Beaufort. In 1924 the federal government had transferred the fortification to North Carolina, which had designated it the state's second state park.

Governmental assistance extended beyond military sites and in the absence of formalized preservation programs could take ingenious turns. This was true for Buck Spring, the 1781 home of Nathaniel Macon, speaker of the U.S. House of Representatives, 1801-1807. In June 1940 attorney John Kerr Jr. of Warrenton reported to Christopher Crittenden of the North Carolina Historical Commission that "Three or four years ago, some woman's organization here bought this place . . . and conveyed title to the county. Then the WPA restored the home and some of the outbuildings. . . . In 1939 I passed a law requiring the State Highway Commission—that is the prisoners kept here in this county—to keep the premises cleaned *up* and *off*" [emphasis by Kerr].

Despite occasional success in using government assistance, North Carolina's old social elites bore the brunt of preserving isolated architectural gems. Amateurs all, they were unorganized on a statewide basis except for some of the women's patriotic groups. Their efforts were concentrated on the local level, and, even so, local preservation efforts were rare. The toll of lost landmarks was heavy. In the decades before World War II, for every landmark that was saved in North Carolina, many others fell into ruin.

In 1939 Archibald Henderson lamented the neglect and ruin of The Grove, a late eighteenth-century mansion at Halifax and the former home of patriot and anti-Federalist Willie Jones.

In his historical text for *Old Homes and Gardens of North Carolina*, published in 1939 by the Garden Club of North Carolina, celebrated mathematician and historian Archibald Henderson noted the loss and listed scores of "lordly demesnes and baronial houses . . . [g]one beyond hope of revival or reconstruction. . . ." Among other then-recent casualties, Henderson cited The Grove, a Palladian-inspired late eighteenth-century mansion at Halifax that had been the home of patriot and anti-Federalist Willie Jones. Henderson observed that the house was still standing in 1914 but in the intervening years had become an "irreparable wreck." In reviewing the lost treasures of the Piedmont, Henderson lamented the fate of Lombardy, the Federal-style house (erected 1799-1801 in Salisbury) of John Steele, comptroller of the treasury under President Washington. Though not demolished, Lombardy had been "modernized out of recognition."

Not cited by Henderson, but equally egregious, was the 1935 stripping of one of North Carolina's finest Federal interiors from Montmorenci, an 1820s plantation house in Warren County. The wooden and plaster decorations and the magnificent spiral stair had been removed to the Winterthur Museum in Delaware.

Henderson also decried the earlier loss of landmarks such as Andrew Jackson's Salisbury law office, razed in 1876. Yet, he saved for last and greatest emphasis Tryon Palace, the combination governor's residence and capitol completed in 1770 in New Bern. That structure's original existence was short-lived. In 1798 fire destroyed the palace except for one wing.

Montmorenci, an 1820s Warren County plantation house, was destroyed by 1941. The photograph above shows the house about 1935. In 1935 the Winterthur Museum in Delaware removed the magnificent spiral stair of Montmorenci for display. The stair is shown at left prior to its removal. Photograph courtesy Henry Francis du Pont Winterthur Museum Library.

Nearly a century and a half later, however, Archibald Henderson was able to strike a responsive chord by urging North Carolinians to reconstruct Tryon Palace as a glorious embodiment of their colonial past. He completed his *Homes and Gardens* text with a stirring challenge to the people of North Carolina: "*Palatium gubernatoris restaurandum est*" [the governor's palace must be restored]. Henderson's message reached a receptive audience. As his words were being published, North Carolinians were finally bestirring themselves to catch up with the Virginians and New Englanders in establishing a statewide preservation organization.

Women's Organizations

The organized preservation movement in North Carolina had its origins in several formative currents in society and government on the state, regional, and national levels. Those currents included American traditions of volunteerism, new roles for women, the drive to validate southern heritage, and the emerging concern of government for historic places.

In the early nineteenth century Alexis de Tocqueville, a French historian who studied American institutions, had recognized the peculiarly American trait of utilizing voluntary organizations to achieve civic and social ends. Excluded from formal avenues of power, American women in particular relied on voluntary associations to achieve a public voice. Contemporaneous with pre–Civil War antislavery and suffrage efforts, the struggle in the 1850s to save Mount Vernon presaged female activism in historic preservation.

As traced by historian Anne Firor Scott in her 1984 study *Making the Invisible Woman Visible*, thousands of women's associations appeared in the nineteenth century, especially in its last thirty years, marshaling energy and activism toward religious, social, and civic goals. As a result, women's concerns and viewpoints entered the mainstream, and women gained confidence in their ability to participate in public affairs.

A prominent example of women's activism in North Carolina in the early twentieth century was the formation in 1902 of the Woman's Association for the Betterment of Public School Houses (WABPS). Founded in the Tar Heel State, the organization enlisted thousands of women in a campaign that spread throughout the southeastern United States to improve the comfort, cleanliness, and appearance of public schools for poor white children.

Historian James L. Leloudis II, in a 1983 article, viewed the WABPS as a phenomenon in which middle-class women sought to modernize the New South and to find a role in life beyond traditional domestic duties. A decline in family size, the availability of commercial products, and movement from the farm to the city gave women more leisure time. Leloudis's study, which reflects a recurring American prejudice against aesthetic concerns, concluded that the women of the WABPS failed to achieve true reform inasmuch as they were "misdirected . . . into an obsession with aesthetics and environmental purity" rather than motivated to address basic social and economic structural problems of the South. Leloudis attributed that failure to the tendency of the women to maintain class biases and traditional notions of femininity.

By the 1930s another organization of middle- and upper-class women in North Carolina was concentrating on aesthetics and community appearance. Strictly speaking,

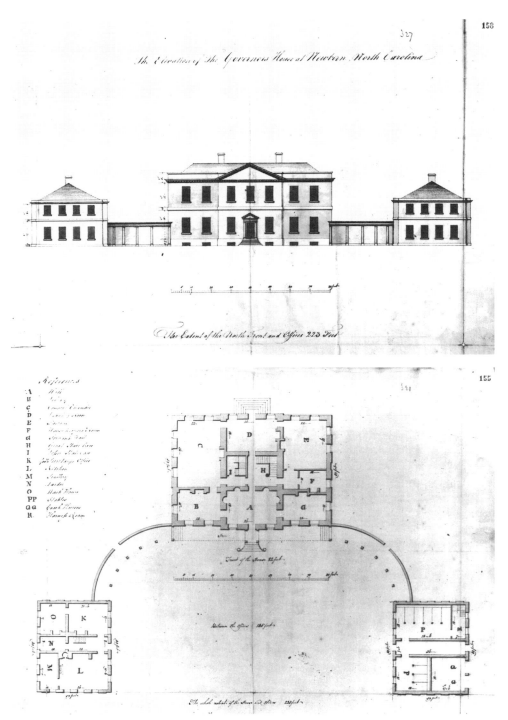

By 1939 the only visible remnants of Tryon Palace were original architectural plans by John Hawks and a wing that survived a 1798 fire. Plans from British Public Record Office; photograph courtesy Division of Archives and History.

In September 1940 the chairwomen of the Garden Clubs of North Carolina met in Raleigh. Preservation leaders pictured above include Minnette Chapman Duffy, seated in the first row, fifth from left; Janie Fetner Gosney, seated in the first row, fourth from right; and Mary Lee McMillan, standing in the third row, fourth from left. Clipping from *News and Observer* (Raleigh), September 18, 1940, Records of the North Carolina Society for the Preservation of Antiquities, Archives, Division of Archives and History, Raleigh (hereafter cited as SPA Records, State Archives).

the Garden Club of North Carolina was not limited to women; as of December 1939, however, thirty-four of its thirty-six officers and committee chairs were female. The interest of the club members had expanded from gardens and landscapes to include the state's architectural masterpieces. In 1938 the garden club worked with the North Carolina Department of Conservation and Development to launch a statewide spring tour of "gardens, old homes, and places of rich historical interest." According to the society page of the April 10, 1938, issue of the Raleigh *News and Observer*, the object of the club's much-heralded "Garden Fortnight and Tour" was to "stimulate interest in the historic treasures of North Carolina, many of which are falling into decadence for lack of interest by influential and civic minded persons capable of restoring them, or callously torn down because public sentiment is not sufficiently aroused to prevent it."

The first Fortnight and Tour, chaired by Janie Fetner Gosney of Raleigh, was a tremendous success. As a result, within a month the club established a restoration committee with Ruth Coltrane Cannon, president of the Garden Club of Concord, as chair. Serving with Mrs. Cannon (at the suggestion of state garden club president Mary Lee McMillan of Raleigh) were McMillan, Gosney, Mrs. Z. P. Metcalf of Raleigh, Mrs. C. A. Penn of Reidsville, Mrs. H. R. Totten of Chapel Hill, and Bessie Gardner Hoey, wife of Gov. Clyde R. Hoey. The Restoration Committee adopted as its first project the creation of a book on North Carolina's historic homes and gardens dating from before 1860. By October 1938 the work of the book committee was well under way.

Ruth Cannon also chaired the book committee. Committee members were Maude Moore Latham of Greensboro and Anna Baker Fenner of Tarboro. Fenner served as secretary and Latham as treasurer and business manager of the committee. Mrs. Latham also supplied crucial financial backing. Joining Cannon and Latham in

In 1938 Ruth Coltrane Cannon of Concord assumed the chair of the state garden club's restoration committee and soon become a leading figure in North Carolina's fledgling preservation movement. Photograph from SPA Records, State Archives.

Maude Moore Latham of Greensboro helped to bankroll the state garden club's *Old Homes and Gardens of North Carolina*, published in 1939. With her daughter, May Gordon Latham Kellenberger, and son-in-law, John A. Kellenberger, she subsequently provided funding for the restoration and reconstruction of Tryon Palace. Photograph courtesy Tryon Palace Historic Sites & Gardens, New Bern. ◂▸

This ghostly image from a frayed newspaper clipping chronicles a milestone in the public appreciation of North Carolina's architectural heritage. Ruth Cannon is shown presenting Gov. and Mrs. Clyde R. Hoey with a copy of *Old Homes and Gardens of North Carolina* in December 1939. Clipping from *Daily Independent* (Kannapolis), December 31, 1939, SPA Records, State Archives.

compiling and editing the entries for the book was Elizabeth Henderson Cotten, assistant to Dr. J. G. de Roulhac Hamilton, director of the Southern Historical Collection of the University of North Carolina.

As indicated above, historical text was supplied by Cotten's brother, Prof. Archibald Henderson of the University of North Carolina, and photographs were taken by Bayard Wootten, North Carolina's most outstanding female photographer. An unofficial editorial board was comprised of Henderson; Cotten; Dr. Christopher Crittenden, the thirty-seven-year-old director of the North Carolina Historical Commission; architectural and art historian Louise Hall of Duke University; and William T. Couch, director of the University of North Carolina Press. The goal, according to Cannon, was to use only "absolutely provable data."

Just in time for Christmas 1939 the University of North Carolina Press published one thousand copies of *Old Homes and Gardens of North Carolina* at ten dollars a copy. Considerable last-minute anxiety attended the printing, in which the dedication was accidentally omitted—much to the chagrin of W. T. Couch. Nevertheless, leaders of the Garden Club of North Carolina expressed great satisfaction with the book and in a formal ceremony proudly presented a copy to Governor and Mrs. Hoey. The book was a limited edition, with the plates being melted after publication. It contained pictures and descriptions of one hundred old homes and gardens selected, in the words of publicist Bill Sharpe, for "their antiquity, historical importance and architectural interest." In keeping with those themes, Archibald Henderson had fittingly concluded his historical narrative with a description of Tryon Palace, North Carolina's most magnificent colonial building, and a call to restore it.

Restricting *Old Homes and Gardens* to high-style examples reflected the universal view of the time that only the oldest and most grand properties in the state were historic. In October 1938 Maude Moore Latham weighed the limitations of that assumption against her own desire to give coverage to all parts of the state. In writing to Ruth Cannon, she observed: "we should have at least one place in every county but [I] am not at all certain that every county has one place of interest."

The production of the book by the women of the state garden club spurred interest in the preservation of the state's most significant historic properties. Given the high level of selectivity, there were so few such properties that their preservation was viewed as presenting no threat to the larger society's devotion to American standards of progress—efficiency, change, and profit making. Nevertheless, the nascent private-sector historic preservation movement of Ruth Cannon and her circle would eventually find governmental and legal support to make historic preservation a force to be reckoned with in North Carolina.

The State Archives and History Movement

By 1939 important steps had been accomplished in creating public historical agencies. In North Carolina and many states of the South, the foundation of the modern state historical agency was laid at the turn of the twentieth century. Though they originally emphasized the preservation of archival materials, state archives and history programs raised a cadre of trained public historians whose interest would encompass historic properties.

In its earliest phase the southern archives and history movement was undoubtedly motivated in part by the desire of white southerners to validate their heritage and cultural traditions in the aftermath of the Civil War and Reconstruction. Some of those southerners evoked an image of an antebellum golden age of civility and order and glorified the "lost cause" of southern nationhood. In the 1993 inaugural issue of Duke University's journal *Southern Cultures*, architectural historian Catherine W. Bishir illuminated this phenomenon as it relates to architectural landmarks. She described North Carolinians involved in historical groups in 1900 as "a statewide network of men and women interested in the histories of their own patrician families and of the state at large, which they usually perceived as one and the same. . . . They codified a lasting version of the state's history that tied Old South to New, interweaving old family heritage, Anglo-Saxon supremacy, and military and political heroism."

The blueprint for North Carolina's archives and history program came from the Cotton Belt. In 1898 Thomas McAdory Owen Sr., a lawyer with a love of history, prevailed upon the Alabama state legislature to create the Alabama Historical Commission (the Alabama Department of Archives and History followed in 1901). In Mississippi, Franklin L. Riley, a former student of Herbert B. Adams, a German-trained practitioner of the scientific school of historical study and himself the holder of a Ph.D. in history from Johns Hopkins University, used the Alabama model to create a historical commission in 1899 and the Mississippi Department of Archives and History in 1902.

North Carolina, led by Raleigh attorney William J. Peele, followed suit in 1903, instituting the nation's third-oldest state historical agency, the North Carolina Historical Commission (which was renamed the Department of Archives and History in 1943 and the Division of Archives and History in 1973). At its annual meeting in 1903, the North Carolina Literary and Historical Association had adopted a resolution requesting the General Assembly to establish a state historical commission. Peele secured passage of the bill creating the commission on March 7, 1903. The legislated duties of the commission were: "to have collected from files of old newspapers, from court records, church records and elsewhere valuable documents pertaining to the history of the State."

The program was enlarged in 1907 with legislative approval of a full-time executive secretary and an additional charge to the commission for the "proper marking and preservation of battlefields, houses, and other places celebrated in the history of the state." The commission's first executive secretary was the former principal of Wilmington High School, Robert D. W. Connor, who in 1934 became the first Archivist of the United States.

The Historical Commission expanded its programs through the years to include the Hall of History (forerunner of the North Carolina Museum of History), established in 1914, and the systematic collection of historical county records, inaugurated in 1915. Its scholarly journal, the *North Carolina Historical Review*, debuted in 1924, and a highway historical marker program began in 1935. The state's archaeological program had its beginning in a 1935 law providing for the preservation of Indian antiquities. By 1940 the agency, in keeping with its original legislative mandate, also developed a research library and amassed and organized a huge archive of public records and private manuscripts.

Beginning in 1933, federal relief programs supplied additional funding and personnel to the commission. With federal assistance, archival records were indexed,

Typical of North Carolina's public history activities before World War II was this unveiling of a memorial plaque to Virginia Dare in the State Capitol on October 24, 1940. Shown (*left to right*) are Gov. Clyde R. Hoey; Mrs. J. F. Hayden of High Point; Miss Mabel Duke Stephenson; Miss Alice H. Parker; Mrs. J. W. Parker of Farmville; and Christopher Crittenden, secretary of the North Carolina Historical Commission.

museum artifacts were cataloged, and archaeological work was undertaken. Christopher Crittenden, secretary and staff administrator of the commission, reported in the agency's biennial report for 1938-1940 that "more than $175,000 (eight times the Commission's biennial appropriation) has been spent on various Works Progress Administration projects with which the Commission has co-operated. . . ." Nevertheless, Crittenden went on to lament that his staff was still inadequate to the task of handling the influx of large collections received during the biennium.

Short of funds and staff, the North Carolina Historical Commission did not develop a program to acquire and preserve historic properties. Before 1940 it owned only one property, Fort Raleigh, site of the first English colony in America. The commission accepted ownership of Fort Raleigh in the mid-1930s only as a way to obtain federal funding for the fort's reconstruction. When the state legislature refused to provide appropriations for the fort's administration and maintenance, the commission in 1936 offered it to the National Park Service, which accepted it as part of the national park system in 1941.

The commission's inability to care for Fort Raleigh no doubt heightened Crittenden's alarm over the state's deteriorating historical places. He realized that the commission did not have the money to solve the problem and in July 1938 used the commission's 1936-1938 biennial report to call for the creation of a private historic preservation society:

The Commission's aid is frequently sought in the care of old houses, of the graves of eminent persons, and of other historic spots, but at present it has no funds for such a purpose. Perhaps the best solution will be the creation of a society to acquire and care for such places. An example of what can be done is furnished by the Association for the Preservation of Virginia Antiquities. Formed half a century ago, this corporation now owns property worth perhaps half a million dollars and is caring for a number of historic old houses, some of which otherwise would have been destroyed. Though the Commission would co-operate in many ways with such an organization, the latter would have a separate and distinct existence.

Three months after making his commission report, Crittenden appeared before the board of directors of the state garden club to urge the creation of a North Carolina equivalent of the APVA. Citing as an example the tenant-occupied "old Gregory Estate near Oxford," he informed the garden club leaders that in North Carolina "There are literally hundreds of these old homes that need attention, care and restoration . . . " and thus implicitly challenged the preservation-minded women of the garden club to create a wholly new statewide historic preservation organization modeled on the APVA.

Early Governmental Preservation Programs

As set forth above, North Carolina's state preservation program began in 1907 with legislation charging the North Carolina Historical Commission with the preservation of historic places. Between 1907 and 1919 the state legislature appropriated funds to nonprofit groups for the preservation of battlefields and historic buildings. In the 1920s the legislature established the Bennett Place Memorial Commission and assigned the administration of Fort Macon to the North Carolina Department of Conservation and Development. An Indian antiquities law of 1935 encouraged private citizens to turn artifacts over to the North Carolina Historical Commission and declared it a misdemeanor to destroy or sell relics found on state lands.

Despite those developments, the North Carolina Historical Commission concentrated on its archival and museum programs in the 1920s and 1930s and did not have the funds to build an active historic preservation component. Not until 1955 did the state's historic preservation program enter its modern era with consolidation in the Department of Archives and History.

Federal laws enacted by 1939 were honorific and applied only to properties of national significance. They included the Antiquities Act of 1906 and the Historic Sites Act of 1935. The Antiquities Act applied only to federally owned land. The more expansive National Historic Sites Act of 1935 authorized the secretary of the interior to acquire and restore historic properties of national significance.

For the first time in the nation's history, the Historic Sites Act of 1935 declared historic preservation to be a national policy. It established the statutory framework for the National Historic Landmark program and the Historic American Buildings Survey (HABS). Despite a narrow focus on nationally significant landmarks, the Historic Sites

Act, in the words of noted preservationist William Murtagh, "heralded the real coming of age of American Preservation. . . . [T]he federal government finally possessed enabling legislation that could lead to coherent planning." Nevertheless, it would be another generation before a comprehensive national preservation program replaced the single-site landmark approach.

Federal historic preservation activity before World War II (as is still the case) centered in the National Park Service (NPS), established in 1916. Armed with new federal powers conferred by the Historic Sites Act of 1935, NPS historians envisioned an expanded chain of national parks with sites representing themes in American history. Sites would be earmarked for inclusion in the park system using data gathered by a great national inventory of historic sites. Yet, the Great Depression smothered those plans by creating a pent-up demand for preservation funding during a period of increasing public concern for historic sites. That demand, coupled with the hope of obtaining federal aid under the Historic Sites Act, unleased a flood of proposals from almost every state for assistance or park designation, making a systematic survey impossible. Eventually the exigencies of World War II abruptly halted expanding federal preservation activity.

Even before the passage of the Historic Sites Act of 1935, pioneering zoning efforts in other states were protecting historic properties on the local level. The South led the way on October 13, 1931, when Charleston, South Carolina, adopted the nation's first local preservation ordinance. The first state law authorizing the creation of a local historic district followed in 1936 with an amendment to the Louisiana constitution providing for the creation of a historic district in the old French Quarter of New Orleans. North Carolina's first local preservation ordinance was adopted in Winston-Salem in 1948 in response to the threat posed by a plan to erect a modern grocery store in historic Old Salem.

In 1939, amid converging trends of greater public- and private-sector activity in historic preservation, North Carolina's social elite, especially its women, determined to save the state's historic places through a private nonprofit organization. In that determination they were following the American tradition of achieving civic goals through voluntary associations. And, in common with other southerners, they sought to validate their heritage. They were also motivated by the encouragement of Christopher Crittenden, the state's leading public historian, as well as by the inspirational examples of the Association for the Preservation of Virginia Antiquities, Colonial Williamsburg, and the Society for the Preservation of New England Antiquities.

Chapter 2:
The Founding

Mrs. Wilmer Comes to Raleigh

In 1939 *Old Homes and Gardens of North Carolina* was published under the direction of Ruth Louise Coltrane Cannon (1891-1965), chairman of the restoration committee of the Garden Club of North Carolina. Mrs. Cannon was a native of Cabarrus County, North Carolina, and daughter of Mariam Winslow and Daniel Branson Coltrane. Her father, a Civil War veteran, was the founder of the Concord National Bank, North Carolina's oldest such facility.

Cannon was the wife of Charles A. Cannon, president and chairman of Cannon Mills Company. She was a wealthy woman who lived her life as a civic leader and benefactor. Moreover, she had graduated summa cum laude from Greensboro College in 1911. A history major, she maintained a lifelong interest in the subject—much to the benefit of the state's historic preservation movement. Ruth Cannon was active in a number of women's and patriotic groups. She held the chairmanship of the Cabarrus County Committee of the National Society of Colonial Dames of America in the State of North Carolina and the presidency of the Dodson Ramseur Chapter of the United Daughters of the Confederacy. She organized the Concord Garden Club, and she and her husband contributed financially to numerous social, educational, and arts organizations.

Work on *Old Homes and Gardens* ignited among North Carolina's cultural and social elite interest in forming a statewide historic preservation organization. Christopher Crittenden, secretary of the North Carolina Historical Commission, fanned enthusiasm by seizing every possible opportunity to urge North Carolinians to form their own version of the APVA: in his July 1938 Historical Commission report; in his October 4, 1938, statements before the state garden club board; and in his October 9, 1938, speech at the unveiling of a historical marker at Fort Fisher.

Although North Carolina garden club members were leaders in the emerging preservation movement, it was not the state garden club but rather the North Carolina Literary and Historical Association that took the initial steps toward formation of a new

Margaret (Mrs. Arthur P.) Wilmer, shown (third from left) with other leaders of the Association for the Preservation of Virginia Antiquities, was president of that organization from 1935 to 1945. Her talk before the North Carolina Literary and Historical Association in December 1938 fired Tar Heel enthusiasm for the creation of the Society for the Preservation of Antiquities (SPA). Photograph (ca. 1935) courtesy Association for the Preservation of Virginia Antiquities, Richmond.

Katherine Clark Pendleton Arrington of Warrenton served as a member the North Carolina Literary and Historical Association's steering committee to create the SPA. She later served as an SPA district vice-president. Photograph courtesy North Carolina Collection, University of North Carolina Library, Chapel Hill.

preservation group. In December 1938 the association devoted part of its annual meeting to a discussion of such a need.

Affectionately called "Lit and Hist," the association, founded in 1900 by the state's social and political leadership, had engineered the 1903 legislation that established the North Carolina Historical Commission—now the Division of Archives and History in the state's Department of Cultural Resources. "Lit and Hist" served as the de facto friends group for the Historical Commission, and Crittenden served as secretary of the association board from 1935 to his death in 1969. The association's meetings were a natural forum for his concerns and those of the commission.

Ruth Cannon presided over that part of the December 1938 Literary and Historical Association meeting devoted to a discussion of whether to form a statewide preservation organization. She had been recruited to do so by the tall and courtly Crittenden, who insisted that he could "think of no one so appropriate for this function." Highlighting the meeting was Margaret (Mrs. Arthur P.) Wilmer, president of the APVA, who attended at her own expense to discuss the work of the Virginians. Cora Vaughan Smith and her husband, publisher Charles Lee Smith, had invited Mrs. Wilmer to Raleigh to stay as guests at their home. Cora Smith had recently married and moved in 1937 to North Carolina from her native state of Virginia. She and Ruth Cannon had been friends since their youth.

Founding Committees and Their Leaders

After an inspiring talk by Mrs. Wilmer, an enthusiastic discussion followed. To Katherine Pendleton Arrington of Warrenton, it seemed "like a Methodist camp meeting." Stirred to action, members of "Lit and Hist" voted "to create a North Carolina society to preserve old houses and the like." A "Steering Committee to create a society to preserve North Carolina antiquities" was appointed, with Ruth Cannon as chair. Committee members were Catherine Albertson of Elizabeth City, Mrs. John Huske Anderson of Raleigh, Katherine P. Arrington of Warrenton, Mrs. William H. Belk of Charlotte, Sally Dortch of Raleigh, Minnette Chapman Duffy of New Bern, Eliza Bellamy Williamson of Wilmington, Adelaide L. Fries of Winston-Salem, Dr. Archibald Henderson of Chapel Hill, Mary Hilliard Hinton of Raleigh, and Lindsay Russell of Wilmington.

The steering committee met on April 28, 1939, in Christopher Crittenden's office on Raleigh's Capitol Square. (The date had been picked so members could also attend a concert by Paderewski that evening.) In convening the committee, Crittenden wrote that he and Ruth Cannon felt the time was right to create the new society and that "this will be one of the most important steps to preserve North Carolina history which has been taken for many years." At the meeting, members reviewed a proposed charter, constitution, and bylaws. Crittenden had prepared those documents, modeled on those of the APVA, before or during the fall of 1938. In November 1938 he sent his drafts to Robert D. W. Connor, Archivist of the United States and former secretary of the North Carolina Historical Commission (1903-1921), for comment.

In a practical step of organizing efficiency (most likely taken at the April 28 meeting), the steering committee delegated its powers to a subcommittee chaired by Dr. Crittenden. Joining Crittenden were Adelaide L. Fries of Winston-Salem and Dr.

Archibald Henderson of Chapel Hill. Probably no nonprofit organization in the history of the state had a team with such high credentials (or IQs) to act as midwife for its beginning.

Charles Christopher Crittenden (1902-1969) was a native of Wake Forest, North Carolina, and the son of Charles Christopher Crittenden Sr., a professor of education at Wake Forest College, and Ethel Taylor Crittenden, who for many years was librarian of the college. The younger Crittenden never adopted the suffix "Jr.," inasmuch as his father died within a year of his birth. Crittenden's maternal grandfather, Charles E. Taylor, was president of Wake Forest College from 1884 to 1905. After earning his undergraduate and M.A. degrees from Wake Forest, Crittenden obtained his doctorate in history from Yale in 1930.

Crittenden was appointed secretary of the North Carolina Historical Commission in 1935, having been assistant professor of history at the University of North Carolina in Chapel Hill. During his career he authored significant books on North Carolina history and built the North Carolina Historical Commission (renamed the North Carolina Department of Archives and History in 1943) into one of the nation's largest and most respected state historical agencies. He helped to found and was later president (1946-1948) of the Society of American Archivists and was also a founder and first president of the American Association for State and Local History. Christopher Crittenden's interests ranged far beyond traditional archival and historical programs. He was a founder and trustee of the National Trust for Historic Preservation and in North Carolina was twice president of the state archaeological society. As the state's leading public historian, he conducted his life's work in accordance with his personal credo, "History for all the people."

Adelaide Lisetta Fries (1871-1949), daughter of Winston-Salem industrialist John William Fries and descendent of four Moravian bishops (including Count Nicholas von Zinzendorf [1700-1760]), was archivist of the Moravian Church, Southern Province, and a prolific writer of books on Moravian history. Her civic and cultural activities included the presidency of the North Carolina Federation of Women's Clubs from 1913 to 1915 and of the State Literary and Historical Association in 1923. Fries had received her M.A. in 1916 from Salem College. In subsequent years she received three honorary doctorates, including those from Wake Forest College and the University of North Carolina, both awarded in 1945.

Archibald Henderson (1877-1963) was a native of Salisbury, North Carolina, and was a man with an astonishing array of intellectual interests. Holder of two Ph.D. degrees, he was Kenan Professor of Mathematics at the University of North Carolina in Chapel Hill. His publications and work in mathematics and mathematical physics brought him into personal contact and friendship with Albert Einstein. His scientific articles were syndicated nationally by the Hearst newspapers. Henderson was also a prolific writer on drama, fiction, and history. He was a friend of George Bernard Shaw and Mark Twain, and he wrote the biographies of each. In 1952 Henderson's literary reputation resulted in his being the first American to be elected a Fellow of the Royal Society of Literature. His enormous collections of research materials eventually enriched the libraries of Yale and the University of North Carolina.

The subcommittee of Crittenden, Fries, and Henderson worked through the spring and summer of 1939 to bring the dream of organization to fruition. They made decisions and recommendations regarding a constitution and policies and recruited charter members and the first slate of officers. Early in the year, Ruth Cannon had disavowed interest in serving as the preservation society's first president. In an undated letter, she wrote: "Am so snowed under with *the* book—don't feel I could ever go into anything big again." She did, however, promise to stand by Crittenden in organizing the new society "until it is in someone's hands after the fundamentals are done—I will help boost."

The Crittenden subcommittee, having the benefit of suggestions made in April by Cannon's steering committee, met on June 8, 1939, on Henderson's front porch in Chapel Hill. There it made final revisions on the corporate documents for the new society. By the middle of June the subcommittee also had recruited Janie Fetner Gosney to serve as secretary for the fledgling organization, which for the interim was called the North Carolina Society for the Preservation and Restoration of Antiquities—leading Fries to write: "What a name!!"

Janie Fetner Gosney (1895-1988) had successfully directed the Garden Club of North Carolina's first statewide tours of historic homes and gardens in 1938. She was the wife of Charles Alfred Gosney, former state representative and, in 1939, a law partner of Kenneth Royall, who later served as secretary of the army. With Cannon out of the picture for the presidency, Janie Gosney superbly fitted a lesser role Crittenden envisioned for a woman. In May 1939 he had written to Fries and Henderson, expressing opinions that would be controversial today:

the Society . . . should be headed by a man, but most of the actual work of organization should be done by some woman, who will be called Executive Vice-President, or something of the sort. The woman should be here in Raleigh, and I believe that I will be able to secure the services of a WPA secretary to assist her. In that way she would be relieved of most of the routine work and at the same time would find opportunity to accomplish a great deal. . . . If we find the right person, our problems will be solved in large measure. It is my idea that the woman selected for this position will go to work immediately, send out the letters to prospective members, and take other necessary steps.

In June 1939 on the porch of "Fordell," Archibald Henderson's home in Chapel Hill, the subcommittee comprised of Henderson, Christopher Crittenden, and Adelaide Fries made final revisions to the organizing documents of the SPA. This photograph (1944) of Henderson relaxing on his porch is from *Archibald Henderson: The New Crichton*, ed. Samuel Stephens Hood (New York: Beechhurst Press, 1949); photograph supplied courtesy Banks C. Talley Jr.

Accordingly, Janie Gosney was quickly put to work in assisting the committee of Crittenden, Fries, and Henderson in their correspondence with other preservationists such as William Sumner Appleton of the Society for the Preservation of New England Antiquities (SPNEA) and Frances A. Wister of the Philadelphia Society for the Preservation of Landmarks.

The return mail brought the North Carolinians sample bylaws, articles of incorporation, and abundant advice, including a strong admonition in August from William Sumner Appleton to "adopt a name that is capable of summing up [the purpose of the society] in one word." Appleton lamented the "great mistake" the SPNEA made in imitating the Virginians by the use of the word "antiquities." He also warned against frittering away energy by trying to work through local chapters and sternly urged the Tar Heels to give priority to preserving existing buildings and to avoid reconstructing disappeared landmarks—advice that would be ignored.

Alston Deas, former president of the Charleston Society for the Preservation of Old Dwellings, likewise wrote Gosney in August, sharing strategic insights from a decade of struggle in South Carolina: "An appeal to the commercial value of the old setting from a tourist standpoint has been of great value. . . . [A]fter all, the first object is to save the buildings. Those who can appreciate them from no standpoint other than a commercial one may come in time to appreciate the value which is inherent in them for themselves alone."

Crittenden immediately took to heart Appleton's warning on the name and urged Fries and Henderson to consider reducing the length of the name of the proposed organization. He also expressed dislike of the word "antiquities" by saying that it "smells

William Sumner Appleton, founder in 1910 of the Society for the Preservation of New England Antiquities (SPNEA), lent a guiding hand to the founders of the SPA. This photograph of Appleton was made in front of SPNEA headquarters, the Harrison Gray Otis House in Boston. Photograph (1929) courtesy SPNEA.

of must, of decayed relics" and cautioned against copying the Virginia association too closely. He advocated the name North Carolina Landmarks Society, modeled on the Connecticut Landmarks Society and suggested by Appleton. It was a choice heartily endorsed by Fries but coolly received by Henderson, who diplomatically acknowledged Crittenden's "eloquent plea." Whatever its name, Crittenden (addressed in correspondence as "C3" by the scientific Henderson) hoped that the new society would be "live and vigorous" and that it eventually would be superior to the APVA.

A Public Appeal

The organizing subcommittee officially appointed Janie Gosney of Raleigh secretary-treasurer on July 26, 1939. On the same day, the subcommittee mailed a broad appeal for public support under the letterhead of the State Literary and Historical Association of North Carolina. The recipients of the mailing were invited to become charter members. In their canvass, Crittenden, Fries, and Henderson sought to stir a response by pointing to the need for "a comprehensive organization to care for houses and other historic landmarks." The subcommittee's declaration that "Persons from other states have sometimes scornfully remarked that North Carolina has no historic places worth preserving" was an unabashed appeal to state pride. The subcommittee bolstered its argument by pointing to hundreds of historic buildings recently surveyed for the *Old Homes and Gardens* project. It called for North Carolinians to restore and preserve for posterity "literally hundreds of fine old houses and other historic landmarks" and to make them known to the nation. Furthermore, it declared North Carolina's history "to be second to no state in the Union."

The organizers also successfully obtained membership lists from social and patriotic groups such as the North Carolina Society of New York and the North Carolina Society of the Daughters of the American Colonists, whose members could be expected to be sympathetic to historic preservation. Individuals responding favorably included Ambassador Josephus Daniels in Mexico, future U.S. senator Willis Smith of Raleigh, and, from Paris, France, Robert Lee Humber, international legal authority and soon-to-be advocate for world federation. Humber, a native of Greenville, North Carolina, returned home in 1940, fleeing the Nazi invasion of France. He became a leader in establishing the North Carolina Museum of Art, and served from 1958 through 1964 in the General Assembly. His handwritten note to Gosney reflected the feeling of many of North Carolina's educated elite: "By preserving these monuments we keep faith with the past and discharge our duty to the future. They are the authentic signets of our true lineage and the building material of our history and destiny."

Joseph Hyde Pratt: "a splendid person for president"

Foremost on the agenda of Crittenden and his subcommittee was a good first team of officers, which they understandably saw as crucial to the success of the new organization. A number of prominent Tar Heels were suggested for president to Crittenden and his subcommittee through the summer of 1939. The committee, after being turned down by Durham banker John Sprunt Hill (1869-1961), approached (on

September 14, 1939) Dr. Joseph Hyde Pratt, former state geologist, who agreed to accept nomination as president.

Pratt (1870-1942), a native of Connecticut (but son of a Confederate officer), received his undergraduate (1893) and doctoral (1896) degrees from Yale. He moved to North Carolina in 1897 as a young mining engineer and in 1899 began a distinguished career on the faculty of the University of North Carolina. He was appointed state geologist in 1906, serving until ill health forced him to resign in 1924. Pratt also rendered a wide variety of services in civic, cultural, and military affairs. From 1905 to 1920 he was secretary of the North Carolina Good Roads Association, and in 1915 he became secretary of the state's first highway commission. A combat veteran of World War I, Pratt received the Distinguished Service Medal as colonel of the 105th Engineers, 30th Division, U.S. Army. The war left him with permanently impaired health, and he required a three-year hospitalization after his return from Europe.

In the years after the war, Colonel Pratt organized and served (1925-1927) as president of Western North Carolina, Inc., to promote tourism in the state's mountain region. Pratt, benignly described by his close friend Archibald Henderson as "an incorrigible 'jinor,'" had held many other organizational presidencies, including those of the North Carolina Forestry Association, the North Carolina Conference for Social Services, and the North Carolina Symphony Orchestra. Pratt's directorships included the National Parks Association. During the New Deal era he served as state engineer for the Civil Works Administration (CWA) and research engineer for the Works Progress Administration (WPA).

Colonel Pratt was a sound choice for the presidency of the antiquities society because he possessed (as recited to him by Crittenden and his subcommittee) prestige, experience, executive ability, knowledge of the state, and genuine interest in historic

Col. Joseph Hyde Pratt, former state geologist and decorated combat veteran of World War I, ably served as the first president of the SPA. Photograph courtesy North Carolina Collection.

preservation. Of particular value were his experience and credibility as an advocate working through nonprofit organizations. Moreover, he enjoyed entrée to agencies such as the National Park Service, which offered the possibility of professional assistance and funding for historic preservation. In a handwritten note to Dr. Crittenden, Ruth Cannon expressed her delight in the selection of Pratt, whom Archibald Henderson had described to her as "a splendid person for president." Reflecting the outlook of the times, she added: "a man is the right one to head it [the new society]."

Founding Day: October 20, 1939

Christopher Crittenden apparently was unpersuasive concerning the matter of the organization's name, for on October 5, 1939, the North Carolina Society for the Preservation of Antiquities (SPA) was chartered with 276 members who had paid a total of $1,500 in dues. The basic annual membership fee was set at two dollars (roughly equivalent to twenty dollars in 1990 purchasing power). Crittenden, Fries, and Henderson signed the charter as incorporators, and the principal office of the SPA was listed as Edenton and Salisbury Streets (the address of the North Carolina Historical Commission) in Raleigh. About the time he filed the incorporation papers, Crittenden gave the press examples of the projects in which the SPA planned to become involved: "interest itself in acquiring the Governor Charles B. Aycock birthplace near Goldsboro, preserve a covered bridge in Lee County, and cooperate in the restoration of Bath."

Incorporation was followed by an organizational meeting in the hall of the house of representatives in the Capitol in Raleigh on Friday, October 20, at 11:00 A.M. Fifty-one people attended, including the three Crittenden subcommittee members, Dr. Pratt, and a goodly representation of North Carolina's philanthropic and social elite. The latter included Mr. and Mrs. John A. Kellenberger of Greensboro and Mrs. Kellenberger's mother, Maude Moore Latham (Mrs. James Edwin Latham), who had helped to finance the inspirational *Old Homes and Gardens of North Carolina*. Ironically, Ruth Cannon was not in attendance. Much to her chagrin, she was already scheduled that day to give a talk on old homes in North Carolina to a Charlotte club.

Dr. Crittenden called the meeting to order and gave a brief review of the organizing of the SPA. In addressing prospective policies (and in ignoring the warnings of William Sumner Appleton), he said that the society was patterned after the APVA and that work would be carried out through branch societies and allied organizations. Not all of Appleton's counsel was discarded, however. Crittenden added that the SPA's first priority would be the preservation of landmarks still standing and that such restorations as Tryon Palace might come later. He completed his remarks by reading letters of support from Ruth Cannon and twenty other prominent individuals such as Josephus Daniels and Robert Lee Humber.

Also addressing the organizers, Archibald Henderson stressed the need for forming the society by ominously quoting an unnamed former governor (probably Cameron Morrison) as saying "there hain't any" when asked what historic shrines remained in the state. Henderson cited as proof of the former governor's error the "more than four hundred and fifty houses" of historical and architectural significance then recently surveyed and photographed by the Garden Club of North Carolina. He

The chamber of the house of representatives in the North Carolina State Capitol in Raleigh was the scene of the founding meeting of the SPA, which took place on Friday, October 20, 1939. Photograph (ca. 1940) from Frances Benjamin Johnston and Thomas Tileston Waterman, *The Early Architecture of North Carolina: A Pictorial Survey* (Chapel Hill: University of North Carolina Press, 1941), 275.

finished by presenting the new society with a catch phrase (and Crittenden with a policy contradiction): his challenge in Latin to rebuild and restore Tryon Palace in New Bern.

Adelaide Fries, known for her felicity of expression, presented the new organization's constitution and bylaws, which were approved. Consistent with the sense of occasion at the meeting, Secretary-Treasurer Janie Gosney read the names of all 267 charter members. The Crittenden subcommittee's nominations of officers, board members, and regional vice-presidents followed; the slate was unanimously approved.

In addition to Pratt (frequently addressed as "Colonel"), the first SPA officers included novelist James Boyd (1888-1944), vice-president, and Janie Gosney, secretary-treasurer. Elected directors were Adelaide Fries, Archibald Henderson, Ruth Cannon, Emily Gregory Gilliam Gary (1867-1962) of Halifax, and Judge Richard Dillard Dixon (1888-1952) of Edenton. Under the SPA constitution Crittenden served as a member of the board in an ex officio capacity as secretary of the North Carolina Historical Commission. Other ex officio members were the SPA officers, the governor of North Carolina, and the heads of the state's Department of Conservation and Development and Highway and Public Works Commissions.

Vice-presidents were likewise elected for each of North Carolina's eleven congressional districts: First, Mrs. W. B. Rodman Jr., Washington; Second, Mrs. Anna Baker Fenner, Tarboro; Third, Miss Gertrude Sprague Carraway, New Bern; Fourth, Willis G. Briggs, Raleigh; Fifth, Rev. Douglas L. Rights, Winston-Salem; Sixth, McDaniel Lewis, Greensboro; Seventh, Eliza Bellamy Williamson, Wilmington; Eighth, George H. Maurice, Eagle Springs; Ninth, Marietta Grier, Statesville; Tenth,

Leaders of the SPA were filled with optimism at the founding meeting of their new organization. Shown at the October 1939 meeting are (*left to right*): Joseph Hyde Pratt, Chapel Hill; Archibald Henderson, Chapel Hill; Janie Fetner Gosney, Raleigh; Adelaide Fries, Winston-Salem; Christopher Crittenden, Raleigh; and Emily Gregory Gilliam Gary, Halifax.

C. W. Tillett, Charlotte; and Eleventh, Mrs. S. Westray Battle, Asheville. Newly elected president Joseph Hyde Pratt closed the meeting with words of thanks, predictions of a great future for the organization, and a forecast (in acknowledging the dominant presence of women in the SPA) that Tar Heel men would become as interested in the movement as the women were.

The October 20 organizers were motivated by a sense of urgency to save North Carolina's vanishing architectural and historical landmarks, as well as by a sense of competitiveness in improving North Carolina's standing as a place of heritage and culture, especially in comparison with Virginia. The society began its first years of existence with high hopes and the support of the state's social elite, renowned academicians, and leading public historian, Christopher Crittenden. It was a beginning filled with optimism and a sense of civic accomplishment, perhaps best summed up by Archibald Henderson in a letter he wrote to Janie Gosney a few weeks after the organizing meeting: "All were very happy to serve in starting something of real import to North Carolina, her history, culture, and posterity."

Chapter 3:
The First Years, 1939-1944

Getting Started

The 1939 constitution of the North Carolina Society for the Preservation of Antiquities declared that the objectives of the new organization were: "to acquire, administer, hold in custody, restore, reconstruct, preserve, maintain, and dispose of historic buildings, grounds, monuments, graves, or other sites, places, or objects, to erect historical markers and monuments, and to take other steps for the purpose of attaining its objectives." Additional objectives included cooperation with public and private organizations and the establishment of branch societies throughout the state.

The presumed visibility and importance of the society in contemporary cultural, economic, and political life manifested itself in the naming of the governor, the director of the North Carolina Department of Conservation and Development, the chairman of the State Highway and Public Works Commission, and the secretary of the North Carolina Historical Commission as ex officio board members. Included as members of an SPA "committee of advisors" were representatives from the North Carolina Folklore Society and the state Congress of Parents and Teachers; such representation suggested a nascent understanding of the broader social and cultural implications of the modern preservation movement.

The evolutionary nature of the organization was evident in the persistence of a nineteenth-century preservation mentality on the part of the founders, who packed the advisory committee with representatives from genealogical and patriotic organizations such as the Colonial Dames, the United Daughters of the Confederacy, the DAR, and the Spanish American War Veterans.

PROGRAMS

of

The State Literary and Historical
Association of North Carolina

The North Carolina Folk-Lore Society

The North Carolina State Art Society

The Archaeological Society of
North Carolina

and

The North Carolina Society for the
Preservation of Antiquities

Raleigh

December 6-9, 1939

Headquarters
Carolina Hotel

*The public is cordially invited to
attend all meetings.*

THE NORTH CAROLINA SOCIETY FOR THE PRESERVATION OF ANTIQUITIES, INCORPORATED

Thursday Afternoon, December 7

2:30 o'clock

(Ballroom, Carolina Hotel)

"The Restoration of Tryon's Palace," Miss Gertrude Carraway, New Bern.

"Coördination of Objectives in Historical and Archaeological Work in North Carolina," Harry T. Davis, Raleigh.

"Restoring the Ancient Town of Bath," A. C. D. Noe, Bath.

"The Society's First Branch—in Guilford County," McDaniel Lewis, Greensboro.

Business meeting.

Thursday Morning, December 7

(Ballroom, Carolina Hotel)

10:00 o'clock

Meeting of board of directors.

11:30 o'clock

Meeting of advisory committee.

The program of the first SPA annual meeting, December 7, 1939, put the restoration of "Tryon's Palace" at the top of the agenda. Program courtesy Division of Archives and History.

SPA leaders conducted their first board meeting during the December 1939 annual meeting. Shown left to right are Margaret (Mrs. Frank) Smethurst, Raleigh, publicity chair; Christopher Crittenden, ex officio board member; Adelaide Fries, board member; Joseph Hyde Pratt, president; Janie Fetner Gosney, secretary-treasurer; Ruth Coltrane Cannon, board member; and Emily Gilliam Gary, board member.

This early mock-up of an Antiquities Society logo was never used. Instead, the society used for its letterhead the obverse of the seal of the Lords Proprietors (see dust-jacket illustration). Mock-up courtesy Division of Archives and History.

The North Carolina Historical Commission provided office space for Janie Gosney, SPA secretary-treasurer, enabling her to begin the work of the society on a businesslike footing. Joining Gosney as members of the first SPA executive committee were Joseph Hyde Pratt and Christopher Crittenden. Initial activity focused on planning and holding the first annual meeting of the SPA, which took place December 7, 1939, in the ballroom of Raleigh's Carolina Hotel. The meeting was scheduled to coincide with the annual "Culture Week" meetings of the State Literary and Historical Association and its allied groups, the North Carolina Folklore Society, the North Carolina State Art Society, and the Archaeological Society of North Carolina. Speakers and topics for the inaugural SPA session included Gertrude Carraway, "The Restoration of Tryon's Palace"; Harry T. Davis, "The Coordination of Objectives of Historical and Archaeological Work in North Carolina"; Rev. A. C. D. Noe, vicar of the historic St. Thomas Episcopal Church in Bath, "Restoring the Ancient Town of Bath"; and McDaniel Lewis (1894-1978), a Greensboro investment banker and civic leader, "The Society's First Branch—in Guilford County."

SPA members approved the following projects: finding and restoring a typical plantation home and outbuildings; acquiring and preserving one or more covered bridges; acquiring, restoring, and preserving an overshot and an undershot waterwheel mill; restoration of the Adam Spach Rock House in Davidson County; restoration and preservation of old fortifications and battlegrounds, including Bentonville Battlefield in Johnston County, Alamance Battleground in Alamance County, and fortifications and Confederate trenches in Halifax, Martin, Craven, and Lenoir Counties; and endorsement, approval, and cooperation in the restoration of St. Thomas Church at Bath, Tryon Palace at New Bern, the clerk's office at Halifax, and the Burgwin-Wright House (then commonly called the Cornwallis House) in Wilmington.

The list was a gauge of what North Carolina's cultural elite in 1939 viewed as worthy of preservation. While high-style buildings were included, they did not predominate. Mills, bridges, earthworks, and a vernacular rock house leavened the mix and belied an absorption with grand antebellum houses and gardens. Irrespective of the nature of its goals, the SPA leadership confidently expected the assistance of government programs and private philanthropy.

Branching Out

An overriding goal was the creation of branch societies. Soon after the organization meeting of October 20, 1939, Joseph Hyde Pratt mailed a packet of information to the district vice-presidents. The packet included the SPA constitution and bylaws; "Circular No. 2, Suggested Procedure in the Formation of Branch Societies"; a statement concerning the responsibilities of district vice-presidents; and a list of charter members. Under the SPA bylaws vice-presidents were assigned the duty of "promoting the organization of branch societies."

Almost immediately (November 24, 1939) the first branch of the society was established in Greensboro under the forceful direction of Sixth District vice-president McDaniel Lewis. One of the first acts of the SPA board in October 1939 had been to grant SPA charter members in Guilford County permission to form a branch society. At the branch organizing meeting, prominent Greensboro attorney Charles A. Hines was elected president. Hines was an important political and civic leader, having served as a member of the Greensboro City Council, chairman of the State Board of Elections, and state senator from Guilford County. He had also managed the last U.S. senatorial campaign of Furnifold M. Simmons.

Colonel Pratt installed Hines and his fellow officers and told the group that the Guilford chapter was "an incentive for creation of other societies upon which success of the parent group will depend." The branch members discussed possible projects,

On November 24, 1939, Greensboro investment banker McDaniel Lewis spearheaded the organization in Guilford County of the SPA's first local branch. Shown left to right are Lewis, SPA Sixth District vice-president; Joseph Hyde Pratt, SPA president; and Charles A. Hines, president of the Guilford County branch. Photograph courtesy Preservation North Carolina, Raleigh.

including the marking and restoration of the "log college" opened in 1767 by Dr. David Caldwell, a Presbyterian minister. Despite the initial enthusiasm, the branch ceased to be active after April 1941.

By December 1939 Alice Parrott of Kinston had accepted chairmanship of the general society's Committee on the Formation of Branch Societies. Janie Gosney felt that the success or growth of the SPA depended "entirely on the formation of branch societies over the state." In order to spur the branches forward, she requested that Margaret Wilmer of the APVA send copies of her organization's constitution, yearbook, and bylaws to SPA vice-presidents for their use in organizing branch societies.

Janie Gosney, as de facto executive director, issued a general directive January 8, 1940, to all the district vice-presidents to start working on establishing local branch societies. She urged them on by warning: "The amount of work accomplished either in preservation or restoration by the Society depends entirely upon the formation of Branch Societies over the State." She also outlined for them the range of projects adopted at the 1939 annual meeting but gave the vice-presidents discretion to investigate other projects locally that would arouse the most interest. A week later, Gosney, describing herself as "itching to really start something," advised Alice Parrott that "If there is nothing in their [vice-presidents'] district to be preserved, a branch society can be formed to help the general society in a state-wide project." Her advice revealed a persistent view that historical resources worthy of preservation were very few in number.

Sixth District vice-president McDaniel Lewis responded promptly to Gosney's January 8 call for branch organization by informing her on January 20 that he had already taken steps for the formation of societies in the other three counties of the district—Durham, Orange, and Alamance—and that it was his "ambition to have a branch in each of them, certainly before the year is gone." On the other hand, Alice Parrott received from one of her committee members, Mrs. Baxter Craighead Davidson of Charlotte, a portent of the subsequent failure of the expansion policy. Mrs. Davidson, mistress of the historic house known as Rosedale, declined to lead local efforts to form subsocieties and noted her own failure to interest several young women in doing so. They were too busy with other civic activities such as the Junior League and hospital drives. In seeking to soften the blow of her rejection, Davidson offered the dubious consolation that volunteers would be found in smaller communities as "people in small towns often find more time for outside work." Seeing little progress in encouraging the creation of new branches, Gosney in March 1940 expressed to Parrott her apprehensions that without such expansion, "enthusiasm in the Society will die."

Nearly a year and a half after the SPA was founded, its second branch was organized in the spring of 1941 in Wayne County with attorney W. A. Dees as president. At the suggestion of Clarence Poe, editor of the *Progressive Farmer*, the Wayne County preservationists chose as their first project the restoration of the birthplace of Poe's father-in-law, Charles Brantley Aycock, "the education governor" (1901-1905). By November 1941 the branch had arranged for the donation by the Aycock family of the house in which the governor had been born, as well as a small parcel of land, and had obtained the donated services of Fayetteville architect Ernest Reinecke. Dees also announced plans for a five thousand-dollar fund-raising drive for the spring of 1942. The Raleigh *News and Observer* characterized restoration of the Aycock house as the leading SPA project statewide.

After the outbreak of World War II, the board of the Wayne County chapter decided to postpone restoration of the Aycock birthplace. Without the momentum of the project, the chapter itself ceased activity. Interest resurfaced in 1949 when local fund-raising efforts and a matching legislative grant culminated in state acquisition of the Aycock site in 1958 and restoration in 1959. Although the postwar efforts were not specifically identified with the SPA, the final restoration owed a great debt to the Wayne County chapter's prewar activity.

In October 1941 Antiquities Society branch expansion reached a high-water mark with the establishment of a third chapter in western North Carolina. The organizational meeting took place at the George Vanderbilt Hotel in Asheville with Pratt, Crittenden, and Gosney in attendance. An SPA press release announced that the purpose of the western branch was to preserve old homes, old letters, and other "antiquities." The first and primary goal of the branch, however, was the development of a cultural museum in the Great Smoky Mountains National Park. Earlier that spring Pratt and Crittenden had joined forces with a western North Carolina museum committee chaired by W. E. Bird, dean of Western Carolina Teachers College at Cullowhee. Together they lined up support

In October 1941 SPA branch expansion reached a high-water mark with the organization of the Western North Carolina Branch of the SPA at the George Vanderbilt Hotel in Asheville. Shown seated left to right are Mrs. E. R. Elmore of Mars Hill; Mrs. S. L. Siler of Franklin; Mrs. R. N. Barber of Waynesville, SPA district vice-president; Joseph Hyde Pratt, SPA president; Mrs. S. Westray Battle; and Mrs. L. E. Fisher, Asheville. Shown standing on the second row are Herbert D. Miles, Asheville; Mrs. Sadie S. Patton, Hendersonville; Janie Fetner Gosney, SPA secretary-treasurer; Christopher Crittenden, secretary of the North Carolina Historical Commission; and George W. McCoy, Asheville. Clipping from *Asheville Times*, October 13, 1941, SPA Records, State Archives.

for a museum of mountain culture from National Park Service officials and the North Carolina congressional delegation.

However, organization of the western branch and the development of the museum soon halted. Charles K. Robinson, editor of the *Asheville Citizen-Times*, refused to accept the presidency of the western branch, and no one of comparable status would step forward. Robinson failed to be moved by Pratt's November 5, 1941, appeal to him in the name of state pride, which contrasted Tar Heel historical markers that said "here stood" to Virginia's, which said "here is." His refusal was doubly disappointing inasmuch as the SPA leadership desired a man to head the western branch in order to avoid (in Crittenden's words) "the impression that the whole thing is a women's organization."

Soon the onset of World War II diverted energy and attention away from the effort to organize SPA branches. In February 1942 Secretary-Treasurer Gosney glumly noted: "I fear that with this war sitting so closely on our tails there is little use trying to organize anything outside of war work." She, Crittenden, and George McCoy, an Asheville leader in SPA western branch activities, reluctantly agreed in March 1942 to defer the organization of additional branches until "this conflict is over" and to make a press announcement accordingly.

Although attempts to organize SPA branches through district vice-presidents were unsuccessful, the vice-presidents themselves would eventually serve—in the absence of chapters—to give the SPA a workable statewide network and local visibility. In October 1939 Christopher Crittenden had undertaken the initial recruitment of district vice-presidents through a mailing to prominent people in the state's eleven congressional districts. Crittenden's letter outlined the duties of vice-presidents under the SPA bylaws: to identify and stimulate local preservation projects, raise funds, and help organize chapters. It was a formidable assignment.

Some candidates immediately refused. Miss Catherine Albertson of Elizabeth City, a member of the SPA formation steering committee, replied on October 9, writing that "The D.A.R. in Elizabeth City are interested in the same line of work as our Society." She "saw no opportunity for raising funds for our programs here . . . [as Elizabeth City was] . . . over organized as to clubs and societies all struggling to raise money. . . ." Likewise, Gordon Gray, publisher of the *Winston-Salem Journal* and the *Twin-City Sentinel*, said that since returning to North Carolina from New York in 1935 he had done little else except solicit funds and wished to "cease and desist . . . for a while at least." Gray nevertheless pledged his support (and indeed in 1962 became chairman of the board of the National Trust for Historic Preservation in America. As chairman of that body he was instrumental in gaining passage of the National Historic Preservation Act of 1966, America's first comprehensive national preservation law).

Of those who initially accepted the district vice-presidencies, several tendered their resignations once they fully realized the difficulties inherent in performing volunteer service in a struggling new organization. Excuses were many. The most original (and humorous) came in November 1940 from a vice-president in the western Piedmont, who resigned on the basis of her pneumonia, floods in her district, her food poisoning, and her preparation for her son's wedding.

Since branches depended on membership, a companion concern for the SPA was the difficulty in attracting members. At the organizing meeting of October 20, 1939, Elizabeth Henderson Cotten of Chapel Hill took the chairmanship of the

The first property acquired by the SPA (1940) was Richmond Hill in Yadkin County. The 1859 brick structure was home to Richmond Mumford Pearson, who served as chief justice of the North Carolina Supreme Court from 1858 to 1878. Clipping from unidentified newspaper, SPA Records, State Archives.

Ayr Mount, built ca. 1814 near Hillsborough by William Kirkland, a native of Ayr, Scotland, was one of at least a dozen historic houses the SPA attempted to acquire by donation in 1940 and 1941. Photograph (ca. 1940) by Frances Benjamin Johnston; reproduced courtesy Library of Congress, Washington, D.C.

Membership Committee. She gamely attempted to interest SPA district vice-presidents in membership recruitment, asking them to assume the chairmanships of membership committees in their districts and to appoint chairs within each county. The results were disappointing. In an undated report of either 1940 or 1941, Cotten reported that only two vice-presidents—Gertrude Carraway and McDaniel Lewis—followed her plan. Direct membership appeals fared no better. Two hundred twenty-five invitations sent by July 1940 to Leaksville-Spray yielded only one member. Gosney complained to Colonel Pratt about the disappointing response of the SPA's generally affluent constituency: "I feel they crawl into their yachts, mountain houses, etc., until fall."

Early Restoration Projects

Richmond Hill

In his November 1941 letter to the reluctant Asheville newspaperman Charles K. Robinson, Joseph Hyde Pratt itemized a number of planned SPA projects, including the reconstruction of Tryon Palace and the restoration of the Adam Spach House in Davidson County, the Hezekiah Alexander House in Mecklenburg County, and Richmond Hill, the 1859 Yadkin County brick house and log law school of Judge Richmond Pearson. Most of the projects were visualized as cooperative ventures with local groups; however, in a policy that was to be repudiated in 1951, the society accepted title in late 1940 to the Pearson property. In the acceptance of ownership, the Tar Heel preservationists sought to follow the Virginia model of property acquisition. Janie Gosney outlined the SPA strategy in a June 1940 letter to Francis Gregory of Leamington, Ontario, owner of Hill Airy, near Oxford, North Carolina: "This Society was organized to do exactly what has been done in Virginia, New England, Philadelphia and Charleston, by similar organizations. The lovely old homes in these states, where the owners do not live in them, have been deeded to these societies and in turn the societies restore them, then they are opened to the public."

Having no money to buy endangered buildings, the officers of the society solicited the donation of at least a dozen historic houses in 1940 and 1941, including Ayr Mount in Hillsborough and the Penelope Barker House in Edenton. Janie Gosney, who made most of the contacts, presented eloquent appeals based on state pride and a chance for donor families to be immortalized in the state's history. Fortunately, perhaps, for the untested SPA, almost all of its requests were denied; however, the Yokley family, furniture manufacturers from Mount Airy, responded by donating to the SPA Richmond Hill—isolated, vacant, and deteriorated—with fifteen acres of land.

Richmond Mumford Pearson (1805-1878) was chief justice of the North Carolina Supreme Court from 1858 to 1878, and his law school was renowned in training a generation of North Carolina's most distinguished lawyers, including six members of the state supreme court and three North Carolina governors. In the summer of 1941 the Antiquities Society prevailed upon the North Carolina Bar Association to undertake a fund-raising drive among the lawyers of the state to restore Richmond Hill as a shrine to their profession. Prominent Salisbury attorney Walter Woodson, former chairman of the local Democratic Party, agreed to lead the campaign. Time passed, however, and

Woodson made no move. He even failed to appear when, in desperation, Pratt and Crittenden converged in August 1941 on his office in Salisbury. In order to salvage the honor of the bar association, its president, future U.S. senator Willis Smith, joined Colonel Pratt in signing an appeal to the lawyers of the state to raise twelve thousand dollars to finance the restoration. Letters went out in the first two weeks of December 1941.

With the attack on Pearl Harbor on December 7, the Richmond Hill campaign sank with the Pacific fleet. Gosney reported to Colonel Pratt in February 1942 that total donations of only thirty-seven dollars did not even "pay for the letters and stamps sent out in December." Of course, more than Japanese aggression influenced the outcome for Richmond Hill. Soon after receiving the appeal, Rocky Mount attorney Kemp D. Battle (1888-1973) wrote Janie Gosney that the lawyers of the state would not raise a fund anywhere near twelve thousand dollars (approximately $104,000 in 1990 dollars) because of "the reduction in income in practicing law in North Carolina." Apparently the depression was still affecting the livelihood of the Tar Heel legal fraternity.

After obtaining the blessing of the Yokleys and the construction supervision of Rev. Douglas L. Rights, president of the Wachovia Historical Society, the SPA in May 1942 spent two hundred dollars to put a temporary roof on Richmond Hill. It then mothballed the property. Gosney and Crittenden hoped that a revived federal Works Progress Administration (WPA) would help restore Richmond Hill after the war.

Instead, with the coming of peace, Tryon Palace and other projects came to the front, and the Antiquities Society lost all track of the Yokleys' contribution. Finally in 1968 the Yadkin County Historical Society furnished the SPA with a photostat of the original deed from the Yokleys. With the photostat came an offer to accept title to the property in order to restore it. At the urging of T. Harry Gatton, SPA president, the transfer was made, and the restoration of Richmond Hill was completed in 1986.

The Adam Spach Rock House

Perhaps the project that rivaled the Pearson House in activity (and frustration) from 1939 through 1942 was the attempted restoration of the Adam Spach Rock House in Davidson County. In 1774 Adam Spach (1720-1801), a native of Lower Alsace, built a combination house and fort in Davidson County fourteen miles south of the Moravian town of Bethabara. The house was constructed of rock and built over a spring on the side of a hill. The Spach House stood intact until about 1925, when its owner removed rock from the wall, causing the house to collapse. The descendants of Adam Spach then purchased the property and donated it to the Wachovia Historical Society, an organization that Colonel Pratt expansively characterized as a "cooperating branch of the NCSPA."

The Spach House restoration was identified as a potential SPA project at the 1939 annual meeting. Adelaide Fries, a Spach descendant, vigorously worked to generate enthusiasm for the project among the SPA leadership. The initiative of the Spach descendants in purchasing the land and providing architectural plans were deciding factors in gaining SPA support. As Christopher Crittenden explained to the press, the purpose of the SPA was to "help those who help themselves." On March 1, 1940, Joseph Hyde Pratt initially requested from Ronald F. Lee, supervisor of historic sites of the National Park Service (NPS) in Washington, D.C., assistance in planning the restoration of the Spach House and asked to meet with Lee in Washington. In the same month, Pratt and Fries also contacted WPA officials in North Carolina for assistance.

No help came from NPS, but in August 1940 the SPA and the North Carolina Historical Commission filed a joint "Works Progress Administration Proposal" for the Spach House restoration in the amount of $13,065. Just five days earlier, the Wachovia Historical Society expressed its willingness to transfer the property to the state historical commission. Such a transfer was necessary because the WPA could assist governmental entities only. Progress seemed assured when in February 1941 President Roosevelt approved the project.

The project sponsors soon learned, however, that it was one thing to obtain presidential approval and another to get the state's WPA bureaucracy moving. State WPA officials immediately placed the project on hold until qualified relief labor in Davidson County became available. In July Janie Gosney appealed to Charles M. Crutchfield, WPA district manager in Winston-Salem, to use his influence "as a North Carolinian" to carry the project through. Finally, in August Crutchfield notified Adelaide Fries that the Spach House restoration could begin after the expected January 1942 completion of a Davidson County office building. Crutchfield cited a reduction in the number of WPA workers as a major cause for the delay in the start-up date.

It is unclear whether the cut in relief workers was a result of waning congressional support for the New Deal, the worsening international situation, or both. In any case, the United States entered the war before the completion of the Davidson County office building, and the Spach House project never began. At the December 2, 1942, meeting of the SPA board of directors, Adelaide Fries reported that the "remaining rocks, bricks,

The outbreak of World War II derailed the SPA's plans to utilize WPA labor in restoring the Adam Spach Rock House, built in 1774 in Davidson County. Photograph from scrapbook in SPA Records, State Archives.

etc. of the Adam Spach House had been put under cover to preserve it for the duration." Thus, with momentum stalled by the war, the fate of the house remained uncertain.

The Hezekiah Alexander House

The SPA's handling of the 1774 Hezekiah Alexander House in 1940-1942 reflected the organization's growing wariness in accepting donated property. The builder of the house, Hezekiah Alexander, was a native of Maryland who migrated to Mecklenburg County, North Carolina, after 1754. He became a wealthy farmer and in 1776 a delegate to the state's Fifth Provincial Congress at Halifax. Waightstill Avery, North Carolina's first attorney general, had also lived in the house. The Hezekiah Alexander House had been one of many historic properties sought by the SPA for donation. Sometime in the summer of 1940 Janie Gosney visited the owner of the house, E. B. Cole, and spent two hours catching fish in Cole's lake while trying to interest him in giving the property to the SPA. But she could not get a commitment and concluded that Cole "was far more interested in the preservation of his *fish*."

A year later the SPA executive committee of Pratt, Crittenden, and Gosney attended a meeting in Charlotte at the invitation of state representative J. B. Vogler, a descendant of Hezekiah Alexander, to consider an offer by Mr. and Mrs. Cole to donate the Hezekiah Alexander stone house and 165 acres to either the SPA or a unit of government. The offer included an additional donation of one thousand dollars

After an unsuccessful attempt in 1940 to acquire the 1774 Hezekiah Alexander House in Mecklenburg County, the SPA supported proposals for restoration by state or local government. This photograph dates from "after [the] 1947 restoration."

by the Coles for architectural plans; nevertheless, the donation of the property was contingent on a commitment to develop the area for recreation. Rather than pursue the offer themselves, the SPA representatives backed a plan for Mecklenburg County to develop the property for a county historical and recreational park.

The Coles' offer continued into the next year and was discussed at the December 1942 SPA annual meeting. By vote the membership directed then president McDaniel Lewis to appoint a committee to study and to lobby the legislature to establish a state or county park on the donated property. Surprisingly, the SPA apparently did nothing. Christopher Crittenden informed the SPA membership at its 1943 annual meeting that he had seen in the newspapers that the Alexander House had been donated to a Methodist organization. Thus, in three years the SPA had gone from actively soliciting the donation of the Alexander House to failing to follow through in advocating governmental intervention.

Tryon Palace: "a Rockefeller will appear"

At the 1939 SPA organizing meeting, Christopher Crittenden announced that the SPA's policy (as urged by William Sumner Appleton) would be to preserve existing structures and to defer reconstructions. In practice the SPA readily followed popular sentiment to restore Tryon Palace, reputedly the finest public building in colonial America. New Bern newspaperwoman, civic leader, and SPA district vice-president Gertrude Carraway had a strong desire for New Bern to emulate Williamsburg. Dr. Fiske Kimball, director of the Philadelphia Museum of Art and member of the Williamsburg Restoration Board, guided Miss Carraway in her efforts.

Through Carraway's persistence and the help of Alexander B. Andrews of Raleigh and of Episcopal rectors in New York, the research staff of the New-York Historical Society in March 1939 found plans of the palace in the society's library. The plans were among the papers of Dr. Francis Lister Hawks, one-time president of the University of Louisiana and a grandson of John Hawks, supervising architect of the palace. Additional plans (and the most complete) were soon found in the British Public Record Office upon inquiry by Christopher Crittenden. In June 1939, at Kimball's suggestion and with Crittenden's help, a WPA project application for federal assistance in excavating the site was drafted (probably by Carraway). As a precondition to providing assistance, the federal government required the city of New Bern as local sponsor to raise fifteen hundred dollars as its contribution to the project—a contribution that Gertrude Carraway agreed to raise from private sources.

By March 1940 Carraway was discouraged and confided to Pratt: "I'm afraid we have a hard row ahead of us as to raising funds. We have not been successful in getting much for the excavation project so far." Both Kimball and Carraway saw the excavation as necessary to "whet the public appetite in a widespread movement to restore the building."

Surprisingly, it was not certain where the palace would be reconstructed. Gertrude Carraway told the SPA membership (at its first annual meeting, December 7, 1939) that "it may be impractical to rebuild the palace on its original site." That difficulty existed because U.S. Highway 70 ran directly over the site. In addition, forty buildings and houses, some of them historic, would have to be razed if the palace were

Gertrude S. Carraway of New Bern served continuously as an SPA officer or board member from 1939 to 1974. She championed the reconstruction and restoration of Tryon Palace. Photograph (ca. 1940) by Bachrach; supplied courtesy Historical Publications Section, Division of Archives and History.

reconstructed. Miss Carraway saw as a possibility the reconstruction of the palace to its original scale on the edge of town. Wherever it was to be located, she envisioned the reconstructed palace, together with the many historic buildings in New Bern, as a great tourist Mecca between Charleston and Williamsburg. At the first annual meeting, she fervently urged the SPA to adopt the reconstruction of Tryon Place as its "one central objective."

A March 1940 visit to North Carolina by the federal Advisory Board on National Parks, Historic Sites, Buildings, and Monuments raised hopes. At a large public meeting in New Bern, the board members declared that Tryon Palace should be reconstructed on its original site. The Historic Sites Branch of the National Park Service recommended that historical research precede any excavation. New Bern native and Norfolk newspaperman Alonzo T. Dill Jr. completed the research (paid for by the SPA) in June 1940. The way was cleared for WPA archaeology, which never began. With approaching war clouds, interest waned, and the WPA was diverted to other projects.

During those discouraging times, hope of a major benefactor remained alive. In regard to Tryon Palace Janie Gosney wrote in December 1940 to Mrs. James A. Fore of Charlotte: "Let's keep talking it, pushing it, and pulling for it, and one of these bright happy days a Rockefeller will appear on the scene."

Rockefeller did not appear, but one of his chief lieutenants did—in the form of Kenneth Chorley, president of Colonial Williamsburg. Early in 1941 Ruth Cannon had visited Chorley's New York offices to make a plea (which proved unsuccessful) for Rockefeller funding of the palace and had recruited him to speak at the SPA's 1941 annual meeting. When Chorley and his wife arrived in Raleigh the following December, North Carolinians placed such great significance on the visit that the Chorleys were made house guests of Gov. and Mrs. J. Melville Broughton and were treated as guests of honor at an Executive Mansion dinner.

Tar Heels were well paid for their hospitality. Waiving his speaking fee, Chorley dispensed sound advice and inspirational motivation in a memorable keynote address at the SPA annual meeting. He emphasized the historical connections between Williamsburg and New Bern and offered arguments in favor of reconstructing the palace based on the structure's historical and architectural importance. Perhaps most beneficially, he emphasized that the reconstruction should be based on accuracy and authenticity, that the best professional advice and services should be secured for the reconstruction, and that the work must be free of commercialism.

Within days of Chorley's address, the United States was at war. As with other SPA projects, the conflict derailed fund raising and development for Tryon Palace. Gertrude Carraway urged that the SPA continue to solicit donations for the proposed Tryon Palace restoration from the state's wealthy citizens so that the money could "be put in bonds until something can be done toward restoration work."

Yet, the impact of Chorley's speech lingered, with profound results. SPA board member Maude Moore Latham, by her own admission, was "enthralled" by it and reread it many times. Since her girlhood, Mrs. Latham had harbored a wish to see the palace reconstructed. On January 26, 1944, she established the Maude Moore Latham Foundation to help acquire the land upon which Tryon Palace stood and to reconstruct, furnish, and maintain the property as a public museum and park. She stipulated that her trust would be terminated January 1, 1954, unless the state or one of its subdivisions acquired the property for restoration.

Ruth Cannon arranged for Kenneth Chorley (*left*), president of Colonial Williamsburg, to be the keynote speaker at the SPA's December 1941 annual meeting. In this November 1941 news clipping, Cannon and Chorley are chatting during the intermission of a concert of eighteenth-century music at Williamsburg. Clipping from unidentified newspaper dated November 17, 1941, in Elizabeth Henderson Cotten Papers, Southern Historical Collection, University of North Carolina Library, Chapel Hill.

The SPA membership jubilantly received the news of Mrs. Latham's gift. Christopher Crittenden told McDaniel Lewis that when he and others were given a confidential preview of Latham's plans at the 1943 annual meeting, "all of us wanted to dance jigs. . . ." Tryon Palace became the central theme of the December 6, 1944, annual meeting inasmuch as, in Crittenden's words, it was "by far the livest [*sic*] development in the restoration field in North Carolina today." At the meeting Gov. Melville Broughton personally emphasized the value the restoration would have in boosting the state's tourist economy. Paul Kelly of the North Carolina Department of Conservation and Development pledged the department's willingness to administer the palace as a unit of the state park system. And Latham reminded those in attendance that "It took both interest and means to start the project and it needs the co-operation of the whole state to complete it."

Thus, it was Maude Moore Latham, a North Carolinian, who had the interest and means to make the restoration of Tryon Palace a reality and who gave the society a much-needed preservation victory in its darkest hour. It had been more likely all along that wealthy Tar Heels like her, and not out-of-state millionaires, would be the answer to the philanthropic needs of the SPA. Mrs. Latham and her daughter, May Gordon Latham Kellenberger, and son-in-law, John A. Kellenberger, proved to be the only large-scale donors to historic preservation during the existence of the SPA, however, and their charitable contributions for historic preservation went almost exclusively to Tryon Palace. (After 1978 the income from the three million-dollar Kellenberger Trust was earmarked for Tryon Palace and preservation projects in New Bern.)

Other Projects: From Archaeology to Civil Defense

Additional projects of the SPA in the early 1940s included the cosponsorship of WPA archaeological excavation at the Frutchey Indian mound (presently part of the ceremonial center at Town Creek Indian Mound State Historic Site) on the Little River, seven miles east of Mount Gilead. In January 1941 Joseph Hyde Pratt sought an additional WPA archaeological investigation of Roanoke Island. Colonel Pratt was fascinated by the possibility that artifacts from the Roanoke colony might be found at sixteenth-century Native American sites.

In May 1940 the SPA arranged to open the Andrew Johnson birthplace to the public with the assistance of the WPA Arts Projects Division. The Colonial Dames had donated the modest gambrel-roofed house to the city of Raleigh, and the structure had been moved several times from its original location. By 1940 it sat beside the armory on the North Carolina State College (now University) campus. Almost six thousand people visited the site between May and December 1940.

In January 1941 the SPA, through Janie Gosney, began discussions with the Jones family of Warrenton, owners of the grave of Anne Lee, daughter of Gen. Robert E. Lee. Gosney sought to curb the vandalism at the grave by suggesting that the Joneses install a high iron fence around the Lee grave site. Although the Jones family was politely responsive, no action was taken.

Concerns increased when the outbreak of the war posed additional dangers for the preservation of historical buildings and documents. In early 1942 the SPA cooperated with the State Defense Committee to plan for the protection of historic

In 1941 SPA leaders sought to stem vandalism at the Warren County grave of Anne Carter Lee, daughter of Gen. Robert E. Lee. Photograph from *State* magazine 8 (August 3, 1940): 1.

buildings in case of enemy attack. Gosney reported in February 1942 to the then-ailing Colonel Pratt that Dr. Crittenden had set up civil defense committees for historic structures in Edenton, New Bern, Wilmington, and Bath. At the urging of SPA president McDaniel Lewis in 1942, a documents protection program was also initiated. A committee was established and a public campaign mounted for historical documents in private hands to be saved from war salvage drives.

Finally, the SPA conducted a limited amount of legislative advocacy during its first years. Its leaders conceptualized the governmental role for historic preservation only in terms of official recognition and ownership of or financial assistance to single-site historic places or museums open to the public. Within that framework, Colonel Pratt, with his many contacts, adroitly and effectively represented the SPA in personal visits and letters to legislative and agency offices.

In May 1941 Pratt sought the help of North Carolina's congressional delegation in an effort (ultimately unsuccessful) to have the Andrew Johnson birthplace designated as a national memorial. Likewise, Gosney fruitlessly pursued the establishment of a historical museum in the Great Smoky Mountains of North Carolina on behalf of the SPA executive committee. On the state level, Colonel Pratt invited forty-five legislators to a meeting in February 1941 in Raleigh's Sir Walter Hotel to secure an appropriation for restoration work; that meeting was canceled, however, because of sickness, bad weather, and conflicting engagements. The SPA did not reschedule the meeting, but Gosney hoped that by the time the "legislature meets in 1943 our work will be well enough known to ask for and secure an appropriation." Unfortunately, by 1943 the society was at a low ebb with war raging, Janie Gosney working for the Red Cross, and Colonel Pratt dead. No legislative appropriations were made.

Service to the Public: Who is the Kingpin?

The public soon learned of the SPA, and requests came for financial assistance and technical know-how. The reality was that the SPA was powerless to save buildings because of lack of funds and staff. The outbreak of war and the loss of government aid for the society's projects exacerbated that condition. Christopher Crittenden, who forwarded many requests to Janie Gosney, must have been relieved to have an organization with which to share the burden of meeting a public demand for which his commission was unequipped to deal.

On December 31, 1939, Rev. Charles Aylett Ashby, rector of St. Paul's Episcopal Church in Edenton, wrote Crittenden that he had read of the formation of the SPA and needed its help in restoring colonial graves. He asked the "name of the kingpin to whom a letter on such a subject should go." Janie Gosney was the kingpin to whom Crittenden turned the query. Apparently at a loss for something to say in reply, Gosney developed one of her stock answers that was as positive as the circumstances allowed. She wrote Ashby in January 1940 that the SPA was too young to have undertaken any restorations but that it planned to do something of a concrete nature soon. She also predicted that an Edenton branch society would be formed and that Ashby should attempt to interest that organization in the restoration of the churchyard.

In the months ahead, Gosney routinely lamented in letters to other supplicants: "If only someone had organized the Society some fifty years ago, as Virginia, then we would be ready for an emergency such as this one. At the present we have very little money. . . ." She also revealed a strong personal commitment and sensitivity to historic preservation that must have increased her frustration in not being able to answer fully local requests for help. In February 1940 she confided to Mrs. Louis Stephens of Dunn: "It grieves me beyond words to hear of the beautiful old houses and buildings in N.C., fallen in decay, being bought by persons from other states and moved from their original location, for some other state to lay claim to and enjoy." And in referring to preservation activity in other states, she concluded: "surely what others have done, we can do." It was during the early months of 1940 that the society, unable to buy properties, began to solicit them through donation.

Unable to provide large-scale financial or technical assistance, the SPA soon improvised a small grants program to local historical and preservation organizations. That program began on September 11, 1940, when the SPA executive committee voted to give one hundred dollars to the park committee of the Halifax Woman's Club and the Halifax Garden Club. The grant, requested by Emily Gilliam Gary, chair of the park committee, was for the "restoration" of the early nineteenth-century clerk of court's office in the historic town. Additional small grants or direct outlays of money for local projects in the early years included total payments of $349 in 1941 and 1942 to restoration architect Thomas Tileston Waterman for a survey, measured drawings, blueprints, and specifications for the 1766 Michael Braun stone house in Rowan County. The Brown-Fisher Families Association owned the house and sought restoration assistance from the SPA.

The Halifax grant of 1940 marked the beginning of what proved to be the most significant, effective, and long-term SPA program—local grants. The fact that for nearly

A 1940 donation in the amount of one hundred dollars for the restoration of the Clerk's Office at Halifax (*top*) marked the beginning of the SPA grants program. Photograph (ca. 1940) by Frances Benjamin Johnston; reproduced courtesy Library of Congress. In 1941 and 1942 SPA grants paid for architectural drawings and specifications by restoration architect Thomas Tileston Waterman for the 1766 Michael Braun stone house (*bottom*) in Rowan County. This photograph of the structure dates from 1955.

fifteen years (until the revival of state grants in 1955) the SPA was the only reliable source for preservation grants in North Carolina magnified the effectiveness of the society's local-grants program and the publicity it generated.

The Great Federal Hope

Depression-era federal relief programs appear to have been widely approved and accepted in conservative North Carolina, especially among the leaders of the state's fledgling preservation movement. As early as April 1939 Christopher Crittenden asked the North Carolina Council of State if the state would accept properties in trust donated to the proposed "North Carolina Landmarks Society." A National Park Service official had informed Crittenden that federal relief labor could be obtained only for developing or maintaining historic property owned by a public agency. Therefore, the society would need to retain administrative responsibility with nominal title in the name of the state. From the beginning, the founders of the SPA anticipated federal aid.

During the summer of 1939 reports from out of state (such as a letter from the Pennsylvania Historical Commission) that many local groups were making "extensive use of the WPA in carrying on restoration" increased expectations of federal largess in North Carolina. At the Guilford County chapter's organizing meeting in November 1939, Joseph Hyde Pratt raised hopes for federal assistance by pointing to the federally assisted historic Dock Street Theater in Charleston, South Carolina. And at its initial meeting, October 20, 1939, the SPA board endorsed WPA archaeological projects under way in North Carolina.

Reality seemed to follow hope in the fall of 1939 when Janie Gosney received the clerical assistance of a WPA worker (who, as it turned out, put the membership list in disarray). In May 1940 WPA assistance enabled the SPA to open Raleigh's Andrew Johnson House. At the December 1942 SPA annual meeting, Christopher Crittenden reported to the board of directors that the SPA had applied to the federal Public Works Reserve Project office for all of the projects in the SPA files. (The federal government established the reserve program under the WPA in order to create a list of public works projects to be undertaken as a means of counteracting any general unemployment caused by the reduction of defense activities at the end of the war.) Throughout the war, Crittenden and his SPA colleagues reiterated their hope for federal postwar assistance for the society's projects.

Yet, federal assistance had a negative side. In February 1941 Janie Gosney complained to William Sumner Appleton about WPA delay and bureaucracy in the Spach House project. She offered the opinion that the three organizations involved in the project—the SPA, North Carolina Historical Commission, and the Wachovia Historical Society—could have restored the Spach House on their own, "but as soon as you say WPA everyone says, Oh! let the government do it." The conservative Appleton replied by condemning the Roosevelt administration and accusing it of stifling local initiative with programs such as the WPA. Uncomfortable with revealing his views, he asked Gosney to destroy his letter.

In addition to federal work relief agencies, the fledgling Tar Heel preservationists also looked to the National Park Service for assistance. The NPS, a federal agency, had technical expertise in historic preservation that the SPA lacked. Its historians were undertaking a national survey of historical sites for inclusion in the national park system. Competing with history-conscious Americans in other states, North Carolinians strove to get as many Tar Heel historic sites as possible under federal jurisdiction. Inclusion assured preservation, added to the state's prestige as a place of heritage and culture, and freed energy and resources for other endangered properties.

Beginning in February 1940, Joseph Hyde Pratt, SPA president, worked to arrange for a visit by NPS officials to North Carolina for an assessment of historical sites for the federal or state park system. As a result, on March 26 and 27 the federal Advisory Board on National Parks, Historic Sites, Buildings, and Monuments made an inspection tour of Fort Raleigh, Kill Devil Hills, Cape Hatteras, New Bern, and Fort Fisher. Advisory board chairman Dr. H. C. Bumpus of Duxbury, Massachusetts, also visited the Bentonville and Alamance battlefields.

At its fall meeting in October 1940 the advisory board adopted a resolution requesting the SPA and the North Carolina Historical Commission to formulate a proposal for the development of a series of national historic sites in the state. Pratt and Crittenden called a public meeting for January 21, 1941, in the downtown Raleigh offices of the North Carolina Department of Conservation and Development. Representatives came from NPS, Conservation and Development, the SPA, and various Tar Heel patriotic and historical groups active in the preservation of the state's battlefields.

Pratt and Crittenden took the information collected at the meeting and quickly prepared a proposal on behalf of the SPA and the Historical Commission. They submitted a "Proposed Program for the Development of National Historical Areas in North Carolina" to NPS in February 1941. The "Program" called for the Park Service to place all NPS military sites in North Carolina under one administrative unit and for the Park Service to acquire Fort Fisher in New Hanover County, Bentonville Battleground in Johnston County, Bennett Place in Durham County, and Alamance Battleground in Alamance County. The plan also contained commitments for the donation of property to the United States for all of the sites except Bentonville, for which Pratt and Crittenden (and presumably the SPA and the Historical Commission) offered to launch a campaign to acquire the necessary land. The North Carolinians especially urged NPS action on Fort Fisher in view of beach erosion that was spreading to the fort itself. They concluded by pointing out that the Park Service did not administer a single Civil War-era site in North Carolina.

In November 1941, after months of silence, the federal advisory board rejected the suggested grouping of sites because of their differing historical themes. The board additionally turned down Alamance Battleground and Bennett Place for the national park system on the basis of lack of national significance. No mention was made of Fort Fisher and Bentonville Battleground. Disposition of those sites remained uncertain until March 1942, when President Roosevelt suspended altogether the NPS site designation program. Viewed as nonessential to the war effort, the NPS became a caretaker organization with a skeletal staff during World War II.

"A great soul passed from our midst"

In its early years the society withstood the loss of initial enthusiasm by many members, the advent of war, and dashed hopes of federal assistance. Those challenges were soon overshadowed by a much greater calamity, however. Joseph Hyde Pratt, who had given energetic and intelligent leadership, fell desperately ill just before the annual meeting of December 1941, causing Gosney's "heart to hit bottom." Pratt received treatment at the Mayo Clinic (where his son Joseph Jr. was a staff surgeon) in February 1942 and died on June 3, 1942.

Colonel Pratt's SPA colleagues loved and admired him and deeply mourned his death. Elizabeth Cotten praised his "genuine nobility of character" and declared that "No native North Carolinian could have loved the state more wholeheartedly, or served it more unselfishly." Archibald Henderson, Cotten's brother and Pratt's close friend of forty-five years, fulsomely eulogized Pratt at the 1942 SPA annual meeting. The grandiloquent Henderson praised Pratt as a "tireless warrior in the Kulturekampf . . . waged in North Carolina in behalf of a better state, a broader outlook, and a finer civilization." Henderson further declared: "With his death a great soul passed from our midst." On the motion of Dr. Crittenden, the organization established a committee to consider a fitting memorial to the society's first president.

Under the SPA constitution, McDaniel Lewis, elected first vice-president in 1940, became president in June 1942 upon the death of Colonel Pratt. Lewis took command of an organization whose principal restoration projects—the Aycock birthplace, Richmond Hill, the Adam Spach House, and Tryon Palace—had bogged down and had been indefinitely shelved because of the national war effort. To make matters worse, the congenitally energetic Lewis was distracted if not enervated by other commitments when he assumed the SPA presidency. A former World War I infantry officer who saw frontline service, the slight, bald, and wiry Lewis had been invigorated by patriotic fervor upon the outbreak of World War II and became immersed in a host of war-related activities that included service as chairman of a Guilford County Selective Service board, chairman of the Guilford County Committee for World War II Records Collection, member of the Greensboro Red Cross board of directors, and continuing duties from prewar days as chairman of the local Armistice Day committee. Those activities coincided with a major reorganization of Lewis's investment banking business, all of which took time away from his SPA responsibilities. In August 1942 Lewis turned down a speaking engagement before a Raleigh DAR chapter, pleading that business demands confined him to Greensboro.

At the December 1942 SPA annual meeting in Raleigh, Lewis was elected president in his own right and was reelected in 1942 and 1943. Lewis felt that the SPA would be unpatriotic if it actively pursued its projects during wartime. (At the same time, he repeated the commonly expressed and comforting opinion that deferred SPA projects would be resumed after the war with the help of an expected "large scale public works program.") At the 1942 annual meeting, Lewis proposed to the membership a scaled-down agenda that included continuing the annual meetings and providing a fitting memorial for Colonel Pratt. Lewis believed that the annual meeting would "more than anything . . . keep alive our work."

One important North Carolina preservationist disagreed with Lewis's minimalist policy, however. Ruth Cannon, who lost a son in the war, later recalled her feelings: "if our sons had gone to fight for the liberty and heritage which is so precious to us, . . . it was the very time that we mustn't let this Society for the great history of our wonderful state lag. . . ." Cannon expressed skepticism over the rationale for reducing programs during the war and concluded that by the early 1940s, preservation had become "something of a fight and people began to scatter." Whether valid or not, Lewis's wartime policy of disengagement (with which everyone except Cannon seemed to have agreed) brought the SPA to a virtual standstill.

The stagnation of SPA programs during the war probably coincided with a time of personal crisis for Janie Gosney. Her husband, Charles Alfred Gosney, a lawyer and former state legislator, had held prominent positions in civic and professional life. He was supportive of his wife's preservation work and helped the SPA with legal issues. Yet, the strains of his law practice led to alcoholism, and this in turn probably prompted separation from Janie later in the decade.

Janie Gosney knew that the reduced wartime activity of the SPA did not justify even her modest salary of fifty dollars a month. Given her problems at home, she must have been concerned about her eventual ability to support herself. After the 1941 annual meeting, she contacted Kenneth Chorley about employment as a hostess at Williamsburg. He was not encouraging, in view of the available local-labor supply in Williamsburg. Finally, at the end of February 1942, she accepted a position organizing classes for the American Red Cross, a job she cheerfully described as "serving our boys and country." She did so with the blessing of Pratt and Crittenden, who were happy to keep her on a part-time basis handling correspondence for the SPA.

Janie Gosney was not the only leader of the state's preservation movement who thought of a career change during the war years. In May 1944 the state nearly lost its leading public historian when Christopher Crittenden quietly lobbied for the presidency of East Carolina Teacher's College in Greenville. At Crittenden's request McDaniel Lewis sent a letter of support to the selection committee, saying that Crittenden "has certainly done his present job well and I feel sure [sic] deserves recognition for larger service." Crittenden's desire for the teachers college presidency and Lewis's view that it was a step up is an indication of the undervalued state of public history professionals at the time.

By the annual meeting of 1944, much of the promise of the SPA of 1939 was unfulfilled. The Virginia model of holding architectural crown jewels through society chapters had utterly failed. Governmental aid, which figured so highly in SPA plans, was buried in an avalanche of wartime priorities. And the persistent and resourceful leadership of Joseph Hyde Pratt was replaced by the more distracted and distant (geographically and operationally) stewardship of McDaniel Lewis. Because of his business commitments, Lewis missed the December 1943 annual meeting. Membership, which stood at 393 at the end of 1941, had plummeted to 86 by the end of 1944.

From a later vantage point, the early leaders of the society appear to have shared a naive view of the burden of property ownership and the difficulty of fund raising. Yet, they should not be faulted. They had few models to look to, and the most prominent on the horizon was Virginia's APVA. Federal and state preservation programs were in their infancy. Pratt and his colleagues could only place their hope in the National Park Service, the WPA, and private philanthropy. Nor can they be faulted for not anticipating America's entry into World War II and its devastating effect on fund raising and their programs. Without the society's early groundwork, it is doubtful that projects such as the Aycock birthplace and Richmond Hill could have been revived years later.

In addition, the SPA created public visibility for historic preservation and stimulated public education. The 1941 SPA meeting, with the dynamic Kenneth Chorley as a speaker, motivated Maude Moore Latham to open her ample pocketbook to the state's most visible and popular preservation project, the reconstruction and restoration of Tryon Palace. Valuable lessons had been learned. Soon peace would come —and with it opportunities for new leaders, programs, and directions.

Chapter 4:
The Cannon Years, 1944-1956

The Women Take Over

On October 6, 1944, McDaniel Lewis took himself out of the running for SPA president, modestly declaring: "Undoubtedly there are others who deserve the honor and who could serve the Society with greater success. . . ." With the completion of Lewis's term in December of that year, the women took the reins of the North Carolina Society for the Preservation of Antiquities. Ruth Coltrane Cannon assumed the presidency, and the indomitable Gertrude Carraway (later described as the queen of England, Winston Churchill, and FDR all rolled into one) was reelected vice-president. With bylaw changes in 1948 removing restrictions on the length of the term of president, Cannon remained in office through early December 1956.

Under Ruth Cannon's leadership the state's wealthiest, most cultured, and socially prominent women dominated the society. Maude Moore Latham (1871-1951) served as a board member until 1950. Succeeding her was Fay Webb Gardner (1885-1969), wife of former governor and undersecretary of the treasury 0. Max Gardner (1882-1947). Fay Gardner was both a socialite and a business executive in real estate and textile manufacturing. Elizabeth Stevenson "Buffie" Ives (1897-1994) of Southern Pines and Bloomington, Illinois, sister of Adlai E. Stevenson II, joined the SPA board of directors in 1953 and followed architect James Alan Stenhouse (1910-1996) of Charlotte as president in 1957. Author Inglis Fletcher (1879-1969) became vice-president under Cannon in 1947.

In the Cannon era other prominent SPA board members included Adelaide Fries, Elizabeth Cotten, and Archibald Henderson, who for years was the lone male on the board. District vice-presidents also included well-connected women such as Katherine Clark Pendleton Arrington of Warrenton, Cora Vaughan Smith of Raleigh, Mrs. Robert

Cecil of Asheville, Jane Henderson Boyden Craige Gray (Mrs. Gordon Gray) of Winston-Salem, and May Gordon Latham Kellenberger of Greensboro. District vice-president Katherine Pendleton Arrington (1876-1958) was a member of the board of Stratford Hall, president of the North Carolina State Art Society, and former member of the state Democratic Executive Committee.

Though they were a preservation oligarchy, Cannon and her circle took significant steps in modernizing the SPA. To cope with a postwar world that was radically different from what they had expected, they found roles for the society other than those envisioned in 1939. At the end of World War II the United States entered a period of sustained economic prosperity. Postwar federal economic stimulus programs with legions of relief workers never materialized. Instead, federal dollars flowed into Cold War military programs and for the rebuilding of Europe. Domestic federal programs were development oriented and centered on highway construction and urban renewal. The predominant government mentality was to bulldoze cultural resources, not restore them. Within the federal government, the National Park Service remained on a starvation budget. New Deal-era plans for park system expansion were not revived.

Likewise, state government offered little in the way of assistance for historic preservation. At the close of the war, the North Carolina State Department of Conservation and Development and the North Carolina State Department of Archives and History (the North Carolina Historical Commission until 1943) were committed to the development of Tryon Palace. The Department of Archives and History provided office space and occasional secretarial services for the SPA, and, because of his personal interest, the department's director, Christopher Crittenden, lent support, encouragement, and advice. Yet, the history programs of the Department of Archives and History were otherwise concentrated on records management, upgrading the history museum, and planning the construction of both a new records center and a new archives and history building.

Thus, the postwar SPA found itself in an economic and political environment in which the vast majority of historic properties were without governmental recognition, protection, or grant assistance and generally viewed as expendable commodities in the marketplace. Stung by the harsh experience of its first years, the SPA took a conservative course in adjusting to postwar realities. It refrained from acquiring property and in 1951, at the insistence of its president, Ruth Cannon, formally rejected the policy of owning property. Instead, in the Cannon era North Carolina preservationists focused on offering financial assistance and information exchange to local preservation groups seeking to acquire and restore historic properties.

Ruth Coltrane Cannon: "a joyous crusader"

Ruth Cannon had a gift for leadership and a vision to match. She knew that for the people of North Carolina to understand their heritage, the state's historic resources needed to be saved. She was an imposing and determined woman, a strong friend, and a formidable adversary. She loved her state, as did her colleagues, in a personal way, signing her annual meeting announcements "Yours for a greater North Carolina." She tied pride in the state to pride in the family homeplace. Cannon and Inglis Fletcher, her friend and longtime vice-president (1947-1956), proudly added the names of their

In July 1944 Charles A. and Ruth Coltrane Cannon attended the christening of the Liberty ship *J. W. Cannon* at a shipyard in Brunswick, Georgia. Photograph courtesy Mariam Cannon Hayes.

respective estates, "Jasmine" and "Bandon Plantation," under their own names on the SPA letterhead.

Ruth Cannon's management style was personal and viewed by some as authoritarian. Yet, for most of her twelve-year presidency, strong leadership was what the society needed. Paradoxically, she issued clear directives, but frequently in undated hard-to-read handwritten letters. She was a pragmatist who knew the limits of what the society could reasonably do. With the experience of Richmond Hill as an object lesson, she opposed property ownership by the SPA.

Cannon's same conservative, clear-eyed approach applied across the board to other areas as well. As he did with Janie Gosney, Christopher Crittenden frequently referred preservation problems to Mary Emma Branch (SPA secretary-treasurer from 1946), asking that the SPA deal with them. Branch would turn to Cannon, who gave pithy and realistic instruction. In response to a request to obtain better care for the grave of the wife of Gen. William Richardson Davie at Halifax, Cannon scrawled as a directive to Branch on the bottom of Crittenden's letter: "get a local DAR member to start interest. . . ." And in response to Crittenden's request to preserve the Henry Clay Oak in Raleigh, Ruth Cannon advised Branch: "this is a matter for the City of Raleigh."

Cannon's buoyant optimism and energy matched her pragmatism. She traveled throughout the state to give advice and encouragement to local preservation groups and was also active in other cultural and historical organizations. She was the first woman to head the Roanoke Island Historical Association, producer of the outdoor drama *The Lost Colony*. She also conceived the development of the Elizabethan Garden at Manteo. In 1949, because of her exhaustive pace, a Raleigh admirer dubbed her "Choo Choo Busy Bee"—an appellation derived from Charlie "Choo Choo" Justice, a University of North Carolina football star of the time.

Cannon's gregarious good humor and boosterism gave sparkle to SPA meetings and enlivened membership communications. In a February 1950 letter to the society membership, she wrote: "You all have been wonderful. . . . We had a marvelous annual meeting with so many projects to be reported that your President had to be on the alert to see that everyone had a chance to enthuse. We really need a day for glowing enthusiasm instead of a three hour meeting."

The full tenor of SPA meetings under Ruth Cannon is best expressed through verbatim transcripts. There are many references to patriotism, state pride, and, above all, to her joy in living in a country in which one could worship God. The Cold War and the loss of a son in World War II may have heightened her patriotic and religious fervor. In 1951 she tied themes of state pride and religion to the common allusion to North Carolina as a vale of humility between two mountains of conceit:

I have just talked at Stanford University about North Carolina and even Mr. Hoover, when he came up didn't accuse me of any humility about North Carolina, but we have been accused of that, so Mr. Wellman who wrote the biography of Wade Hampton came up afterwards to me and said, "Have you read Bunyan's 'Pilgrims Progress' lately?" I had to admit that I had not. He said, "Do you know what took place in the Valley of Humility?" and I had to ask him what. And this is what he said, and I think we in North Carolina must remember this constantly. In the Valley of Humility pearls were found. I heard the whisper of angels, and I found my God.

Well, certainly we in North Carolina are so grateful for the freedom that we possess here in North Carolina, the freedom to worship our God, to carry forth the heritage that has been handed down to us, and so may we in the Valley of Humility carry the banner that is our rightful heritage.

At the annual meeting in December 1952, Ruth Cannon touched upon similar themes. She said that America's strength was in proportion to the depth of its traditional roots, that we must sometimes die for freedom, and that the SPA was on "a crusade for the preservation of history in North Carolina."

The leadership qualities of Ruth Cannon and her first vice-president, Gertrude Carraway, exempted them from Christopher Crittenden's reservations concerning women in positions of authority. The original SPA constitution limited the president's term to three consecutive single years. Yet, as the annual meeting for 1947 approached, Crittenden was concerned that without continued guidance by Cannon's strong hand, the society might founder. Miss Carraway's refusal to seek the office because of her obligations as state regent of the DAR reinforced Crittenden's concerns. Therefore, in October 1947 Crittenden proposed to Cannon that the SPA constitution be amended to allow her to serve five years instead of three. He wrote that he and Mary Emma Branch could not think "of any one else . . . as enthusiastic and efficient in this position."

On motion of Gertrude Carraway, the SPA removed the constitutional bar of term limitation at the December 1947 annual meeting, and the road was open for an extended Cannon presidency. Under Cannon, the grants program was increased and the revolving loan fund and Cannon Cup Awards were established. Society membership grew by elevenfold from its 1944 level, reaching 980 in 1949. Former SPA president

McDaniel Lewis reflected the feelings of many when he wrote Cannon in December 1948: "You have done exceedingly well in arousing interest as attested by the large attendance and the wonderful programs [at the 1948 annual meeting]. The society and the state are indeed grateful to you." Bruce Cotten, writing to Cannon from Baltimore in April 1949, was more matter-of-fact: "you have rescued this Society from early extinction. . . ."

A Quiet Departure and Secretarial Successions

Janie Gosney's Red Cross employment continued after the war. She also remained active at reduced hours as secretary-treasurer of the SPA and as a member of the executive committee. The part-time nature of her duties threw more of the operational burden upon Crittenden. Gosney soon left the SPA, however, and Charlie Huss Lovejoy (a woman), collector of records at the Department of Archives and History, became secretary-treasurer in November 1945. The change occurred without fanfare, and no indication of the reasons for Janie Gosney's departure was recorded in the society records. Gosney possibly found it too hard to divide her time between her new duties as a Red Cross caseworker and her SPA job. She had worked twenty hours a week for the SPA at fifty dollars a month. It is likely that Crittenden recruited Charlie Huss Lovejoy, inasmuch as she was a member of his staff. In any case, Ruth Cannon approved of the new secretary-treasurer, noting that Lovejoy "loves history."

Janie Gosney had given the SPA the operational and administrative strength it needed to survive in its early years. Despite Crittenden's apparent prejudice against women in executive positions, she held him in high regard and defended him when he angered Maude Moore Latham in January 1941 for failing to acknowledge a donation. In smoothing things over, she explained to Latham that Crittenden was simply absentminded and alluded to his respect for women intellectually. At the same time, she characterized his dealings with women as "very thoughtful."

Economic necessity probably pulled Gosney, who was obliged to concentrate on earning a living, away from the SPA. The string of setbacks the society suffered in its first years, including the death of the much beloved Colonel Pratt, may have eroded her enthusiasm. By February 1946 Gosney had moved to Asheboro, North Carolina. By long-distance telephone she guided Charlie Huss Lovejoy through the preparation of the SPA's income tax return for 1945 and requested news of the society's progress. In 1949 she dropped her society membership and apparently never again participated in its activities. Beginning in 1950, at the age of fifty-five, she spent the rest of her working career as a receptionist for the State Capital Life Insurance Company in Raleigh.

Charlie Huss Lovejoy left the SPA at the end of April 1946 and moved out of state. In May of that year Joye E. Jordan, another member of Crittenden's staff and administrator of his department's Division of Museums, replaced Lovejoy briefly. Jordan's service was also short-lived, and Crittenden himself served through the remaining spring and summer of 1946 as acting secretary-treasurer. In September 1946, deflecting Ruth Cannon's desire for a volunteer secretary, he recruited Mary Emma Parker Branch of Raleigh to be the SPA's paid secretary-treasurer. Branch was a DAR officer, a genealogist, and the wife of Dr. Ernest A. Branch, a dentist and member of the staff of the state board of health. Mary Emma Branch would serve the SPA for twenty years.

The Virginia Model Fades Away

The Virginia model of holding property through chapters had foundered in the war years. There was not enough interest on the local level for chapter formation, and the property-holding experience with Richmond Hill was an operational cold bath. Still, the Virginia model did not die at once. After the war there was some movement toward chapter formation in three places—Hillsborough, the southwestern Piedmont's Eleventh Congressional District, and Moore County—though by 1947 none had come to fruition.

Additional property ownership was still a possibility in October 1945 when Crittenden extended an offer on behalf of the SPA to accept title to the endangered eighteenth- and early nineteenth-century Nash-Kollock School in Hillsborough. Title was never transferred, and the society did not make another such offer for at least another decade. In February and March 1946 the SPA refrained from acquiring the James Iredell House in Edenton on the then-likely chance that it would continue to be used as a private dwelling. Iredell was a justice of the Supreme Court of the United States from 1790 to 1799. The DAR subsequently acquired the house in 1949 with the assistance of a twenty-five-hundred-dollar loan from the SPA Revolving Fund, established the previous year. Much hoped-for assistance from the lawyers of the state never materialized, and the DAR transferred title to the site to the state of North Carolina in 1951. In recent years the science of dendrochronology (the dating of old wood through the analysis of tree-ring patterns) indicates that the Iredell House was not standing during James Iredell's lifetime.

The restraint exercised by the SPA was consistent with a new de facto policy of not owning property. According to Charlie Huss Lovejoy, the SPA by February 1946 had "evolved" a policy of assisting local organizations through its grants for acquisition and restoration but not for maintenance. The SPA encouraged local groups to raise funds and to acquire properties themselves. Accordingly, in May 1946 the SPA executive committee made a grant of two hundred dollars to the Moore County Historical Association to help it purchase the early nineteenth-century Shaw House, built by Scottish settlers at Southern Pines. The Moore County group, lead by SPA Eighth District vice-president George Maurice and local activist Elizabeth Stevenson Ives, had proven its mettle by raising five thousand dollars on its own and by Ives personally securing a ninety-day option on the house. Cannon attended the March 22, 1946, organizing meeting of the Moore County Historical Association. She reported to Crittenden how struck she was by the "sincerity and enthusiasm" of Elizabeth Ives.

The death knell for the Virginia model of property ownership began sounding at the December 1948 annual meeting of the SPA. Crittenden led an agonizing discussion on how to dispose of the rapidly deteriorating Richmond Hill law school, donated to the society in 1940. He pointed out that there was not enough standing timber on the Richmond Hill tract to cut in order to raise funds for restoration. Ruth Cannon firmly held that the society was not in a position to raise funds for restoration and that it should not own properties. No decision was made, and the matter was turned over to a committee for further study and recommendation. Adelaide Fries was appointed committee chair, and Crittenden and Cecil Long of Newton (and national president general of the United Daughters of the Confederacy) served as members.

The issue dragged on for another three years, slowed by the death of Fries in 1949. Finally, at the December 1951 annual meeting, the membership confirmed by unanimous vote the policy of not owning property. At that meeting Crittenden reviewed the history of the Richmond Hill project, including the prewar donation, and asserted: "now the situation has changed, and the policy of the Society today is not to own properties, but simply to contribute funds to local groups that are seeking to own property like this, as it is pretty well off the beaten track, and so your Committee, of which Mrs. Long is Chairman, and of which I am a member, feels that is best to return the property to the family."

Significantly, in its vote the society members did not intend to rule out all future ownership of historic properties. They could not have done so even if they had wanted to, because the SPA constitution still listed property ownership as an "object" of the organization. Ruth Cannon explained, however, that nonownership was the right policy for her presidency because it kept the SPA free of management burdens and also because SPA funds were kept free to benefit a greater number of local projects:

Dr. Pratt had hoped that we might own places and, of course, I think that would be wonderful. Maybe some day the Society will have a President who will know how to do it. They do in some other states, but it hasn't seemed feasible, so if you and I discuss some time would we like to have you give us a place, we are going to say no because we want you to do it yourselves, then you will have the curator, you have the responsibility and where this has worked in other places, it has worked wonderfully. . . . When you see that we gave . . . [out] more in the $200 donations and had more restorations, I believe you will think that we are doing the right thing. We are helping a great many more by spreading out our interests.

For the rest of Cannon's long tenure as president, the SPA acquired no additional properties. The society instead concentrated on assisting restoration efforts of local groups through grants, loans, advice, and moral support.

Prewar Projects in the Postwar Era

Richmond Hill

Except for Tryon Palace, shelved SPA projects remained stagnant after the war. Much hoped-for federal aid and work relief programs never materialized. In 1948 (and as stated above) Richmond Hill, the SPA's only property, having been neglected since 1942, reemerged as the topic of anxious deliberation. Returning from Blowing Rock to Raleigh in August 1948, Christopher Crittenden stopped to see the house and had to walk a mile to reach it. He was shocked by its deplorable condition and estimated that it would cost twenty thousand dollars (roughly equivalent to $111,200 in 1990) to restore. Doubting that the society could raise that amount, he recommended to Ruth Cannon and the SPA membership that the property be given back to the Yokley family of Mount Airy, which had donated it before the war.

At the 1948 annual meeting Adelaide Fries accepted appointment as chair of the Richmond Hill committee. In June 1949 she reported to Cannon that her committee had yet to recommend a course of action. She was troubled by the ethics of the SPA's returning the property in such a ruinous state, having accepted it as a gift. The seventy-eight-year-old Fries died five months later in November. At the December 1951 annual meeting, Fries's replacement, Cecil Long of Newton, announced that the committee recommended that the property be returned to the donors. After discussion, the membership voted unanimously to return it and to adopt a policy of not owning property. Nevertheless, it took no action to transfer Richmond Hill back to the Yokley family. The house again drifted out of the society members' collective consciousness.

The Adam Spach Rock House

The war had forestalled WPA construction assistance to the Spach project, but with the return of peace, prospects looked promising for reconstructing the eighteenth-century rock house and fort. The project's biggest booster within the SPA, Adelaide Fries, gave an optimistic report at the society's December 1947 board meeting. She said that the title to the Spach House site had been transferred back from the Department of Archives and History to the Wachovia Historical Society. She also announced that funding was available and that restoration of the structure was being planned. Following Fries's death two years later, however, another Spach descendant, a Mrs. Donnell, informed the SPA membership at the December 1949 general meeting that reconstruction would not occur: "Instead of restoring it as it was in the beginning, I think it has recently been decided *to restore it as a ruin,* and at a recent reunion of the family we decided that was better." Apparently, no stabilization of the ruins ever occurred. The site gradually deteriorated into archaeological remains in the form of a cellar hole and stone rubble. The Wachovia Historical Society still owns the property.

The Hezekiah Alexander House

In 1940 the SPA sought to acquire the Hezekiah Alexander House, but by its annual meeting of 1942 the society had backed away from acquisition and supported efforts to turn the house and land into a state or local park. The last report during the war was that the house had been donated in 1943 to the Methodist Church.

SPA files from the Cannon years reveal little about the Alexander House except that it was the subject of a two hundred-dollar grant in May 1949. In August 1949 the *Charlotte Observer* reported that the house was "being restored by the Mecklenburg County D.A.R. with Mrs. E. C. Marshall as chairman of the restoration committee." The house was definitely out of the danger zone by that time. The Hezekiah Alexander Foundation, which leases the property from the United Methodist Church, presently maintains and operates the property as a house museum.

Tryon Palace

The establishment in 1944 of the Maude Moore Latham Foundation and the state's acceptance of Mrs. Latham's challenge to acquire the site of Tryon Palace for reconstruction and restoration all but assured the property's development. The following year the General Assembly authorized $150,000 for acquisition of the palace site, despite the spirited opposition of businesses and property owners in the project area, who called the proposed reconstruction "a pig in a poke." The legislature also established the Tryon Palace Commission to oversee the reconstruction and management of the resulting facility.

Momentum increased in 1949 when the General Assembly voted an additional $77,000 for acquisition of real estate. In the same year, May Gordon Kellenberger announced at the SPA annual meeting that her mother, Maude Moore Latham, was making an additional donation of $121,000 worth of rare English eighteenth-century furniture to the state for Tryon Palace. According to Ruth Cannon, the collection was "marvelous, beyond words." In 1951 the palace commission hired William Graves Perry of Boston to be the architect for Tryon Palace. Perry was highly qualified, having been the principal architect of the Williamsburg restoration.

The SPA stayed closely involved with the Tryon Palace reconstruction. Under the terms of the Latham trust, the SPA and the North Carolina Department of Archives and History had to approve in writing the plans and specifications of the project. By the summer of 1950 the state's Department of Conservation and Development was busily buying up property for the palace, and state attorney general Harry McMullan worked with Gertrude Carraway to obtain the SPA's review and approval of the plans at its August board meeting in Blowing Rock.

Ruth Cannon personally raised money for the palace by carrying a contributors book to every meeting she attended. After paying one dollar, donors signed their names in the book. In October 1952 Cannon proudly wrote in the SPA annual meeting announcement that William Graves Perry was the scheduled speaker and joyfully added that work on the palace had "really begun." Two and one-half years later, as her presidency was winding down, she reported to the SPA membership from her sickbed in June 1955 that "the wings of Tryon Palace have been completed and the center section is well underway [sic]." At Ruth Cannon's last meeting as president in 1956, May Gordon Kellenberger set 1958 as the date for opening Tryon Palace to the public.

The Grants Program

From 1940 to 1974, almost all of the state's most important landmarks benefited from a $200 incentive grant from the society, which donated a total of approximately $19,056. During the Cannon years, assisted properties included St. Thomas Church in Bath, the House in the Horseshoe in Moore County, the Oval Ballroom in Fayetteville, and the Charles Brantley Aycock Birthplace in Wayne County. Among the most significant properties receiving aid through the years were the Bellamy Mansion in Wilmington, the Thomas Wolfe Memorial in Asheville, and the eighteenth-century Chowan County Courthouse, the latter two being National Historic Landmarks. In

Original members of the Tryon Palace Commission posed with Gov. R. Gregg Cherry (seated) in the governor's office at the State Capitol in Raleigh on November 6, 1945, during the first meeting of the commission. They included the core of SPA leadership. Shown left to right are state senator D. L. Ward, New Bern; R. Bruce Etheridge, director of the State Department of Conservation and Development; Atty. Gen. Harry McMullan; state senator Carroll P. Rogers, Tryon; Mrs. Paul L. Borden (later Mrs. William E. Stroud), Goldsboro; Mrs. J. Wilbur Bunn, Raleigh; Mrs. James Samuel Mitchener, Raleigh; Mrs. John A. Kellenberger, Greensboro; Mrs. P. P. McCain, Sanatorium; former governor J. Melville Broughton, Raleigh; Mrs. Elizabeth Dillard Reynolds, Winston-Salem; Miss Gertrude S. Carraway (partially obscured), New Bern; Maude Moore Latham, Greensboro; Miss Virginia Horne, Wadesboro; Ruth Coltrane Cannon, Concord; Minnette Chapman Duffy, New Bern; Katherine Pendleton Arrington, Warrenton; Judge R. A. Nunn (representing L. C. Lawrence, mayor of New Bern); Elizabeth Henderson Cotten, Chapel Hill; Judge Richard D. Dixon, Edenton; and Rev. Robert L. Pugh (representing George W. Ipock, chairman of the Craven County Board of Commissioners). Absent were three ex officio members—Christopher Crittenden, director of the State Department of Archives and History; Mayor Lawrence; and Mr. Ipock— and eight of the first members: A. H. Graham, Hillsborough; U.S. senator Clyde R. Hoey; Mrs. William Henry Belk, Charlotte; Mrs. E. L. McKee, Sylva; Mrs. J. Laurence Sprunt, Wilmington; Mrs. Andrew Burnet Stoney, Morganton; S. Clay Williams, Winston-Salem; and Dr. Fred Hanes, Durham. Photograph courtesy Tryon Palace Historic Sites & Gardens.

In 1949 Maude Moore Latham donated furnishings valued at $121,000 to the state for Tryon Palace. At the 1949 SPA annual meeting, May Gordon Latham Kellenberger presented the gift on behalf of her mother to George Ross, director of the State Department of Conservation and Development. Also pictured are (*left to right*) Gertrude S. Carraway, John A. Kellenberger, Mrs. Roland McClamroch, Roland Mumford, and Ruth Coltrane Cannon. Clipping from *Raleigh Times*, December 1, 1949, SPA Records, State Archives.

In 1955 Ruth Cannon jubilantly reported to the SPA membership that "the wings of Tryon Palace have been completed and the center section is well underway [*sic*]." Photograph courtesy Tryon Palace Historic Sites & Gardens.

TOP: A 1951 SPA grant assisted the restoration of the 1784 Salem Tavern at Old Salem. The photograph shows the building in 1956. CENTER: A 1955 SPA grant assisted the restoration of the ca. 1818 Oval Ballroom in Fayetteville. BOTTOM: A March 1956 SPA grant was earmarked for the grand colonnaded Bellamy Mansion, completed in Wilmington on the eve of the Civil War. This view of the mansion is from 1953. Photograph at center by Tim Buchman from Catherine W. Bishir, *North Carolina Architecture* (Chapel Hill: University of North Carolina Press, 1990), reproduced by permission and supplied courtesy Preservation North Carolina.

an early but unusual grant for documentary preservation, the SPA in 1948 donated one thousand dollars to assist the State Department of Archives and History in the purchase of the Carolina Charter of 1663 from a dealer in England for ten thousand dollars. The society discouraged grants for cemeteries and made them to groups, not individuals.

The manner of awarding grants was not consistent during the Cannon presidency. Although the board of directors and the membership discussed grants and voted on them at annual meetings, the president, acting alone, personally approved many others. There were no formal application process and criteria. Grant awards reflected the personal subjectivity of Cannon and her colleagues; yet, by and large, their judgments were sound, and the vast number of grants went to well-administered projects involving significant properties.

Under such a system there were bound to be a few unusual, if not questionable, awards. In December 1951 Cannon's guest of honor at the 1950 Blowing Rock tea, Sir Evelyn Wrench, founder of the English-Speaking Union, requested that the SPA make a two hundred-dollar grant for the repair of St. George's Church, Gravesend, near London. According to tradition, Pocahontas is buried there. Cannon, who was then head of the Roanoke Island Historical Association, instructed Branch to make the grant on the basis that "this is a good contact with England for our Elizabethan Garden." In another instance Cannon directed that funds be sent to aid an outdoor drama dealing

A 1948 SPA grant in the amount of one thousand dollars to the State Department of Archives and History assisted in the acquisition of the Carolina Charter of 1663. It was the largest grant made by the SPA outside of the revolving fund.

with the Battle of Kings Mountain. In short, the grants were not always directed toward sites important in North Carolina history or to historic preservation per se.

On balance, the SPA performed a critical service in the postwar years as the state's only reliable source of preservation grants. The awards gave valuable recognition and encouragement. In December 1952 Edenton's Penelope Barker Association had depleted its funds. Upon receiving a two hundred-dollar grant within eight days of requesting it, Mrs. J. H. Conger, secretary of the association, sent a letter of gratitude to Mary Emma Branch in which she remarked: "The house being in such poor condition and the cost of building being so high, we had become somewhat discouraged with the tremendous task that we had undertaken. Your gift however gave us a much needed boost in morale."

Beginning in 1955, the state made additional grant assistance for North Carolina preservation projects available on an annual basis. A legislative act (drafted by staffs of the Department of Archives and History and the Department of Conservation and Development) authorizing a state Historic Sites Commission preceded the grants. The measure probably arose from a legislative study committee urged by Crittenden in February 1949. Pursuant to the act, the General Assembly created a Historic Sites Commission in 1953 to develop criteria for state grants to local historic projects.

Nevertheless, state grants did not flow until the General Assembly reorganized state government in 1955. In addition to transferring the state's historic sites to the then newly created Historic Sites Division of the Department of Archives and History, the 1955 legislature established a grants-in-aid program of special appropriations for the restoration of non-state-owned property. Almost all of the first recipients included such SPA-assisted properties as Hope Plantation (home of early nineteenth-century governor David Stone) in Bertie County; Bentonville Battleground; the House in the Horseshoe in Moore County; the Penelope Barker House in Edenton; and Historic Halifax, which the state acquired in 1965.

In addition to the properties mentioned above, the Department of Archives and History provided state aid in 1955 for the Bunker Hill Covered Bridge in Catawba County. Yet, the introduction of state grants by no means obviated the need for the SPA grants program in following years. The society's incentives grants—with no criteria, no cumbersome procedure, and a turn-around time of mere days between application and receipt of funds—continued to play an important role. Moreover, the SPA grants were not inconsiderable: in the early 1950s two hundred dollars was equivalent to one thousand dollars in 1990 purchasing power.

Although the legislation that established the state grants program did not come from the SPA, Crittenden had credited the SPA in 1949 with generally arousing interest in legislative action for preserving historic sites and buildings in North Carolina. In addition, key SPA members played important individual roles in the 1953 state Historic Sites Commission, appointed by Gov. William B. Umstead. Future SPA president (in 1956) James A. Stenhouse of Charlotte was appointed chairman of the commission. SPA board member (and also future president) Elizabeth Stevenson Ives of Southern Pines served as a commission member.

In 1954 Ruth Cannon looked back with satisfaction at the performance of the SPA grants program. In her April report to the membership she listed forty projects assisted by society grants since 1940. Rhetorically refuting claims that she was overly enthusiastic and wore rose-colored glasses, Cannon pointed to the list of projects, saying that even she could not "exaggerate the moving enthusiasm over the staggering facts of the 'Spade work that has been done' and the overwhelming joy in the 'Fruition that seems to lie just ahead.'"

The 1948 Restoration Revolving Fund: "I do want us to do the most good for restoration with our money"

Complementing the grants program was an innovative revolving loan fund established in 1948. It was probably the first such fund in America. During the 1947 annual meeting, Ruth Cannon proposed that the fund be created and that loans be made from it at a small rate of interest to "organizations planning to secure and care for historic sites or buildings." Her idea was adopted with a modification urged by Adelaide Fries that funds "be made available only to local groups which had already started a project, and where the local people themselves had made a contribution."

The fund was started with $6,000 from the general SPA treasury (approximately $33,400 in 1990 dollars) in July 1948 and was generally maintained at $5,000. It was kept in the Cabarrus Bank, Concord, with the bank's president (and Ruth Cannon's husband), Charles A. Cannon, serving as its custodian and manager. Total loans and grants from the SPA revolving fund eventually amounted to $28,700 (approximately $139,000 in 1990 dollars).

Loan payments were plowed back into the fund in order to "revolve" to other projects. Charles Cannon said in a November 1955 letter to SPA vice-president Inglis Fletcher that a true revolving fund would not make loans but would be directly involved in real estate transactions with the sale proceeds revolving back to the fund. In any case, Ruth Cannon wanted the society "to do [with the fund] the most good for restoration with our money." Certainly, preservation loans provided a critical service for cash-starved nonprofit groups in North Carolina working to save historic structures.

Implementation of the revolving fund came in 1949 with a loan in the amount of $2,500 at 2 percent interest to the Edenton Tea Party Chapter of the DAR, which acquired the James Iredell House for $15,000. The New Bern Historical Society Foundation received a loan in 1954 in the amount of $2,500 for the restoration of the Attmore-Oliver House, the oldest section of which dates from between 1790 and 1800.

In his November 1955 letter to Inglis Fletcher, Charles Cannon additionally reported a $2,500 loan to the Moore County Historical Association for the purchase of the ca. 1770 Philip Alston House, otherwise known as the House in the Horseshoe. Cannon also listed revolving fund grants for which it had "no notes or reason to expect any repayments." Those nonrecoverable grants from the revolving fund clearly reflected the dominant interests of Ruth Cannon and included fund allotments to the Roanoke Island Historical Association for remodeling a stage setting and for the "Elizabethan Garden projects." Charles Cannon stated that the society put a total of $8,500 into the SPA fund. Of that amount, $6,097.41 was left, $5,000 of which was in the form of notes of $2,500 each from the Moore County Historical Association and the New Bern Historical Association, leaving $1,097.41 in cash. Because of the depletion of the fund balance, Ruth Cannon felt that the fund should not be publicized. In the cautionary words of her husband to Inglis Fletcher, "we have no desire to stir up requests for loans."

The first loan from the SPA revolving fund was made in 1949 to the Edenton Tea Party Chapter of the Daughters of the American Revolution for the restoration of the Iredell House, shown here as it appeared in 1905.

Preservation Battles

True to its name and the ideals of its founders, the SPA and its members tried to stem the tide of demolition that swept the state and nation amid the renewed prosperity that followed years of economic depression and war. Of the many preservation battles that occurred during the Cannon years, some of the most significant occurred in North Carolina's oldest and most historic communities.

Edenton

In June 1945 the historic character of the old colonial city of Edenton received a double threat. The Chowan County commissioners planned to raze the county jail, built in 1825 (but then believed to have dated from 1769), and plans for a new Belk-Tyler department store threatened the eighteenth-century Penelope Barker House. SPA First District vice-president and superior court judge Richard Dillard Dixon joined forces with fellow Edenton residents Penelope S. McMullan, Margaret S. Davis, and Inglis Fletcher to fight the demolitions.

On June 21, 1945, Dixon notified Christopher Crittenden that an immediate crisis was averted. The county commissioners deferred building a new jail to the next fiscal year. Dixon also received a promise from W. H. Belk in Charlotte to preserve the Barker House. At Ruth Cannon's suggestion, the SPA formed a committee in August, with

Dixon as chairman and Fletcher and Davis as members, to study the Edenton situation and make long-term recommendations to the SPA. In May 1946 Inglis Fletcher and her husband, Jack, reported to Ruth Cannon that the Penelope Barker House would be permanently preserved on a long-term basis by moving it to another site for use as an antiques shop. With the immediate danger to the Barker House and the jail removed, the Dixon committee ceased activities without making any recommendations. (Also in 1946, Dixon left for Nuremberg, Germany, where he served as a war-crimes trial judge until 1948.)

Fortunately, serious threats to either structure never reappeared. The Barker House did not become an antiques shop and remained on its original Broad Street site until 1952. Haywood Phthisic then purchased it and offered it to the community on condition that it be removed. Three Edenton civic organizations—the Business and Professional Women's Club, the Junior Chamber of Commerce, and the Women's Club—raised the funds necessary to move the structure to a picturesque location on a spit of land extending into Albemarle Sound. The SPA assisted by donating two hundred dollars to help with restoration after the move. In 1956 the civic clubs formed the Barker House Association and used the house for their meetings and as a community building.

Historic Edenton, Inc. (an arm of the Edenton Historical Commission), opened a visitor center in the Barker House in the mid-1960s and in 1968 inaugurated a tour program that operated from the house. From the 1970s to 1992 the North Carolina Division of Archives and History managed the visitor center in the Barker House and the Edenton tour program in exchange for office space. In 1992 the state completed

In 1945 Edenton members of the SPA acted to save the eighteenth-century Penelope Barker House from possible demolition for a department store. This photograph of the Barker House on its original site probably dates from the late nineteenth century.

its own visitor facility. The Edenton Historical Commission is presently preparing the Barker House for use again as a community building.

Hillsborough

A less satisfactory conclusion occurred in Hillsborough in attempts to save the Nash-Kollock School from demolition in the late 1940s. The frame school complex consisted primarily of an eighteenth-century one-story east wing believed to be the oldest structure in the town and a two-story west section added in 1817. (Original ownership of the east wing was popularly and erroneously attributed to Isaac Edwards, secretary to Gov. William Tryon; the actual owner of the entire house, however, was Frederick Nash, chief justice of the North Carolina Supreme Court from 1852 to 1858, who made the property his home for fifty years.) Soon after Nash's death his daughters Maria and Sally Nash and their cousin, Sarah Kollock, converted the building into a prestigious boarding school for young women and operated it until 1890.

In 1940 SPA member Jessie G. Parker moved to Hillsborough and was captivated by the history of the vacant and deteriorating structure. She soon launched an all-out campaign to save it. Parker's objective was for the SPA to acquire the school and to use it as a community center. Accordingly, she urged establishment of an Orange County SPA chapter to oversee the property. SPA leaders rallied to Parker's support.

The Nash-Kollock School (shown with its students about 1875) in Hillsborough operated from 1858 to 1890 as a prestigious boarding school for young women. Photograph courtesy Historic Hillsborough Commission.

Through Christopher Crittenden, the SPA in October 1945 offered to accept title to the endangered school building. At the same time, in a speech before the Hillsborough PTA, Ruth Cannon urged the formation of a local chapter and adoption of Parker's plan.

Sadly, Parker's sense of urgency was not widely shared locally. Ann Strudwick Nash, member of the prominent Nash family, had rebuffed Parker's 1944 request for a public statement in support of "restoring and preserving the old school building as an example of the architecture, life, and teaching of its day." Against the backdrop of World War II, Nash coolly replied that she thought money would be better expended for war relief than for historic preservation.

Despite such setbacks, Parker's campaign gained enough momentum that by October 1946 she was able to offer the property owner, Henry S. Hogan, one thousand dollars in cash as an initial installment. Parker's hopes were soon dashed, however, by a group of Orange County citizens seeking a site for a farm cooperative warehouse and store. Control of the old school building and its spacious grounds fell into the hands of former lieutenant governor (1933-1937) Alexander H. "Sandy" Graham, scion of a prominent Hillsborough family and member of the first Tryon Palace Commission. Graham removed the building's priceless woodwork and arranged for the building and land to be sold—only ten days after Parker's offer—to the Durham Farmers Mutual Exchange cooperative.

In January 1947 Parker, sleepless from worry over the farm cooperative's determination to demolish the building, made a frantic and impassioned appeal for aid from the SPA. In her frustration she decried the lack of state laws to protect historic houses from destruction.

Society records give no indication of a response. The organization's shift to a policy of not accepting property would have weakened its negotiating power, but probably no action could have saved the landmark in the face of a determined property owner. Many years passed before Hillsborough established a local preservation commission. The Farmers Exchange demolished the Nash-Kollock School building in February 1947 and erected in its place a nondescript cinder block warehouse. Graham installed the structure's exquisite woodwork in his 1898 Georgian Revival house, Montrose, on the outskirts of Hillsborough. Ironically, in 1964 Ann Strudwick Nash published *Ladies in the Making*, a lovingly written history of the Nash-Kollock School, which she had attended.

The Durham Farmers Mutual Exchange demolished the Nash-Kollock School in February 1947 despite plans advanced by SPA member Jessie G. Parker to use the complex adaptively as a community center. Photograph by Eleanor Bell; reproduced courtesy Historic Hillsborough Commission.

In a few people, at least, the demolition elicited an intense and extended sense of loss. Visiting the site soon after the razing, May Gordon Kellenberger, SPA district vice-president, experienced an "indescribable sadness" and lamented the "great loss to the state." With nearly twenty years of hindsight, Ann Strudwick Nash in *Ladies in the Making* eloquently praised Jessie G. Parker for her "valiant fight" and acknowledged the missed "prospect for a rich contribution to the cultural life of historic Hillsborough. . . ."

Advocacy for Governmental Planning and Protection

During the Cannon years, the SPA and its members urged local and state government to preserve and protect historic buildings under their jurisdiction and control. In 1947 Cannon forcefully spoke out on behalf of the SPA against a plan by a legislative study committee to alter the classic Greek Revival exterior of the State Capitol. The radical proposal called for adding massive new wings to the existing building and caused such an outcry that the plan was dropped. At its annual meeting of 1948 the SPA passed resolutions praising the State Department of Conservation and Development for preserving Fort Macon and beseeching the mayor and city council of Wilmington to save the Greek Revival-style Thalian Hall from destruction.

In the late 1940s, the society gradually turned from its emphasis on single-site landmark preservation to a realization of the need for comprehensive architectural surveys and governmental planning controls as a means of preserving historic resources. Jessie G. Parker, the embattled Hillsborough preservationist and SPA member who in 1947 fought to save the Nash-Kollock House, that same year called for a statewide law to prohibit the destruction of houses more than one hundred years old. At the 1947 SPA annual board meeting, vice-president Inglis Fletcher deplored the continued destruction of the state's historic buildings. At her urging and upon the motion of Christopher Crittenden, the SPA resolved "to present a request to the Department of Conservation and Development that they make a survey of old buildings, and that the state legislature be asked to place some restrictions on indiscriminate destruction of these landmarks of history."

Fletcher, an Illinois native with Tar Heel roots, was well traveled by the time she moved to North Carolina from California in 1944. From 1940 to 1964 she produced a series of twelve historical novels based on North Carolina's colonial and Revolutionary War-era history. She had seen much of the world, and perhaps her travels gave her more of an experimental frame of mind when it came to saving historic properties. In October 1947 Fletcher expressed to Ruth Cannon the hope that a qualified state board of restoration architects might be established "to pass upon plans for any alteration of any building that antedates 1847 (100 years). . . ." Fletcher felt that it was "no use in trying to treat these depredations locally" and that it would "take statewide movement to have any effect on local authorities." She concluded that Americans needed to follow European models of architectural review.

The following year, the SPA established a committee (with a budget of two hundred dollars) comprised of Fay Webb Gardner (chair), Estelle Smith, and Susan Graham Erwin Ervin (widow of Congressman Joseph Wilson Ervin). The society

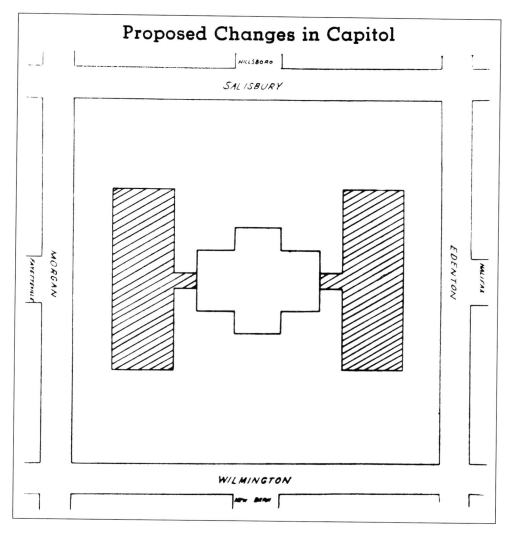

Proposed Changes in Capitol

In 1947 the SPA vigorously opposed plans by the state to expand and modernize the North Carolina Capitol. Proposed additions to the Capitol in the form of north and south wings are represented here. Clipping from *News and Observer*, January 14, 1947, SPA Records, State Archives.

charged the Gardner committee with asking the General Assembly to create "safeguards against the indiscriminate destruction of old landmarks." In January 1949, through the assistance of Sir Raymond Streat and a Mr. Wilks, the legal adviser for the Manchester Cotton Board, the committee obtained copies of English preservation statutes. In February, Ronald F. Lee of the National Park Service sent Susan Graham Ervin a summary of the law of historic preservation in the United States. Concerned over a possible proliferation of piecemeal proposals being introduced in the legislature, Crittenden suggested to interested state senators and to Susan Ervin that a legislative study committee on historic preservation be appointed to prepare a report for the 1951 General Assembly.

As mentioned above, the combination of those initiatives undoubtedly helped to achieve an expanded role in 1955 for the State Department of Archives and History in operating a new state grants program, in administering state historic sites, and in providing advisory assistance to the public in historic preservation projects. Nevertheless, comprehensive state planning and protection laws for historic preservation were not enacted until the early 1970s.

Culture Week

At the beginning of the sixth year of the presidency of Ruth Cannon, page one of the December 1, 1950, Raleigh *News and Observer* proclaimed: "Crusaders for the glory of North Carolina's proud past made their annual pilgrimage to the Sir Walter Hotel here yesterday. Led by their determined but jolly president, Mrs. Charles A. Cannon of Concord, the mostly feminine membership of the North Carolina Society for the Preservation of Antiquities stormed the city in the second day of the current culture siege."

The decades of the 1940s through the 1960s were the heyday of "Culture Week," during which the members of all the state's literary, arts, and historical groups converged in early December at Raleigh's Sir Walter Hotel. There, from Wednesday through Friday, they held their annual meetings, with each organization having its own special day. Thursday was set aside for the SPA. In the morning, the society held a business meeting, during which representatives from local preservation organizations gave progress reports. In the afternoon a luncheon, featuring a speaker, took place. In the late afternoon, SPA members enjoyed tea and a reception at the Executive Mansion with all of the other Culture Week participants. In the evening the society held its general meeting, which included presentation of Cannon Cup awards and a combination of activities that frequently included special speakers and entertainment such as historical skits and music. Beginning in the late 1940s, the SPA concluded its full day of activity with a reception about ten o'clock in the evening.

By 1950 restoration activity had increased throughout the state to the point that reports were crowding the agenda timetable. In ordering the membership to limit presentations to one minute, Ruth Cannon added in her inimitable way that "all must be prepared to rave briefly but to hand in full reports. . . ."

Culture Week and the programs of the SPA were intellectual as well as social affairs. The morning business meeting, the noon luncheon, and the evening annual session all featured experts who presented lectures on a wide variety of topics on history, architecture, and historic preservation. Speakers included nationally known figures in historic preservation such as Kenneth Chorley (1941), president of Colonial Williamsburg; Ronald F. Lee (1948), chief historian of the National Park Service; and Richard H. Howland (1958), president of the National Trust for Historic Preservation.

In April 1994 Dr. H. G. Jones (who succeeded Christopher Crittenden in 1968 as director of the Department of Archives and History) observed that a transcendent benefit of Culture Week was that at least one time each year the state's social and political elite sat through hours of learned papers and cultural progams, absorbing uplifting information. Sometimes the state's senior political figures themselves made presentations. In 1944 Gov. J. Melville Broughton spoke to the SPA membership on

The North Carolina Society
FOR THE
Preservation of Antiquities, Incorporated
"HER HERITAGE"

Number Life Members 330

Number Annual Members 640

Dear Wonderful Members:

A touch of glory for us all lies in the marvelous awakening in North Carolina to the preservation of our Heritage.

The inevitable consequence of elation - backed up by works - is, as you saw in our spring letter, the wonderful list of places that we have helped by an initial donation or loan: Tryon Palace, Edenton, Old Salem, Bath, Halifax, et cetera, et cetera. Funds for this cooperation come from memberships so be sure yours are paid up and bring in other members. Get out our list and rejoice. Yet, there are great numbers besides in which just our enthusiasm is playing a moving part. This list will be sent you on request.

Our morning meeting at 10:00 A. M. at the Hotel Sir Walter, December 2, 1954, will be given over to a short business session, election of officers, and to hearing members tell of their pet projects. Mr. James Stenhouse, Chairman Historic Sites, will speak on the preservation of St. Thomas Church in Bath and of the Alston House in the Horse Shoe in Moore County. As last year, slides will be shown of places being restored in North Carolina. Come and marvel at our treasures. Dr. Crittenden, State Director of Archives and History, tells us they can show many more this year. But we will stop for lunch!

Make reservations early for our Luncheon ($2.50 per plate) at 1:00 P. M. in the Cafe Garden of the Sir Walter. The program will center around the grand plans for the preservation of the town of Halifax. A special treat will be hearing Chancellor Robert House discuss the Halifax Resolves, April 4, 1775. "Liberty is not inherited - one must Work, Fight, - and there are those who have Died - for It." We hope also to have Senator Sam Ervin speak to us.

In the afternoon we will be the guests of Governor and Mrs. Umstead at a Tea at the Governor's Mansion.

Our night meeting will be at 8:00 in the Ball Room of the Hotel Sir Walter. At this meeting the president will recognize the new life members, and Paul Green will present the Charles A. Cannon Awards. The program, in charge of Miss Gertrude Weil, will be on the restoration of the home of our great Public Schools Governor, Charles Brantley Aycock, in Wayne County. At the reception immediately following the meeting, the officers and life members of the Society will receive.

"In God We Trust."

Yours for North Carolina,

Ruth Coltrane Cannon

Ruth Coltrane Cannon, (Mrs. Charles A.)

October 15, 1954

"To Preserve and Revere our past is to insure our future"

Ruth Cannon filled her communications to the SPA membership with buoyant optimism and memorable phrases. Her October 1954 letter announced the SPA program for Culture Week. Letter from SPA Records, State Archives.

the state's interest in the restoration of Tryon Palace, and at the same session former governor J. C. B. Ehringhaus delivered a talk titled "Ancient Albemarle." In 1946 former ambassador Josephus Daniels presented a program on Joseph Hewes, a North Carolina signer of the Declaration of Independence.

The SPA made a special effort to make the programs more accessible to all of its members. In the early part of Ruth Cannon's presidency, the luncheon was limited to life members, whom she treated. At the suggestion of Mary Emma Branch in 1948, the luncheons were put on a fee basis and opened to the annual members, who Branch hoped would learn more about the society.

Culture Week was "old home week" for North Carolina's elite, who looked forward to seeing old friends and acquaintances during the annual pilgrimage to Raleigh. It was a pageant of a rarefied world. Though engaged in civic causes and public life, upper-class women remained strongly bound to a traditional emphasis on matters of fashion and style. They vied with one another over who wore the most elegant dress and accessories, including the ubiquitous orchid corsage. Cannon was very particular in matters of proper dress and would inspect all the female speakers to assure that hat, gloves, and overall attire were fitting to the occasion. Likewise, male presidents of the society and male Cannon Cup winners knew that they must wear black tie to please "Mrs. Cannon."

The young women of the Department of Archives and History, pressed into service by Christopher Crittenden to help with arrangements, dubbed the handsome and theatrical Katherine Pendleton Arrington "Lady Arrington." Always arriving late, Arrington would enlist the staff women to help her make final adjustments in her ensemble in the ladies' lounge. Then, ignoring the entreaties of her junior helpers to enter the meeting through the rear door, Arrington would grandly sweep through the most conspicuous entrance for all to see.

At other times of the year the Cannons hosted SPA receptions and formal teas in Blowing Rock and at their eighteenth-century country home, "For Pity's Sake," which they had painstakingly restored in rural Cabarrus County. Those social and fund-raising events attracted many distinguished visitors. This was especially true of the Blowing Rock teas, once cited by the Raleigh *News and Observer* as among "the state's most brilliant social occasions." Over the years, Blowing Rock tea guests included important

In the 1940s and 1950s, North Carolina newspapers gave prominent coverage to Culture Week activities. In 1955 the Raleigh *News and Observer* depicted SPA leaders discussing the society's 1955 program for Culture Week. Shown left to right are Elizabeth Stevenson "Buffie" Ives, Southern Pines; Inglis Fletcher, Edenton; and Mary Emma Branch, Raleigh. Clipping from *News and Observer*, December 2, 1955, SPA Records, State Archives.

Culture Week and SPA programs were intellectual as well as social affairs. In 1950 J. C. Harrington of the National Park Service addressed this assemblage of people at the annual meeting of the SPA in the Virginia Dare Ballroom of the Sir Walter Hotel in Raleigh. Clipping from *Daily Independent* (Kannapolis), SPA Records, State Archives.

politicians, British aristocrats, and Edith Bolling Galt Wilson, wife of Woodrow Wilson. Such gatherings were not entirely social, however, and customarily were preceded by a business meeting of the SPA board.

Crittenden's old fear that the society would appear to be a "woman's organization" was realized—especially so on the occasion when he was mistakenly addressed as "Madam Chairman" at the 1955 annual meeting. The social aspects of the organization were very much associated with women and their then-customary society page activities. Female dominance also extended to the business part of the annual meeting. Aberdeen lawyer J. Talbot Johnson, who attended the 1949 annual meeting, expressed the wish that more men would participate, adding: "I am sure they would profit thereby, and thus relieve the shyness of the few men who do attend."

Much of the society's activities were relegated to the social page, which probably hobbled its credibility in the Darwinian world of real estate, finance, and politics, in which the fate of historic properties was ultimately determined. It was predominantly a woman's organization and suffered from the prejudicial view that women's activities and concerns were not all that important. Yet Culture Week was a significant educational event in which the Tar Heel elite gave common allegiance to the civilizing forces of art, literature, and history.

Mr. and Mrs. Charles A. Cannon

At Home

Monday, the fourth of August

from three until six o'clock

The Summit

Blowing Rock, North Carolina

Mrs. Woodrow Wilson   R.S.V.P.

The Raleigh *News and Observer* termed the SPA teas in Blowing Rock hosted by the Cannons as among "the state's most brilliant social occasions." This card (*top*) served as an invitation to one such event. In 1948 Mrs. Woodrow Wilson headed a list of prominent people who attended the Cannons' SPA Blowing Rock tea. Shown left to right in the newspaper clipping at bottom are Fay Webb Gardner, Shelby; Ruth Coltrane Cannon, Mrs. C. V. Henkel Sr., Statesville; and Mrs. Woodrow Wilson. Clipping from *Blowing Rocket* (Blowing Rock), August 20, 1948, SPA Records, State Archives.

The Cannon Cup Awards

In 1948 Ruth and Charles Cannon established the Cannon Cup Award for achievement in historic preservation. Ruth Cannon insisted that the award be named after her husband, Charles A. Cannon. The Cannon Cup quickly became a coveted honor and an excellent public relations device. Names of award recipients were engraved on a silver bowl displayed in the state history museum (then called the Hall of History). Recipients additionally received individual replicas of a "camp cup" used during the American Revolution by Ruth Cannon's ancestor, Col. Beverly Winslow of Virginia. For years, playwright Paul Green presented the Cannon Cup Award on behalf of the society.

The first recipients of the Charles A. Cannon Award in 1948 posed proudly with Ruth Cannon, donor of the award, in the foreground. Shown left to right are Cora Vaughan Smith, Raleigh, who received the award on behalf of her husband, Charles Lee Smith; Adelaide Fries, Winston-Salem; Christopher Crittenden, Raleigh; Gertrude Carraway, New Bern; Paul Green, Chapel Hill; Maude Moore Latham, Greensboro; Dr. Douglas Rights, Winston-Salem; and Inglis Fletcher, Edenton. Dr. Archibald Henderson of Chapel Hill was absent. Clipping from *News and Observer*, n.d. (but probably November 1948), SPA Records, State Archives.

Although the award was putatively that of the SPA, Ruth Cannon did the selecting. The award was limited to categories of historical research, preservation, and restoration but it often recognized a broader range of achievement that defied definition. Most of the winners included mainstream preservationists such as Christopher Crittenden, Gertrude Carraway, and, posthumously, Joseph Hyde Pratt; however, other recipients were more difficult to pigeonhole, among them movie producer Cecil B. deMille (in 1954) and bandleader Kay Kyser (1956) of Chapel Hill, who, according to SPA news coverage, had worked "with the Roanoke Island Historical Association."

No one objected to Ruth Cannon's dominant voice in the award selections and the idiosyncratic process, inasmuch as the Cannons established and paid for the awards—no one, that is, except McDaniel Lewis. In a polite but persistent manner, Lewis began writing to Mary Emma Branch and Ruth Cannon to suggest that the Cannon Cup Award be opened to a public nomination process with criteria and a selection committee. He also had the temerity to suggest, "as [the SPA's] only living ex-president," that the society generally was operating with insufficient attention to its bylaws or constitution.

Pictured among recipients of the 1952 Cannon Cup is James Alan Stenhouse of Charlotte (*second from left*), who was Ruth Cannon's hand-picked successor as president of the SPA in 1956. Shown left to right are Kermit Hunter, Chapel Hill; Stenhouse; May Gordon Latham Kellenberger and John A. Kellenberger, Greensboro; Ruth Cannon; master of ceremonies Paul Green, Chapel Hill; Miss Virginia Horne, Wadesboro; and an unidentified man (possibly Laurence Sprunt of Wilmington) partially obscured by Miss Horne. Appearing at right in a damaged portion of this photograph (not shown here) are Clara Byrd of Greensboro, a man who appears to be George Ross of Raleigh, and Richard Walser of Raleigh.

At first, neither Branch nor Cannon replied to Lewis's letters. Finally, Lewis evoked a coldly furious blast from Ruth Cannon in June 1956 when he questioned a 1955 Cannon Cup Award to Robert Frazier of Greensboro, Lewis's hometown. Lewis complained that Frazier was "never known to be active in the work of our Society or its objects." Dictating her reply to a nurse, the invalid Cannon pointedly reminded Lewis of the dramatic drop in membership during his presidency and of his missing his second annual meeting as president in 1943. She dismissed his charge of constitutional impropriety by curtly declaring: "I do not have a copy of the Constitution and By-laws." Addressing the Cannon Cup, she defiantly added: "As for the rules and procedure under which the Cannon awards are made, I make them myself and pick the ones I think should have them. As for Mr. Frazier getting a cup, I gave him one because he was good enough to write the history of my father's life."

In a possible effort to palliate or even shame Lewis, she also informed him that he was going to get a cup and that she would be glad to consider any Cannon Cup Award nominations from him. In his reply, Lewis politely declined the award "under the circumstances" and defended his record as SPA president on the basis of the war emergency. He repeated his call for the society to be operated according to its constitution and bylaws and for the Cannon Cup Award program to be administered on the basis of open selection and stated rules of procedure. In words that must have stung, he added that until such procedures were implemented, "The Cannon awards . . . will not rank with other similar awards. One of the recipients told me it was the least valued honor of many this person had received, because there was no well defined method of award published and understood by the public." Ruth Cannon never responded, but Lewis had made his point. Still, no Cannon Cup Award criteria were drafted for another ten years.

Membership: "a permanent nucleus for the society to prosper"

Ruth Cannon emphasized membership development. In the second year of her presidency she told Crittenden of her desire for "a permanent nucleus for the society to prosper and ever to continue." When she took command of the foundering SPA in December 1944, its membership rolls were at a skeletal 86, down from 393 at the end of Colonel Pratt's second term. By January 1946, membership had shown a healthy recovery to 265, with 209 annual members and 56 life members. That recovery was the likely result of Cannon's emphasis on membership development and an increase in SPA activity under her presidency—activity that included the revival of the grants program and the Tryon Palace project. Moreover, Ruth Cannon's social prestige gave SPA membership instant respectability and status. According to Joye E. Jordan, director of the state's division of museums during Cannon's presidency, belonging to the Antiquities Society "became the thing to do."

Under Cannon, membership reached its peak in December 1950 with 270 life and 872 annual members, for a total of 1,142; thereafter, the numbers crept downward to a total of 923 in December 1956, the end of her presidency. Significantly, annual membership had dropped to 575, whereas life membership rose to 338. Since annual memberships were the principal source of SPA income, their relative decline in numbers did not augur well for the society's future financial stability.

Other Projects:
Fundamental Constitutions to the Silver Screen

In 1946 Christopher Crittenden had been among the first to propose creation of a national organization patterned after the English National Trust. His idea came to fruition in 1949 with the formation of the National Trust for Historic Preservation in America. The SPA was a sponsoring organization at the founding of the trust, and Crittenden became a trustee.

Also in 1949 Ruth Cannon, acting in the name of the SPA, acquired an original copy of a 1682 summary (possibly by John Locke) of the 1669 Fundamental Constitutions of Carolina and presented it as a gift to the North Carolina Department of Archives and History. She purchased it for the society for $346.50 from a Philadelphia dealer in rare books and fine art. In 1950 Cannon's interests extended to motion pictures. She unsuccessfully entreated North Carolina native Cecil B. deMille to make a motion picture about the Tar Heel State. DeMille tactfully declined through an assistant, saying that making such a picture was "a privilege he will have to deny himself" because of other production commitments; however, deMille did accept Cannon's invitation to join the SPA, becoming a life member in April 1950. Despite his reluctance to put his home state on film, deMille received a Cannon Cup in 1954.

While President Cannon labored unsuccessfully to have North Carolina immortalized on film, her predecessor and sometime Cannon Cup nemesis McDaniel Lewis labored unsuccessfully to have Col. Joseph Hyde Pratt immortalized on canvas. Lewis never forgot the society's promise to honor the memory of its first president. Nothing had come of the 1944 resolution to establish a memorial, although Cannon had awarded a Cannon Cup to Pratt posthumously in 1949. Given Lewis's view of the Cannon Cup as an empty honor, he no doubt considered it insufficient to satisfy the 1944 resolve.

In late 1955 Lewis moved ahead with a plan to honor the society's first president with an oil portrait for display in a place of honor in some appropriate place such as the state's Hall of History. He consulted with the State Department of Archives and History and the University of North Carolina Library to confirm that no known oil portrait of Colonel Pratt existed. At Lewis's request, Archibald Henderson obtained a photograph from Pratt's widow, Harriet White Peters Pratt, to use as a model for an oil portrait. Henderson also obtained a commitment from Harriet Pratt that both she and her stepson, Dr. Joseph Hyde Pratt Jr., would contribute liberally toward the cost of the painting. But Lewis's efforts soon ran into the strong opposition of Ruth Cannon, who withheld society cooperation and support. Cannon dismissed the plan, declaring that "There would be others we would have to get if we start that." The project then languished. Cannon's irritation with Lewis over his criticism of the Cannon Cup put her in no mood to support any ideas coming from him.

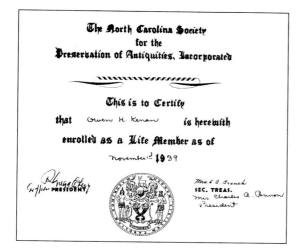

The early emphasis on life memberships eventually sapped the SPA of needed annual income. This life membership certificate was signed by Gov. R. Gregg Cherry in the 1940s for Owen H. Kenan of Kenansville. Certificate from SPA Records, State Archives.

In 1949 the SPA purchased and donated to the State Department of Archives and History a 1682 manuscript summarizing the 1669 Fundamental Constitutions of Carolina. In this news clipping SPA vice-president Inglis Fletcher studies the manuscript. Clipping from *News and Observer*, December 2, 1949, SPA Records, State Archives.

The Avant-garde Meets the Old Guard

McDaniel Lewis was not the only person in North Carolina to displease Ruth Cannon. Henry L. Kamphoefner, described by the Raleigh *News and Observer* as a "tough, cantankerous architect and educator," came from Oklahoma in 1948 to initiate the School of Design at North Carolina State College. Kamphoefner, a nationally recognized proponent of modern architecture, immediately stirred controversy in a speech before the Virginia Chapter of the American Institute of Architects by declaring that Colonial Williamsburg had been "catastrophic" to progress in architecture.

Kamphoefner attended the SPA's 1949 annual meeting in the company of Morley Williams, professor of landscape architecture at the School of Design (and landscape architect for Tryon Palace). He received a frosty reception. Ruth Cannon told Kamphoefner that she was charmed by his wife even though Cannon did not "think much of what . . . [he] was doing." An unidentified male member of the SPA then confronted Kamphoefner and said: "Well, I am surprised to see you here. I thought you were anti-antiquity." In response, Kamphoefner testily refused to shake the man's hand.

At Cannon's prompting, dramatist Paul Green introduced Kamphoefner to the SPA membership; but when Kamphoefner tried to explain his remarks concerning Williamsburg, Cannon cut him off by insisting that it was not necessary for him to do so, adding that "we're going to be good." But soon Cannon had to leave, and in her absence Green insisted that Kamphoefner be heard. The design school dean then explained that he respected the architecture of Colonial Williamsburg, supported its restoration, and backed historic preservation in general. He felt, however, that the Georgian style represented by Williamsburg should not be used as a model for contemporary architecture and that to do so retarded architectural progress. In that sense, Kamphoefner viewed Williamsburg as "catastrophic."

Kamphoefner blamed the press for sensationalizing his remarks out of context. He presented the progressive philosophy of his school while acknowledging the importance of historic preservation to the field of architecture: "Now, we believe in the School of Design that architecture is creative, it is living, it is dynamic. Architecture is moving on, it is progressing, and . . . we can do better. . . . [W]e teach our students to know something about Gothic and classical and Egyptian architecture. We teach them to respect the old architectures of the past in our school, and they learn many lessons. . . . [W]e will do better things because of the things that you are doing, and that's the story I wanted to put over today."

Henry L. Kamphoefner (*right*), shown in May 1950 with Frank Lloyd Wright on the campus of North Carolina State College, underwent a baptism by fire at the 1949 SPA annual meeting. Photograph courtesy Prof. Robert P. Burns, School of Design, North Carolina State University.

Kamphoefner's words had their desired effect. Christopher Crittenden, who chaired the meeting in Cannon's absence, spoke for all in acknowledging the reasonableness of the dean's statement: "It seems to me that there is no real conflict at all. You are working with regard to architectural developments today, and as I understand it, you are not in the least opposed to preserving these old places. You are in favor of the documentation of our architectural and cultural heritage. So are we, and I feel everyone of us will go along with you in what you are interested in today."

Thus Henry Kamphoefner, the brilliant proponent of modern architecture, achieved rapprochement with the architectural traditionalists of the SPA. Cooperation and good relations existed thereafter between the society and the School of Design, which acquired an international reputation under Kamphoefner's twenty-five-year leadership.

"Releasing her responsibilities"

At the age of sixty-three Ruth Cannon suffered a stroke while visiting in California and was confined to her bed for much of 1955 and 1956. Because of her illness, she missed both the 1954 and 1955 annual meetings and made her May 1956 membership report from Warm Springs, Georgia, where she was undergoing muscle therapy. She kept track of SPA activities with the help of her husband, Charles, who handled her correspondence.

In view of Cannon's poor health and her disability, she did not continue as president after 1956. Sensitive to her attachment to the society, Charles Cannon seemed delighted (according to Elizabeth Stevenson Ives) that his wife was "releasing her responsibilities." Cannon hand-picked as her successor Charlotte restoration architect James A. Stenhouse and asked Mary Emma Branch to continue as secretary-treasurer. The selection of Stenhouse pleased Crittenden, who, once again, wanted a man as SPA president. In turn, Stenhouse chose as his vice-president one of his clients, Sally Labouisse of Charlotte, an heiress of the Cameron family and owner of Fairntosh Plantation in Durham County. She was vice-regent for North Carolina of the Mount Vernon Ladies Association of the Union.

At the 1956 annual meeting, Ruth Cannon appeared for the first time since 1953, barely able to speak because of her disability. She was showered with accolades, including those of Gov. Luther Hodges, who came to pay tribute to her. After nomination by Gertrude Carraway and a "spirited oration" by Ives, Cannon was voted honorary president for life amid "a tremendous burst of enthusiasm on the part of the members." Ives, grateful for Cannon's encouragement and friendship over the years, spoke eloquently for all: "I can't think there is a woman anywhere in America who has done in the same gallant, charming, intelligent, loving way what she has done for restoration. . . . [I]n devotion to Ruth Cannon and what she has done for the State, we must keep the work of the society alive and vital." "[S]he has enriched my life, she has enriched my generation; and my gratitude to Ruth Cannon will never end."

Chapter 5:

An Organization of Interest, Not of Wealth, 1956-1970

New Leaders: "they are going to make me President"

James Alan Stenhouse, a forty-six year old Charlotte architect, was Ruth Cannon's hand-picked successor. He brought solid credentials to the SPA presidency. Stenhouse had cofounded the firm of J. N. Pease and Company, one of the largest architectural and engineering firms in the nation. Among his civic and avocational achievements, he had been the first chairman of the North Carolina Historic Sites Commission; founder and first president of the Mecklenburg Historical Association; and, in 1952, winner of a Cannon Cup for *Journeys into History*, a booklet on historic sites in Mecklenburg County.

One of Stenhouse's postwar clients was Cannon Mills. Ruth Cannon shared his interest in history and encouraged him to publish his writings on historic sites. He fondly recalled in later years that he and Cannon used to ride out into the countryside "looking for places in her big limousine with the chauffeur driving. . . ." When Stenhouse was appointed the first chairman of the North Carolina Historic Sites Commission in 1953, he personally inventoried seven hundred historic places throughout the state, traveling more than three thousand miles in the process. He was proud of that effort, considering it to be the first systematic survey of historic sites in North Carolina. As a practicing architect, he designed mostly contemporary structures but out of pure enjoyment also handled historic restorations, claiming in 1955 that he "never made a cent of money from it."

Later comments by Stenhouse revealed ambivalent feelings about the SPA and its leadership during his presidency. Although he considered Ruth Cannon a "dear friend," he felt that she exercised too great a control over the society. He was also disenchanted with the SPA membership, which he viewed as "more like a social club," with members primarily interested in the heritage of their own families.

James Stenhouse served one term as SPA president and declined renomination, as did his vice-president, Sally Labouisse. Stenhouse explained to McDaniel Lewis that he stepped down because he felt he was unable "to get my feet on firm ground in the Society." He cited the demands of his business as the likely cause. During his term, Stenhouse's principal goal was to encourage the compulsory teaching of American history in the public schools.

Elected at the December 1957 annual meeting to succeed Stenhouse and Labouisse were Elizabeth Stevenson Ives (1897-1994) and her vice-president, Edmund H. Harding of Washington, North Carolina. At the urging of Christopher Crittenden, Ives told the assembled SPA members that her brother, Adlai, had called her two nights before from Washington, D.C. When he asked what she was doing, she answered: "I am going to Raleigh Thursday to the Antiquities Society meeting with all the ladies, and they are going to make me President." He responded: "Good, good. I'm glad somebody in the family made it."

Elizabeth Ives had first come to North Carolina in 1920 with her mother to winter at Southern Pines. In 1939 her husband, Ernest Linwood Ives, retired from the U.S. Foreign Service. They settled on the 115-acre Paint Hill Farm near Southern Pines and resided in a historic log house, which they restored. They divided their time between there and the Stevenson family home in Bloomington, Illinois. Ives soon became interested in her North Carolina ancestral roots and active in many historic preservation projects. She was a founder of the Moore County Historical Association, a recipient of the Cannon Cup in 1949, and a member of the special Historic Sites Commission established by the General Assembly in 1953. In 1967 Pres. Lyndon B. Johnson appointed her to the national Advisory Council on Historic Preservation, established by the National Historic Preservation Act of 1966.

Ives lived abroad for many years with her husband, who was posted in Europe, Asia Minor, and South Africa. She was very impressed with the importance of historic architecture in European culture. For many summers she and her husband rented the Villa Caponi in Florence. From her European forays, particularly in Florence, she developed a feeling that structures should be saved for their beauty as well as for their historic value.

Regal of mien and silver of tongue, Ives was viewed as a "powerful person of great influence and a strong will." Anyone who had the misfortune of irritating her soon learned how strong her personality was. In responding to her complaint concerning the engraving of the Cannon Cup for the 1960 annual meeting, a "shocked and distressed" Raleigh jeweler, C. E. Bowman, protested: "never have we received as critical a complaint as yours." In October 1966 Ives vehemently objected to the proposed award of a Cannon Cup to James Craig, a furnishings specialist who displeased her while working with the Historic Bath Commission. In protest, she wrote to awards chair Alice Slater C. Guille of Salisbury, threatening to "resign from the

In March 1954 Elizabeth Stevenson Ives, SPA president, 1957-1960, and her brother, Adlai Stevenson, shared a laugh with U.S. senatorial candidate and former governor W. Kerr Scott in the Carthage school gymnasium at a reception sponsored by Moore County Democrats. Shown left to right are Mrs. Ives, Adlai Stevenson, Scott, and an unidentified man.

Antiquities Society" and to make "the statement public that I am resigning." James Craig never received a Cannon Cup.

Yet, Ives was a warm and caring person who made many friends. She gave freely of her time, traveling throughout the state to spur local preservation efforts with wise counsel and inspiring and motivating eloquence. Sometimes she performed volunteer services, as when she served as chair for the Friends of Hope Committee. John E. Tyler II, who spearheaded local efforts to save Hope Plantation, an endangered Bertie County landmark, remembered Ives as "very cosmopolitan" and one of the most interesting women he ever met. Frequently on the move, Ives gave eight speeches in the first four months of 1959. She viewed that activity as a means of boosting membership, which stood at 1,170 in early 1959, the highest ever to that time. Among her new recruits was her brother, Adlai, a life member. Lura Self Tally, who later served the SPA as president, lauded Ives for having "lit the lamps for many projects throughout our State."

Being from outside the state, Ives was sensitive of the need to assure Tar Heel natives of the genuineness of her interest, as well as those of other non-natives such as fellow Illinoisan Inglis Fletcher. At the close of the 1956 annual meeting, she asked all who were not native to North Carolina to raise their hands and declared: "We are all interested in this state, no matter where we were born, and interested in helping to preserve these things." Elizabeth Stevenson Ives served two terms until December 1960. Thereafter, she continued to share a dominant role in SPA affairs with Ruth Cannon and after Cannon's death in 1965 was probably the most influential voice in SPA councils until she stepped down from the board in 1968.

Edmund Hoyt Harding (1890-1970), vice-president for both of Ives's terms, succeeded her as president in December 1960. Harding was from Washington, North Carolina, and was a professional humorist and public speaker. Beginning in the late 1940s with R. Gregg Cherry, each governor designated him "North Carolina's Ambassador of Good Will." Harding's involvement in historic preservation began in 1955 when he became the leader of a movement to preserve historic Bath, North Carolina's oldest town. His talents, humorous and musical, greatly enlivened SPA meetings.

Harding served one term and was succeeded in November 1961 by his vice-president, Lura Cowles Self Tally of Fayetteville. Tally, a native of Raleigh, was a public school teacher and guidance counselor. Her husband (whom she later divorced) was Joseph O. Tally Jr., mayor of Fayetteville from 1949 to 1953. Lura Tally's preservation

In 1966 the Historic Bath Commission presented Edmund Hoyt Harding (SPA president 1960-1961) an award for distinguished service. To Harding's right is Mrs. Fred W. (Emma Neal) Morrison, vice-chair of the Historic Bath Commission.

In December 1963 Lura Self Tally (*left*) and Elizabeth Stevenson Ives admired floral table decorations for Culture Week at the Sir Walter Hotel in Raleigh. Tally was completing a two-year term as SPA president. Photograph courtesy Mrs. Tally.

Daniel M. Paul, SPA president, 1963-1964, carried out his duties during half of his term by long distance from Atlanta, where he served as head of the field office of the U.S. Department of Commerce. This photograph shows Paul as a 1931 graduate of North Carolina State College. Photograph courtesy Special Collections Department, North Carolina State University Libraries.

activities began during her presidency of the Fayetteville Woman's Club when she spearheaded efforts to save the Federal-style "Oval Ballroom," a Fayetteville landmark. Becoming involved with the SPA, she served from 1958 to 1961 as co-chair of the society's Minuteman Committee, a grass-roots network designed to save endangered historic properties throughout the state.

During her two-year presidency, Tally worked with the School of Design at North Carolina State College to initiate a survey of North Carolina's historic buildings. She enriched SPA meetings with references to history and literature. At the 1962 annual meeting she employed the words of Francis Bacon—*Antiquitas Saeculi Juventus Mundi* [the age of the Centuries in the Youth of the World]—to make the point that the task of the SPA was "to preserve some of the best architectural products, historical and artistic, of the youth of our State. . . ." Beginning in 1973, Tally represented Cumberland County for twenty years in the North Carolina General Assembly.

After serving two terms as society vice-president under Tally, Daniel M. Paul (1910-1996), managing director of the North Carolina Chain Store Council, assumed the presidency in December 1963. Paul, a native of Pantego, was a 1931 graduate of North Carolina State College at Raleigh. He subsequently served as agricultural agent for Granville County and then as alumni secretary for his alma mater. Paul, married to Isabel Hoey, daughter of U.S. senator Clyde R. Hoey, was a World War II naval hero of the Pacific theater; he commanded a tanker ship that Japanese planes sank after four days of bombing and strafing.

Paul achieved some minor savings by ordering SPA stationery without the names of officers and board members on the letterhead. He also sought to increase membership by having district vice-presidents solicit members of other cultural organizations. Tall and aloof, Paul served as president for a year, the last six months of which was by long distance from Georgia. He left the chain store council in July 1964, having received an appointment by U.S. secretary of commerce Luther Hodges to head the department's Atlanta field office.

Paul was probably relieved to have his transfer to Georgia remove any possibility of his serving another term. He enjoyed a good working relationship with his successor, Lillian Moore Robinson, whom he highly recommended. And he especially held Carraway and Tally in high esteem. Yet, in a cautionary note to president-to-be Robinson, it was clear that he chafed under the dominating influence of Cannon, Ives, Branch, and other female leaders of the SPA, whom he collectively considered to be "battle axes," requiring "the utmost patience."

Paul's special disdain was reserved for Mary Emma Branch, who was accustomed to operating under the informal direction of Cannon and her circle of socially prominent women, all of whom Branch held in affectionate regard. Paul complained to Robinson that although Branch "is a dedicated soul . . . she is totally irresponsible about anything that does not conform with her ideas." He added that since he had his own office facilities, he "called on Mrs. Branch very rarely."

Dan Paul's vice-president, Lillian Moore Robinson (1906-1991), of Littleton, succeeded him as president in December 1964. Robinson's vice-president was Henry J. MacMillan of Wilmington. Robinson was born in Wellston, Ohio, but was a descendant of the prominent Moore family of the Cape Fear region. After coming to North Carolina in 1926, she taught school in the 1920s and 1930s. When her husband, Horace Palmer Robinson, became an invalid, Robinson assumed the management of his farms and businesses. By the 1960s she was farming in Halifax County and was president of the Littleton Sales Company, a large wholesale distributor of products for area stores. She led preservation efforts in Littleton and spearheaded efforts by the Littleton Woman's Club to restore Person's Ordinary, an eighteenth-century tavern. Under her presidency the SPA initiated a massive membership drive in 1966.

Under Lillian Moore Robinson, SPA president from 1964 to 1967, the society initiated a massive membership drive. This photograph of Robinson dates from 1952. Photograph courtesy Blair R. Beasley.

Robinson's vice-president for her second term was T. (Thomas) Harry Gatton, who later humorously described himself as a "two-mule farm type" from Iredell County; Gatton became president of the SPA in 1967 at the age of forty-nine and served three terms to December 1970. Described as "super smooth, knowing every law in the book, and as one to whom everyone deferred," Gatton had spent ten years in Washington and had served as executive secretary to U.S. senator Sam J. Ervin Jr. In 1960 he succeeded Jesse Helms as executive director of the North Carolina Bankers Association. Gatton's leadership in historical activities began in 1961 with his appointment by President Kennedy to the American Battle Monuments Commission, which oversaw U.S. cemeteries overseas. He served on the commission throughout the 1960s.

Harry Gatton's statewide historical and preservation volunteer work began in earnest in 1965 when he was appointed to the Executive Board of the North Carolina Department of Archives and History. Later in that year Gatton was elected vice-president of the SPA. He came to the attention of the society through his restoration of the historic Farmville Plantation in Iredell County. Mrs. S. R. "Tempie" Prince of Reidsville served as vice-president during Gatton's first two terms, and Virginia Ford Zenke of Greensboro served as vice-president during his 1970 term. While Gatton served as president, he spent most of his time raising funds and attempting to revamp the society's programs to fit new service needs.

Future SPA president T. Harry Gatton met Pres. Franklin D. Roosevelt in December 1938 at the University of North Carolina. Gatton was then secretary of the Carolina Political Union, a student group that had invited Roosevelt to speak at the university. Shown in foreground left to right are Roosevelt; Sam Hobbs, a UNC student from Alabama and member of the political union; and Gatton.

As a favor to Ruth Cannon, Mary Emma Branch had agreed to stay on as SPA secretary-treasurer beyond Cannon's presidency. Following Cannon's death in December 1965, Branch retired in early 1966 after serving twenty years under six presidents. The board sent her a resolution expressing appreciation for her "long and faithful service." She continued to serve in a volunteer capacity, chairing the Governor's Reception Committee for Culture Week in 1967.

Christopher Crittenden viewed Branch's departure as providing the society "a fine opportunity to upgrade and expand its programs." He recommended that Jane A. Holliday of Raleigh be hired to work as part-time secretary-treasurer and that she be directed "to launch immediately an aggressive membership campaign." Crittenden further urged that Holliday be charged with seeking "other ways to develop a broader and more effective program." His expectations of Holliday were reminiscent of the de facto executive directorship of Janie Gosney twenty-five years earlier.

Holliday had a year of college and had worked as a secretary for state geologist Jasper L. Stuckey and for North Carolina State College. Her husband, Joseph, was principal of Needham Broughton High School. In March 1966 the SPA hired Holliday, whom Crittenden had characterized as "a fine and competent new Secretary-Treasurer," on a two-month trial basis. In June the society extended the trial period to the annual meeting in December. Crittenden provided an office and equipment for her in the Archives and History Annex Building on the corner of McDowell and Lane Streets in Raleigh. Holliday's position was generally titled secretary-treasurer, although in keeping with the greater management role reserved for her she was also called the executive secretary.

Jane Holliday efficiently helped to plan and execute membership and fund-raising drives during the Robinson and Gatton years. Yet, as time went on it was clear that her priorities as a homemaker overshadowed her SPA service. In 1968, citing child and family responsibilities, she declined an opportunity provided by Gatton to attend a week-long preservation planning course for preservation professionals at the Institute of Government of the University of North Carolina. She left the SPA in 1969 to devote more time to her family. Upon her departure, Gatton praised her highly, acknowledging his reliance upon her leadership.

T. Harry Gatton, SPA president from 1967 to 1970, strove to improve the society's financial condition and to update the society's programs. He is shown with Gertrude Carraway during Culture Week in 1969.

Barbara Barnes, administrative assistant for the Literary and Historical Association, succeeded Holliday as secretary-treasurer on an acting basis during the summer of 1969. In September, Nancy Adams assumed the secretary-treasurer position on a full-time basis but remained only a short while. Sharon Sandling, a staff member of the Department of Archives and History, served as acting secretary-treasurer in 1970 until she was officially given the position at the December annual meeting. She also served as editor of the SPA's quarterly newsletter *Antiquities*. Sandling also worked for the North Carolina Literary and Historical Association, inasmuch as in April 1970 the board authorized the hiring of a secretary on a shared-time arrangement with "Lit and Hist" on a sixty ("Lit and Hist")-forty (SPA) basis. The two organizations paid the state for the positions.

Holliday's hiring in 1966 was indicative of the close working relationship between the SPA leadership and the North Carolina Department of Archives and History. Out of town for a week, Gatton left the interviewing to Crittenden and historic sites chief William Samuel "Sam" Tarlton. Crittenden also hired Stephanie Swain to work on the SPA membership drive through the summer of 1967, when Holliday was on leave. Sometimes Tarlton himself carried out SPA staff duties in organizing the society's annual meetings.

In 1968 the SPA's founder, longtime adviser, and friend, Christopher Crittenden, retired as director of the Department of Archives and History, having served since 1935. His health was poor, and he was growing weary from the demands of administering what had become a large and complex agency. He told his successor, Dr. Houston Gwynne "H. G." Jones, that he was "tired of the whole bloomin' thing!" Yet, he stayed on as Jones's assistant director and served as a liaison to the legislature and various state commissions. Jones, born in 1924 in Caswell County, had been state archivist since 1956. As a young graduate student going to school on the G.I. Bill, he had worked summers in the late 1940s as editor and reporter for the *Blowing Rocket* of Blowing Rock. He covered SPA events for the newspaper and became a friend of Ruth Cannon.

As Crittenden's successor, Jones became an ex-officio member of the SPA board by virtue of his position. Everyone concerned continued to favor Crittenden's participation on the board. On the motion of Fay Webb Gardner, the SPA honored Crittenden at the December 1968 board meeting by appointing him an advisory member of the board of directors. He died in October 1969, the last of the three original incorporators of the society.

Loans and Grants

SPA loans and grants continued as a major program element during the late 1950s and the 1960s. Receiving assistance were a number of significant and varied properties, among them Hope Plantation in Bertie County, the Montague Building at Mars Hill College (Madison County), Bentonville Battleground (Johnston County), the Cupola House in Edenton, and Blandwood in Greensboro; the latter three properties have since been designated National Historic Landmarks. Grants diminished in frequency, however: from eight in 1950 to one or two each year in the 1960s. Nevertheless, the enduring value of SPA grants remained undiminished, as was amply demonstrated in a 1964 gift in the amount of two hundred dollars to the Beaufort Historical Association. In 1963 SPA president Lura Tally had encouraged association president (and then Beaufort mayor) John D. Costlow to apply for a grant of "seed money" for restoring historic buildings in the heart of the then decaying town that (as Costlow later observed) "time had passed but . . . hurricanes had devastated." The Beaufort group used the money to develop a brochure on its long-term objectives. Serving as a catalyst, the brochure undergirded a successful fund-raising drive for initial acquisition of early buildings. Costlow later credited the single SPA grant as the spark that led to the revitalization of the historic coastal community and the generation of millions of dollars in economic return.

In May 1958 a loan of twenty-five hundred dollars from the SPA revolving fund helped the Beaufort County Historical Society save the eighteenth-century Palmer-Marsh House at Bath. The Bath restorationists were more fortunate than previous borrowers: When the state acquired the Palmer-Marsh property in December 1964, the SPA generously canceled the historical society's debt at the suggestion of Charles Cannon, revolving fund custodian. Cannon made the recommendation because the state could not legally assume the debt. President Dan Paul readily agreed, noting that "this money has nobly accomplished the purpose for which it was appropriated."

In 1958 and 1959 a major infusion into the revolving fund came from Edith Bailey Dent of Southern Pines and Greenwich, Connecticut. Dent's friend, Elizabeth Stevenson Ives, persuaded her to make a gift in the amount of eight thousand dollars to finance a Tar Heel restoration project. The SPA executive committee attempted to steer Dent toward the Bath restoration, but she was more interested in reconstructing the Bennett house near Durham, where in 1865 Gen. Joseph E. Johnston surrendered to Gen. William T. Sherman. Because the Bailey family was involved in the North Carolina textile industry, Dent preferred to assist a site near "a mill village."

Elizabeth Stevenson Ives surveyed the audience before speaking in 1957 at memorial exercises at Bennett Place in Durham. Photograph by Jim Sparks, *Herald-Sun* Papers, Durham.

The reconstruction of the Bennett house and kitchen was completed by December 1960 at a total cost of nearly fourteen thousand dollars. Fortunately, the exact dimensions of the original house had been recorded by Durham architect Raymond Weeks, whose widow donated the plans. Sam Tarlton, historic sites superintendent of the Department of Archives and History, used photographs and existing drawings to develop plans and specifications for the reconstruction. Additionally, SPA Minuteman Committee chair Lura Tally of Fayetteville helped locate old lumber for reuse in the rebuilding. Dent's eight thousand-dollar donation was applied to the reconstruction of the house. An additional gift of five thousand dollars from the heirs of Samuel T. Morgan, who formerly owned the property, complemented Dent's donation; it was applied toward work in the structure's kitchen. (The Morgan heirs also donated the remainder of the thirty-acre site as a state park.)

The highly visible and popular Bennett Place reconstruction was the last project assisted by the SPA revolving fund. After the death in 1965 of Ruth Cannon, Charles A. Cannon did not want to continue as custodian and in July 1966 turned the fund, which then had a balance of $8,710.97, over to the SPA. The society put eight thousand dollars of the fund into a savings bond and the remainder into a savings account. The SPA revolving fund ceased operation.

In the 1950s and 1960s the grants and technical-assistance services of the North Carolina Department of Archives and History, provided by Sam Tarlton and his staff in the Division of Historic Sites, complemented the society's financial-assistance

The reconstruction of the Civil War-era farmhouse of James and Eliza Bennett (originally spelled "Bennitt") as part of Bennett Place State Historic Site, completed in 1960, was the last project assisted by the SPA revolving fund. This photograph of the restored farmhouse dates from 1962.

programs. During that same period, Christopher Crittenden as director and McDaniel Lewis as chairman of the department's Executive Board guided the department. The agency grew from eight employees in 1932 to ninety in December 1962, with a corresponding increase in its biennial budget from $11,315 in the 1934-1935 biennium to $576,714 in the 1962-1963 biennium. In 1962 the North Carolina Department of Archives and History was among the six leading state programs in the nation in the size of its budget and staff.

The beginning of a systematic and professionally managed state grants program in 1955 created an additional source of financial and technical assistance for local projects. The restoration of Person's Ordinary, the eighteenth-century tavern located in Littleton, is illustrative of the value and impact of the expanded assistance program. In April 1957 the SPA gave the project two hundred dollars, which was quickly followed in June by a two thousand-dollar state grant pushed through by legislator John Kerr Jr. The Littleton Woman's Club, sponsor of the restoration, received another two thousand dollars from the state in 1958. In addition, Sam Tarlton, head of the historic sites division of the Department of Archives and History, provided technical assistance to the restoration project.

The SPA and legislative grants enabled the Littleton Woman's Club, led by Lillian Moore Robinson, to complete the exterior restoration and interior plastering. In 1959, with funds exhausted and the project "at a standstill," the SPA gave Robinson's group another two hundred-dollar grant, which the Littleton preservationists agreed to match with the proceeds from a pancake supper. Elizabeth Stevenson Ives explained the additional grant by declaring that the Littleton project "is the kind of thing we ought to do, when we find a serious group of people working so hard." Her confidence was well founded: The Littleton preservationists raised $733 with their pancake supper and the sale of calendars in 1959.

In 1958 the SPA established a special annual grants program through the North Carolina Federation of Women's Clubs for the chapter that accomplished the most for historic preservation. Lura Tally announced the annual award program at the May 1959 federation meeting in Pinehurst. At the June 1961 federation conference the SPA presented its first award of fifty dollars and a certificate of merit to the Woman's Club of Edenton for projects involving removal of paint from the Chowan County Courthouse and production of a promotional film.

The Smith Richardson Foundation of Greensboro greatly expanded available preservation grants in North Carolina from 1965 through 1967 by providing a total of one hundred thousand dollars to be administered by the Department of Archives and History. In announcing the grants at the December 1964 SPA annual meeting, Christopher Crittenden said that they had to be matched and would be awarded according to the axiom "God helps those who help themselves."

In 1966 the state grants program overwhelmed the small preservation staff of the Department of Archives and History, and the department and the state's Historic Sites Advisory Committee declared a moratorium on state grants for 1967 and 1968. SPA grants continued in the interim as the only source for new funding for local projects. Soon the SPA grants program would more closely resemble governmental programs with the adoption of criteria for merit selection. At the December 1970 SPA board meeting, H. G. Jones had noted the lack of formal criteria. Board member Nicholas B. Bragg of Winston-Salem responded by suggesting that a committee be appointed to develop criteria for grant awards and agreed to head it.

Culture Week: "relegated to the . . . back page"

Through the 1950s and 1960s Culture Week continued to serve the SPA as a primary forum for the exchange of information and the dissemination of public education. A high point came in 1958 when the governor's reception was moved to Friday to accommodate attendance by former president Harry S Truman, who, in honor of the 150th anniversary of the birth of Andrew Johnson in Raleigh, spoke on Johnson at the meeting of "Lit and Hist" on that same evening. During the turbulent 1960s, Culture Week began to lose its prominence. In the 1950s it had been an important social event profusely covered on page one by the Raleigh *News and Observer*. But by the late 1960s Culture Week was, in the words of Jack Tyler (SPA president 1970-1972), "relegated to the second paragraph of the back page."

Along with its allied organizations, the society had been stung by a February 4, 1968, *News and Observer* editorial by Jonathan Daniels, who lampooned Culture Week as a "dilapidated circus of culture . . . with the same old ladies and gentlemen . . . inbred, elderly and unexciting." Just two weeks before the editorial appeared, the Culture Week coordinating committee had shown its loyalty to Raleigh by rejecting a Charlotte bid to host the 1968 event as part of that city's bicentennial celebration. Within days of the editorial, an angry Crittenden sent out a mail ballot to members of the coordinating committee, who reversed their previous vote. The site of Culture Week was changed to Charlotte, even though Crittenden had been looking forward to hosting sessions in the auditorium of the newly completed Archives and History/State Library building in Raleigh.

Yet, Jonathan Daniels had told the truth concerning the ages of most participants in the SPA and its sister organizations. Three days before his editorial appeared, the executive committee of the Literary and Historical Association had met to plan its

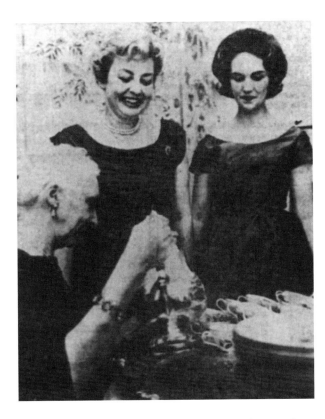

Janet Quinlan Crittenden (*left*), wife of Christopher Crittenden, poured tea at Culture Week in 1962 for Virginia Camp Smith (Mrs. Charles Lee Smith Jr.) and Susan Ehringhaus (*right*). Clipping from *Raleigh Times*, December 6, 1962, SPA Records, State Archives.

Culture Week program. It pinpointed the need to make sessions more interesting, "particularly for people under fifty years of age." Friendly critics at the last meeting had commented that "Lit and Hist" "seemed like a Golden Age Club."

Undoubtedly motivated by Daniels's barbs, Crittenden followed up in March by urging all the Culture Week groups to bring in younger people. Nothing could have pleased the senior stalwarts of the SPA more. Al Honeycutt Jr. of Crittenden's staff remembered years later how the older members rejoiced to see the influx of young men working in the state historic sites program and attending SPA meetings.

Additionally, not all young people found "the same old ladies and gentlemen" unexciting. In the 1960s, E. Frank Stephenson Jr., a young preservation activist in Murfreesboro, was "thrilled" to be in the company of the Culture Week participants, many of whom were well known and accomplished. Stephenson felt that a strong camaraderie existed among those in attendance, and, knowing that he had saved historic buildings, North Carolina's old social elite treated him as an equal. Despite its aging membership and declining appeal, SPA Culture Week programs continued a tradition of fine speakers of national stature that included Walter Muir Whitehill, director of the Boston Aethenaeum (1966); Carlisle H. Humelsine, president of Colonial Williamsburg (1967); and Charles C. Wall, resident director of Mount Vernon (1969).

The Cannon Cup: Reformation and Renewal

After the presidency of Ruth Cannon, the Cannon Cup continued to serve as the society's flagship award. Gradually, rules and a more formal application process were added. Through the late 1950s and the 1960s, McDaniel Lewis had doggedly continued his calls for reforming the Cannon Cup procedures. He contacted each new president that followed Ruth Cannon and urged the adoption of criteria, an open nomination process, and award selection by a committee. Yet, as long as Ruth Cannon was still active, SPA leaders were slow to move in a direction that might offend her.

Lewis motivated President Elizabeth Stevenson Ives enough to raise the issue of award selection before the executive committee at its April 1958 meeting at the home of Ruth Cannon. The cryptic committee meeting minutes reported: "Mrs. Ives inquired whether in the past there had been a committee to select the winners of the Charles A. Cannon awards, and Mrs. Cannon replied that there had not been . . . [any] . . . such committee." No action was taken. In 1958 the number of Cannon Cup Award winners was reduced from six to five. For the sake of economy, Ives convinced the society to establish five as the limit. The prestige of the award continued unabated, with the governor presenting the cups in 1959 and 1962.

By October 1960 rules for the awarding of Cannon Cups supposedly had been adopted. In that month, McDaniel Lewis requested from Ives a copy of the rules and the names of the awards committee. Ives responded within days with the names of the committee, comprised of Ruth Cannon, James Stenhouse, Lillian Robinson, Lura Tally, and Alice Slater Guille of Salisbury. Although Ives did not send a copy of the rules, she added that the committee had decided that awards should be only for restoration and preservation work and not for historical literary work and that in 1961 the number of awards would be reduced from five to four.

The persistent Lewis quickly replied in early November, urging that the membership receive copies of the rules for the Cannon Cup Awards, be informed of the identity of the award committee, and be informed that the society itself had been paying for the awards. Society records contain no copy of a reply to Lewis from President Ives; however, in response to Lewis's criticism, Ruth Cannon decided once more to pay for the cups. After Ruth Cannon's death in 1965, Christopher Crittenden, acting on behalf of the SPA, invited her husband, Charles, to continue to award the cups. Through his personal secretary, T. C. Haywood, Cannon declined, observing that the pervasive identification of the award with his wife made their continuance "inappropriate" in light of her passing.

The leaders of the SPA were not about to let a popular awards program die. They took it over completely and proceeded to reform those elements that had long elicited criticism. In September 1966 the board of directors finally adopted comprehensive "criteria, rules and procedures" for the nomination and selection of award winners. Under the new rules, drafted by Christopher Crittenden, Sam Tarlton, Sally Labouisse, and Gertrude Carraway, the SPA followed the suggestion of Elizabeth Ives and renamed the award the "Ruth Coltrane Cannon Cup Awards." The preamble to the rules candidly (but gingerly) acknowledged that there had not been "clear and generally understood guidelines or procedures for awarding the cups," and that that shortcoming "should now be remedied, especially since Mrs. Charles A. Cannon, who took such a close interest in them and guided the nominations each year, is no longer with us."

Great Houses in the Balance: "Get together and do it yourselves"

During the 1950s and 1960s many grass-roots efforts were undertaken with the encouragement and aid of the SPA. Citizen groups attempted to save, with varying degrees of success, historic places such as the Old Salem Historic District in Winston-Salem; the Calvin Jones House in Wake Forest; the General Gregory House "Fairfield" near Elizabeth City; Hope Plantation (the Gov. David Stone House) in Bertie County; and Little Manor (Mosby Hall) and Person's Ordinary, both in Littleton. Almost all such groups and similar ones throughout the state received SPA grants and a visit and encouragement from the SPA leadership. Representative cases of local efforts that involved the SPA were those of Fairfield near Elizabeth City, Little Manor in Littleton, and Blandwood in Greensboro. In one instance, a historic structure was saved; in the other two, important buildings were lost.

Fairfield (the Gen. Isaac Gregory House), Elizabeth City

In a large field in Camden County and across the Pasquotank River from Elizabeth City stood Fairfield, the stately eighteenth-century Georgian brick mansion of Revolutionary War general Isaac Gregory. During the 1950s local preservationists

Fairfield, the Camden County home of Revolutionary War general Isaac Gregory, was eventually lost. This photograph of the house was made in July 1971.

100

formed the General Isaac Gregory Antiquities Society of the Albemarle to save the house. In 1959 Lura Tally told the SPA membership that Fairfield was the type of fast-disappearing landmark that could otherwise serve as tourist attractions for the state and that "immediate steps must be taken to keep them."

SPA president Edmund Harding visited Fairfield in June 1961 and met with the owners, who offered the property to the society. Although Harding was enthusiastic about the offer, the SPA never accepted title. Shortly after his visit, Harding had Mary Emma Branch send the General Gregory group a grant in the amount of two hundred dollars. By 1964, however, Fairfield was reported to be deteriorating rapidly. The General Gregory Antiquities Society was ultimately unsuccessful in raising sufficient interest and funds. Giving up the effort in 1968, the group returned (with $34.54 interest) the grant it had received from the SPA in 1961. Had the local society been more vigorous, the SPA revolving fund more active, and the state grants program not under a moratorium, perhaps Fairfield (and other Tar Heel landmarks lost at the time) could have been saved.

Little Manor (Mosby Hall), Littleton

Lillian Moore Robinson, who became SPA president in 1964, led efforts in Littleton to save Little Manor, also called Mosby Hall, one of the finest pedimented Federal-style houses in the Roanoke region of North Carolina. The earliest section was built after 1780 by Revolutionary War patriot Thomas Person, and the massive front was added after 1804 by Person's nephew, state senator William Person Little. The house was renowned for its Adamesque detailing. In the 1960s it was not in danger of demolition but was rapidly deteriorating.

In April 1958 the SPA executive committee asked Lillian Robinson and the Littleton Woman's Club to develop suggestions for action. At the December 1958 annual meeting Robinson happily reported that she and her colleagues had persuaded William T. Skinner, the owner of Little Manor, to stabilize the historic mansion by boarding up its windows and repairing the roof. Sometime, probably in the late 1950s, when she was president, Elizabeth Ives had visited the house and Littleton, where she

Little Manor (Mosby Hall), shown here as it appeared in 1954, was one of the finest Federal-style houses in the Roanoke region of North Carolina. SPA presidents Lillian Moore Robinson and Elizabeth Stevenson Ives encouraged its owner to stabilize the deteriorating structure. Nevertheless, the property was eventually lost.

gave a speech. She "charmed and delighted" the locals, according to Skinner, who wrote Ives a full report on his attempts to repair and stabilize Little Manor. After Skinner's death in 1964, however, efforts to save the house stagnated, and the property continued to deteriorate under Skinner's heirs. Because of the architectural significance of Little Manor, the state successfully nominated it for inclusion in the National Register of Historic Places in 1973. Today the structure is a ruin.

Blandwood, Greensboro

In the saving of Blandwood, the 1844 Italian Villa mansion in Greensboro of Gov. John Motley Morehead, the SPA successfully applied its policy of encouraging people to carry out local preservation efforts. Greensboro interior designer Virginia Ford Zenke attended her first SPA meeting during the presidency of Elizabeth Stevenson Ives. Mrs. Zenke hoped to find assistance in preserving Blandwood. With that goal in mind, she asked Ives if the SPA planned to restore the homes of former North Carolina governors. Zenke was surprised when the patrician Ives slapped her on the back and cheerfully exclaimed, "Get together and do it yourselves!"

And that is what Virginia Zenke and her colleagues in Greensboro proceeded to do. Aiding them was an SPA committee appointed by Ives that successfully worked to have the legislature establish the John Motley Morehead Memorial Commission in 1959. Elizabeth Stevenson Ives also worked to find qualified and interested people to serve as members of the commission. Later, in the 1960s, she helped in a personal way by pouring tea at the first major fund-raiser social in the unrestored Blandwood.

Between 1966 and 1968 the Greensboro Preservation Society raised $110,000 for the acquisition of Blandwood. That sum, combined with a HUD grant in the amount of $100,000 to the city of Greensboro, enabled the municipality to purchase Blandwood from Guilford College and donate it to the John Motley Morehead Memorial

By the time of this 1970 photograph, the restoration of Blandwood by the Greensboro Preservation Society was well under way. A 1967 SPA grant assisted the project.

Commission. The Greensboro Preservation Society immediately commenced restoration and carried it through to completion. A grant in the amount of $200 from the SPA, awarded in December 1967, assisted the project. Preservation Greensboro, Inc. (formerly the Greensboro Preservation Society), presently operates Blandwood under a cooperative agreement with the John Motley Morehead Memorial Commission.

Tryon Palace: "a fine house and not a museum"

The dream of reconstructing and restoring Tryon Palace had spurred the formation of the North Carolina Society for the Preservation of Antiquities. With the commitment of wealthy donors and the state, the palace restoration continued apace toward a successful completion and was the premier success story of the SPA. At the 1958 annual meeting May Gordon Latham Kellenberger reported that the furniture was secured, curtains were being hung, and the rooms were completed except for pictures and small objects. The anticipated opening date was spring 1959.

Kellenberger also summarized the philosophy of the Tryon Palace restoration for the SPA membership: "Please remember the restoration is a fine house and not a museum. It has been returned to the fine house and capitol building it was. . . . [T]he restoration should be made to enrich the lives of the people of North Carolina and we have strived to make it come back alive to every North Carolinian and every school child in North Carolina."

The triumphal opening of Tryon Palace occurred over the course of a week beginning April 8, 1959. Kellenberger, chair of the Tryon Palace Commission, was immediately obliged to soothe the feelings of SPA members who were either not invited

The dream of reconstructing and restoring Tryon Palace was finally realized in 1959. Photograph of reconstructed palace courtesy Tryon Palace Historic Sites & Gardens.

or who felt underrecognized at the opening celebration. In a May letter she thanked Elizabeth Stevenson Ives and the SPA for reprinting Marshall De Lancey Haywood's *Governor Tryon of North Carolina* (which was being sold at the palace gift shop) and explained why there was not a "special day" set aside for the SPA. Kellenberger related that the original idea for a special day of recognition for all the groups that helped in the restoration was scrapped as the "the list grew and grew, and we realized that such an event would kill us all—not to mention what it would have done to our treasury!"

Therefore (as she continued to explain), the three "special days" were limited to people and groups associated with state government; the Tryon Palace Commission, New Bern, and that community's Swiss heritage; and the palace's connection with the British government. Interestingly, in addition to the SPA, American patriotic groups such as the Colonial Dames and the DAR were not afforded "special day" treatment. Of course, key people such as Elizabeth Ives and her husband, Ernest, as well as the Cannons, attended the opening. Other SPA leaders such as Christopher Crittenden, Elizabeth Henderson Cotton, Fay Webb Gardner, and Inglis Fletcher were members of the Tryon Palace Commission. McDaniel Lewis attended in his capacity as chairman of the Executive Board of the Department of Archives and History.

Even with the opening of the palace, much remained to be done with the grounds. Landscape architect Morley Williams reported in December 1959 that no evidence of

Gov. Luther H. Hodges spoke at opening ceremonies for the restored Tryon Palace in April 1959. May Gordon Latham Kellenberger is shown on the front row. Photograph courtesy Tryon Palace Historic Sites & Gardens.

a garden had been found. Therefore, a landscape of the period 1760 to 1770 was re-created, and an effort was made to find old plant varieties. By 1964 the grounds and formal gardens were open throughout the year, although they were still in a state of "continuing development."

Equally important to the interpretation of the complex was the quality of its holdings. In 1964 May Gordon Latham Kellenberger considered the palace's rare book collection to be "one of the greatest and most authentic assets of the restoration." In Kellenberger's view the library and its period furniture, paintings, and artifacts gave Tryon Palace great potential as an educational institution. Annual visitation was nearing 140,000 people, with all fifty states and sixty-eight foreign countries represented. The palace had received much publicity, which stood to be increased further by a film highlighting the complex.

In October 1966 Tryon Palace and May Gordon Kellenberger won national recognition among preservationists. At its annual meeting in Philadelphia, the National Trust for Historic Preservation presented its highest honor, the Louise du Pont Crowninshield Award, to Kellenberger for outstanding achievement in historic preservation and interpretation.

Publication of Haywood's
Governor Tryon of North Carolina

As the Tryon Palace restoration neared completion, thoughts turned to generating public interest in the opening. In one effort to achieve that interest, the SPA and the publications committee of the Tryon Palace Commission jointly reprinted Marshall De Lancey Haywood's 1903 volume *Governor William Tryon and His Administration in the Province of North Carolina, 1765-1771*. Although Haywood had written *Governor Tryon* more than a half-century before, Christopher Crittenden felt that the volume was "still timely." The SPA agreed to underwrite the expense of republishing the book, and the Tryon Palace publications committee pledged its best efforts in promoting sales of the reprint. Charles Cannon viewed the publication project as an opportune way to publicize Tryon Palace during the 1959 legislative session.

In April 1958 Cannon, acting on behalf of the SPA, authorized Edwards and Broughton Company of Raleigh to print the new edition for $2,500. The SPA executive committee decided that the book should contain pictures of Maude Moore Latham, Ruth Cannon, John and May Gordon Kellenberger, the interior and exterior of the palace, and the palace garden and that it should also include a foreword or introduction by Elizabeth Stevenson Ives, president of the society.

Ives counted on having the book out by Christmas, but additional suggestions from the Cannons concerning acknowledgments and the content of the foreword dashed that hope. Ives was also surprised to receive a suggested foreword by May Gordon Kellenberger, even though Christopher Crittenden had been assigned to draft a foreword for Ives's signature. Moreover, Ives was loath to make the book a "telling of the whole story of the restoration," believing that Gertrude Carraway (by then the director of Tryon Palace) could do that later in a separate book. Charles Cannon, by contrast, wanted the book to contain at least "a short explanation as to . . . [by whom]

and why the palace was rebuilt," arguing that such an explanation would be apt inasmuch as the book was to appear about the same time the palace opened.

In order to settle what she termed "a confused and troublesome situation," President Ives put the matter before the SPA board of directors at its December 1958 meeting. At the suggestion of Charles Cannon, a compromise was achieved by adding a small appendix containing information on the restoration of the palace. The book was finally published, and one thousand copies were delivered to the Crab Apple Shop in Raleigh, owned by Mrs. Marshall De Lancey Haywood (widow of the author), who assumed responsibility for the distribution and sale of the books.

Governor Tryon of North Carolina sold moderately well, but by 1964 there remained a goodly number of unsold copies. Charles Cannon arranged for the surplus of unsold books to be disposed of by sale to an unnamed source in 1964 at two dollars a copy, which eliminated the existing publication loss of $911.25 to the society. The SPA did not make a profit on the book, but it had not expected to do so. At the 1964 annual meeting May Gordon Kellenberger, chair of the Tryon Palace Commission, expressed her gratitude to the SPA for publishing *Governor Tryon*. In reflecting on the impact of the reprint, she pronounced the "excellent and readable book" a "great contribution, not only to Tryon Palace, but . . . perhaps to the whole country."

Advocacy: "we had done our little bit"

In the post-Cannon years the SPA continued its push toward greater governmental planning controls for the protection of historic resources both in government and private ownership. It also called for state funding of preservation projects. New issues, such as the highway construction boom of the 1950s and America's technological race with the Soviet Union, confronted preservationists and shaped advocacy.

The launching of the Soviet space capsule *Sputnik* generated a cry for greater emphasis in science in American schools. At the December 1957 annual meeting the SPA membership adopted a resolution urging the General Assembly to make the teaching of American and North Carolina history compulsory. Society president James A. Stenhouse called for such action, saying: "we want to make sure that history is not one of the subjects that is dropped when more scientific subjects are taught." At the 1957 annual meeting, members also expressed concern over the impact of construction grants under the Federal-Aid Highway Act of 1956 on North Carolina's historic resources. Thirty-two billion dollars had been appropriated to build forty-one thousand miles of new highway throughout the nation. In regard to North Carolina's participation in the federal program, the SPA membership resolved "That our North Carolina State Highway Commission be requested in planning and constructing highways to make every effort to preserve undamaged our historic sites, together with ample surrounding land in each case, and . . . that our President be authorized and requested to appoint a committee to take this matter up with our Highway Commission and to remain constantly alert during the coming year to take all necessary measures to protect our historic sites from damage or loss as a result of highway construction."

Highway names and beautification also occupied the 1957 SPA agenda. At the urging of James Stenhouse, the society went on record in favor of naming the North

In August 1951 U.S. Highway 29 was opened amid great fanfare, which included a ribbon cutting by Gov. W. Kerr Scott. Post-World War II highway construction spurred by the Federal-Aid Highway Act of 1956 alarmed North Carolina preservationists concerned over the potential impact of new roadways on historic sites and the state's natural beauty.

Carolina segment of a proposed superhighway linking the Midwest to Florida after U.S. presidents Andrew Jackson, James K. Polk, and Andrew Johnson so that, in the words of Stenhouse, "tourists from Ohio will realize for the first time in their lives that there were presidents born in states other than Ohio and Virginia."

SPA stalwart John A. Kellenberger strongly felt the need to keep the proposed highways free of billboard clutter. At the 1957 annual meeting, Kellenberger voiced outrage that one of North Carolina's senators (unnamed by Kellenberger except to say that he was a former governor, which pointed to W. Kerr Scott) was backing a bill to allow billboards on the proposed interstate system. The SPA passed a resolution offered by Kellenberger that billboards despoiled the view of nature and distracted drivers. The resolution, seconded by Ruth Cannon, requested the North Carolina congressional delegation to oppose any legislation "permitting erection of any commercial sign or billboards in and along our national highways."

In 1959 a statewide bond referendum that included funding for historic preservation raised the hopes of SPA members and prompted Christopher Crittenden to ask society members to contact their state legislators. The more than $30 million measure included $250,000 for eleven historic places, many of which had been the subject of past society involvement. The eleven sites prospectively earmarked for state aid were: Alamance Battleground, Alamance County; Town Creek Indian Mound, Montgomery County; the Charles B. Aycock Birthplace, Wayne County; the Zebulon B. Vance Birthplace, Buncombe County; Brunswick Town, Brunswick County; the Palmer-Marsh House, Beaufort County; Fort Fisher, New Hanover County; the Old Stone (Braun) House, Rowan County; Temperance Hall and

Literary Society, Scotland County; the James K. Polk Birthplace, Mecklenburg County; and the Daniel Boone Homeplace, Davidson County.

The bond referendum was narrowly defeated by a statewide vote of 54,613 against to 51,870 in favor. Urban areas tended to favor the bond measure, and rural areas opposed it. Unfortunately for those properties for which legislative requests for grants had been incorporated into the bond bill, defeat of the referendum left project sponsors without hope of any state assistance for the year. The Rowan Museum, for one, had to borrow funds to acquire the 1766 Braun House, a leading example of the state's early Germanic architecture. The imposing stone house was almost sold for a "road house." Fortunately the SPA stepped in to aid the museum that year with a grant in the amount of two hundred dollars.

As they had done since the late 1940s, SPA leaders continued to agitate for comprehensive statewide protection laws for historic properties. In December 1960 the society unanimously approved a resolution offered by Fay Webb Gardner calling upon Terry Sanford, the incoming governor, to initiate a study of landmarks legislation and recommend suitable legislation. Part of the justification Gardner cited for the resolution was that historic attractions boosted North Carolina's third-ranking industry, tourism, by $775 million annually. The society submitted the resolution to Sanford early in 1961. He passed it on to a legislative committee, but no bill was reported out. The SPA resubmitted the resolution to Governor Sanford after its December 1961 annual meeting, again without perceivable results.

At the 1961 meeting Elizabeth Stevenson Ives added her forceful voice for governmental protection of historic properties. In a speech titled "What We Should Be Doing Now," she offered a Cold War perspective on preservation-related legislative goals:

We must know that although . . . it is possible in one moment there is a force that can destroy us all, we must believe we can survive and go on, and we will not be panicked. Every bit of vitality that we put into restoration will pay.

I really believe that the fundamental requirement will be in getting legislation passed. We as individuals in a community can save one little house or perhaps two houses, but unless there is going to be an overall plan and the law is on our side, we can only go so far. The rest of us on our humble projects will have to count on better legislation. We will have to count on our representatives and our particular attention to what has to be done. . . . If the individual does not care and does not occupy himself with these things, the people they put in office will not either. A commission must pass on old buildings before they are touched in Italy, France and Quebec. This is the thing we have to see is done in this great country.

Within two years action commenced on protective legislation for Tar Heel historic properties. The 1963 General Assembly directed its Legislative Council to study the need for historic zoning and to recommend legislation for the 1965 General Assembly. In 1964 momentum increased when the SPA membership approved a resolution drafted by Christopher Crittenden that endorsed a "tentative draft" of a bill prepared by the staff of the Institute of Government at the University of North Carolina. The proposal would have authorized all municipalities to designate historic districts and establish historic district commissions with the authority to review proposals for exterior changes to historic structures and to delay demolitions for sixty days.

The 1965 initiative allowing all local governments to establish and protect historic districts and landmarks did not pass. Although the measure failed, the SPA resolutely adopted a motion by Emma Williamson Hendron of Wilmington at the December 1965 annual meeting "that the Society go on record as favoring historical zoning legislation for the entire State of North Carolina."

The 1965 session had not been without its victories, however. The comprehensive proposal backed by the SPA helped set the stage for an important law enacted that year to protect four of North Carolina's most historic communities. The impetus for the measure came from a legal challenge to Winston-Salem's 1948 ordinance protecting the Old Salem historic district; the ordinance and the district were the first of their kind in the state. The city called upon Robert E. Stipe and Philip P. Green Jr., both of the Institute of Government, to block the suit by drafting a special legislative act authorizing the designation and protection of Old Salem. Stipe and Green modeled the 1965 bill on Arkansas legislation. The municipalities of Edenton, Halifax, and Bath joined Winston-Salem in promoting and being named in the bill. By 1970 five other municipalities had come under the provisions of the enabling legislation.

Thus, North Carolina followed a quickening trend toward legislation authorizing the designation and protection of local preservation districts and landmarks, a means of noncompensatory protection and control first initiated in 1931 in Charleston, South Carolina. Stipe soon drafted bills that would enable all municipal and county governments in the state to enact preservation ordinances; the bills were enacted into law in 1971 and 1973. Likewise 1973 saw the passage of the Archives and History Act, a comprehensive law drafted by Stipe in consultation with H. G. Jones. The act required that properties listed in the National Register of Historic Places be considered in state-level planning and development through mandatory consultation between state agencies and the North Carolina Historical Commission.

The direct involvement of the society in the passage of state preservation laws of the 1970s was secondary to that of the Department of Archives and History and the staff of the Institute of Government at the University of North Carolina. Nevertheless, the advocacy of the SPA was key in raising the awareness of governmental leaders and in making the ultimate passage of preservation protection legislation a reality.

In the late 1960s and early 1970s, the expansion of state preservation protection laws in North Carolina and other states coincided with a strengthening of federal preservation legislation. By 1970 a very limited number of North Carolina properties were being protected by the National Historic Preservation Act of 1966. Under that law, federal agencies undertaking or funding projects in North Carolina were required to consult with the staff of the Department of Archives and History in an effort to avoid or reduce adverse effects of their programs on properties listed in the National Register of Historic Places. Projects assisted by the federal Departments of Housing and Urban Development and Interior, as well as the Appalachian Regional Commission, were "routinely referred to the staff of Archives and History for review and comment concerning their effect upon historic preservation."

As of July 1970, however, only forty-seven North Carolina properties were listed in the National Register, and only 2,210 were listed nationally. Since federal environmental protection for historic preservation was tied to properties listed in the National Register, few properties stood to be protected by the National Historic Preservation Act. That state of affairs, coupled with the small number of communities in North Carolina with landmark controls (nine by 1970), meant that no effective protection yet existed for the vast majority of the state's historical resources.

Nevertheless, governmental involvement was in its ascendancy, and Tar Heel preservationists were heartened and honored when in April 1967 Pres. Lyndon Johnson appointed one of their own, Elizabeth Stevenson Ives, to the President's Advisory Council on Historic Preservation. The National Historic Preservation Act of 1966 established the council to advise the president and Congress on historic preservation and to comment on federal undertakings affecting National Register properties.

In addition to legislation, Ives sought greater SPA influence over the state budgetary process. In November 1961 the SPA board unanimously approved her proposal that incoming president Lura Tally ask the legislative Advisory Budget Commission to notify the SPA "when they were recommending appropriations for historic sites and preservation." Society records do not reveal the results of the proposal.

Advocacy tended to focus on broad-based issues of governmental planning and policy. Yet, there were instances in which the SPA lent its weight to support local preservation causes. In 1959 SPA president Elizabeth Ives sent the Statesville City Council a vigorous protest of that body's plans to destroy a 1789 wall of the historic Fourth Creek Burying Ground as part of a road-building project. (Ives, who had an ancestor buried in the cemetery, had been alerted by SPA district vice-president Marie Long Land.)

In 1966 President Lillian Robinson contacted the president of Liggett and Myers Tobacco Company to urge restoration of the Richard Bennehan House, a late eighteenth-century Federal-style dwelling in Durham County that formed part of the Stagville plantation, which the company owned. Liggett and Myers later donated Stagville to the state as a historic site.

SPA advocacy extended beyond state boundaries. At the urging of history professor Chalmers G. Davidson of Davidson College, the society in 1968 came to the aid of its old role model and rival, the Association for the Preservation of Virginia Antiquities. The APVA opposed plans of the Virginia Department of Highways to encroach upon historic Tuckahoe plantation, where Thomas Jefferson spent part of his boyhood. Galvanized by an article in the *Richmond News-Leader*, Davidson, who believed Tuckahoe to be "one of the great treasures of the South and the Nation," enlisted the "prestige" of the SPA to demonstrate to Virginia officials that interest in preserving the plantation extended beyond the borders of the Old Dominion. Responding with enthusiasm to Davidson's request, SPA president Harry Gatton dispatched a letter of protest to Virginia governor Mills Godwin, with a copy to the chairman of the Virginia State Highway Commission. When the Virginia highway department backed down, Jane Holliday wrote Gatton: "I felt so proud that we had done our little bit. . . ."

The Minuteman Committee: "We let the British win in that skirmish!!"

At the suggestion of Christopher Crittenden, President Ives in 1958 created the Minuteman Committee, a rapid-response network to be on the alert for destructive threats to historic properties and to work with other nonprofit groups and the Department of Archives and History to secure necessary funds and materials to save endangered landmarks. Named cochairs were Lura Self Tally of Fayetteville and Mrs. Ralph P. Hanes of Winston-Salem.

The Minuteman Committee served as the grass-roots network for SPA efforts in support of the 1959 state bond referendum that included funding for historic preservation projects. In reporting at the December 1959 annual meeting on the defeat of the bond issue, Lura Tally lamented: "We let the British win in that skirmish!!" Society records do not reveal whether the committee was instrumental in saving any specific landmarks, although the 1959 and 1961 SPA minutes credit committee members with having sent to the North Carolina State College School of Design lists of buildings, for which measured drawings were to be executed by architectural students. The committee also helped locate old building materials for reuse in projects such as the Bennett Place reconstruction near Durham.

Although the Minuteman Committee sparked some enthusiasm, SPA records do not mention the body after 1961. Perhaps the need for its services was lessened somewhat by the growth of the state's Division of Historic Sites, whose staff helped the SPA keep track of threats to historic properties throughout the state. Moreover, with neither the funds to acquire endangered properties nor protective laws to undergird its advocacy on behalf of historic preservation, the Minuteman Committee offered little more in the way of rapid response than the existing network of SPA district vice-presidents and members.

Policies of the Times: Schools of Hard Ownership

The SPA was a volunteer organization with only a part-time secretary. With limited financial and staff resources, it could not afford to go in all directions at once. Selectivity was necessary for the greatest impact. Accordingly, scarce SPA grant money went only to groups, not individuals, and then only to recipients such as the Littleton Woman's Club that had shown a willingness to raise money and display initiative. Likewise, the Cannon Cup awards were eventually limited to projects or personal achievements that pertained only to preservation.

Through the 1950s and 1960s the consistency of SPA advocacy aided the society's effectiveness. The SPA leadership continually urged the passage of legislation enabling government to designate and protect historic properties. It also supported grass-roots efforts against harmful actions by local governments. Beyond those major areas of concern, continuity was less evident. For example, although one theme of James Stenhouse's presidency was the teaching of history in public schools, succeeding presidents did not raise the issue of school curriculum. Under Ives, in April 1958 members of the SPA executive committee refused to become involved in a campaign to name a highway for Bennehan Cameron (1854-1925), railroad executive and industrialist from Durham County. Their consensus was that "the Society has enough duties and problems without getting into the highway naming business."

Yet, as recently as December 1957, the SPA had called for sections of a proposed north-south interstate highway through the western Piedmont to be named for former presidents of the United States from North Carolina. At the December 1959 annual meeting, the society wisely declined to become involved in a dispute over the moving of a Confederate monument from the Chowan County Courthouse in Edenton. The teaching of history, the naming of highways, and the location of monuments were relevant but peripheral issues that did not greatly affect the society's public standing or impact one way or another.

The SPA maintained its post-World War II centralized organizational structure, which had represented a break with the original Virginia model of organizing and operating through branch chapters. In confirming that policy in April 1958, the executive committee decided to encourage the Littleton group, which was attempting to save Little Manor, to form an independent organization to cooperate with the SPA but not to be a chapter of the society.

The greatest mistake the society made in the 1950s and 1960s was to break with its policy against property ownership. Obviously, examples of direct ownership abounded in other areas of the country, where the practice was effective and useful in saving historic properties. But in the 1940s the SPA had shown itself to be woefully lacking in sufficient financial and operational resources to own and manage property, and there was nothing to indicate greater capacity to do so in the 1950s. Even though the society had voted in 1951 to dispense with property holding, the question reemerged in 1958 when Edward and Blanche Benjamin of Greensboro and New Orleans offered to donate to the SPA the Greensboro site of a historic log college operated by Rev. David Caldwell from 1767 to 1822. Famous North Carolinians such as Archibald D. Murphey and John Motley Morehead had been educated at the school. James G. W. MacLamroc, Greensboro attorney and historian for Guilford County, had encouraged the Benjamins to preserve the site. MacLamroc was a society member and a former district vice-president. Edward Benjamin's plans for the site did not involve a reconstruction but rather the placement there of a commemorative bronze tablet, as "at Jamestown."

The discussion of the proposal at the 1958 annual meeting revealed a surprisingly limited corporate memory. President Ives declared that the Benjamin offer presented a novel situation "because we have never taken title to property and it would mean amending our by-laws." Apparently forgetting that the SPA constitution authorized property holding, Christopher Crittenden likewise cautioned that acceptance would require an amendment to the society's constitution and recommended that a committee be appointed to investigate the matter and report to the executive committee, which could then act on the offer. No mention was made of Richmond Hill, owned by the SPA and silently falling to ruin in a remote area of Yadkin County. Soon a committee was appointed, with SPA life member Fielding Fry of Greensboro as chairman and Mrs. W. F. Roberts of Salisbury, Dean H. H. Cunningham of Elon College, former Greensboro mayor Robert H. Frazier, and Greensboro residents Burke Davis, John Harden, and James G. W. MacLamroc as members.

Stacked with Guilford County history enthusiasts, the Fry committee, not surprisingly, recommended acceptance. In October 1959 the Benjamins' Starmount Company transferred title to the Caldwell school site to the SPA. The deed restricted the use of the land to a memorial to David and Rachel Caldwell. Fielding Fry reported at the 1959 SPA annual meeting that title to the 1.65-acre site of the Caldwell log school had been delivered and announced that the committee hoped to mark the site with a bronze tablet. In addition, it was reported that Dr. E. Lawrence Lee Jr., professor of American colonial history at The Citadel, had conducted preliminary archaeological work at the school site. Lee, who attended the annual meeting, said that he had found stone foundations and eighteenth- and early nineteenth-century artifacts.

Lee's archaeological work was followed in 1960 by that of state archaeologist Stanley South, who found the basement of the Caldwells' second house. The Benjamins subsidized South's work. In October 1960, with Elizabeth Ives present, the SPA dedicated the marker at the site of the Caldwell log college. For the remainder of the 1960s the Caldwell site remained unimproved and seemingly forgotten.

Ironically, in March 1965 an old ghost of a project in the form of Richmond Hill reappeared before the startled leaders of the SPA. Jimmie R. Hutchens, president of the Yadkin County Historical Society, wrote President Lillian Robinson, announcing his group's desire to acquire and restore Richmond Hill. After several years of sporadic correspondence (and after Jane Holliday could not find the deed in the SPA files), Hutchens furnished the SPA with a photostat of the 1940 deed showing SPA ownership. With the photostat came an offer to accept title to the property in order to restore it. Upon the recommendation of society president Harry Gatton and that of Crittenden and Holliday, the SPA board unanimously accepted Hutchens's terms and in October 1968 deeded Richmond Hill to the Yadkin County Historical Society.

The Caldwell property remained in SPA custody, however. In a replay of Richmond Hill, the SPA could not actively manage the Caldwell property and failed to make arrangements for local oversight. The property became unkempt and overrun with brush. Yet, unlike Richmond Hill, the Caldwell site was not conveniently located out of public view, and the denouement of the situation was bound to bring bad publicity. In October 1969, with a headline that began with the words "Disgraceful Neglect," the *Greensboro Record* ran a feature article on the Caldwell site. It was a public relations nightmare in which reporter Jim Schlosser took the SPA to task:

> With the tremendous emphasis today on reconstruction, restoration and preservation, it seems incredible one of North Carolina's most important historical sites could fall into a disgraceful state of neglect.
>
> But it has happened to the Dr. David Caldwell property off Hobbs Road in Greensboro. . . .
>
> The property today is in a jungle-like condition and is hardly a fitting memorial to the memory of Dr. Caldwell. It is owned by the North Carolina Society for the Preservation of Antiquities.

Schlosser suggested options for the Caldwell site that included transfer to a Greensboro museum or agency to convert the site into a public park with interpretative markers or reconstructed buildings. He had interviewed Harry Gatton, SPA president. The politically adroit Gatton took the most positive stance he could, saying that the society welcomed the "attention being focused on this important piece of property." The beleaguered SPA president disarmingly admitted the limits of the SPA's financial ability to manage or rehabilitate property: "You must remember the Society has no funds for restoration purposes. The purpose of the Society is to encourage the preservation of historical tracts. In other words, we simply try to keep the axe and bulldozer from destroying the tracts."

In February 1970 Gatton appointed a special committee on the Caldwell property with himself as chairman. Members were Virginia Ford Zenke and William J. Moore of Greensboro and Raymond F. "Ray" Pisney, assistant administrator of the Division

In 1969 former SPA Sixth District vice-president James G. W. MacLamroc inspected the "jungle-like" Caldwell log college site in Greensboro. Newspaper clipping from *Greensboro Record*, October 1, 1969, SPA Records, State Archives.

of Historic Sites and Museums of the Department of Archives and History. In April 1970 the SPA board of directors approved the committee's recommendation that the property be given to an appropriate group in Greensboro to preserve the site. Yet, at the same time, the SPA allowed James MacLamroc time to try to interest Burlington Industries in funding the development of the property as a historic site. (The Caldwell school site was adjacent to the corporation's home office.)

Disposal of the property was made easier when in 1970 the city of Greensboro dropped its claim against the society for a decade's worth of unpaid property taxes. By the end of Harry Gatton's last term as president in December 1970, the SPA board determined that if MacLamroc failed to interest Burlington Industries in the Caldwell school site, the society would offer it to the city of Greensboro for use as a park.

Other Projects: Portraits at Home and Abroad

In the late 1950s McDaniel Lewis continued his efforts to have the SPA honor Joseph Hyde Pratt with an oil portrait. Lewis contacted Pres. Elizabeth Stevenson Ives, who raised the issue at the April 1958 executive committee meeting at the home of Ruth Cannon. Predictably, no action was taken. Lewis continued to press the issue to no avail.

In the same year, the undiscouraged Lewis also tried without success to prod Archibald Henderson into writing the history of the formation of the SPA. Lewis then attempted to enlist Elizabeth Ives to pursue the matter with Henderson. Failing to stir the action of others, Lewis wrote his own one-and-one-half-page account of the beginning of the society. He presented his history in a speech to the Tryon Palace Commission in June 1960 and later sent a copy to SPA officers Ives, Harding, and Tally. Perhaps following up on Lewis's efforts, Christopher Crittenden suggested at the December 1964 board meeting that the SPA publish a history of itself as part of its twenty-fifth anniversary. Again, no action was taken.

Ever since research was compiled in the 1930s for *Old Homes and Gardens*, interest continued in surveying North Carolina for its historic architecture. At the

1961 annual meeting, upon the motion of Mrs. Roy Harrell of Elkin, district vice-presidents were assigned the responsibility "for promoting inventory-taking within their districts." Mary Emma Branch was directed to write each chairman of the county boards of commissioners, asking for cooperation in gathering "a complete list of all historic buildings."

During her two-year presidency, Lura Tally worked with the School of Design at North Carolina State College and the National Trust for Historic Preservation to launch a survey of North Carolina's historic buildings. At its December 1962 meeting the SPA board allocated two hundred dollars for the survey and drawings. Under the survey project, teams of architectural students made studies and measured drawings of significant buildings throughout the state. School of Design student William A. Brogden transferred the information to more than one hundred forms. Lura Tally proudly took the completed forms to the 1964 annual meeting to show them to the board. The forms were then filed with the National Trust for Historic Preservation.

In the 1960s the society began to look beyond Culture Week for additional opportunities to educate North Carolinians through conferences. A chance came in 1963 when North Carolina celebrated the three hundredth anniversary of the granting of the Carolina Charter by King Charles II. As part of the celebration, Old Salem sponsored in April the first North Carolina Conference on Preservation and Restoration. The SPA cosponsored the meeting with the North Carolina Department of Archives and History and the National Trust for Historic Preservation.

In November 1965 the SPA played a prominent role in planning and participating in the annual meeting of the National Trust for Historic Preservation, which took place in Raleigh. True to form, Edmund Harding employed his trademark "entertaining verses" in introducing former SPA presidents to the assembled preservationists. President Lillian Robinson warned the former presidents ahead of time to "be prepared for the worst when you take your bow."

In 1966 the society rendered an international service to the U.S. Department of State. Dudley W. Miller, officer in charge, Yugoslav Affairs, wrote the SPA in March for assistance in locating a photograph of North Carolinian Richmond Pearson (son of North Carolina chief justice Richmond Mumford Pearson), who was designated minister to Montenegro in 1907. The American ambassador to Yugoslavia, C. Burke Elbrick, was assembling pictures of all the American ambassadors and ministers to Yugoslavia and to Serbia and Montenegro before the establishment of Yugoslavia. State Department personnel had combed the Library of Congress and other institutions in Washington but could not find a likeness of Pearson. Jane Holliday obtained permission from the University of North Carolina to copy a photograph of Pearson that appeared in *Editor in Politics*, by Josephus Daniels, published by the University of North Carolina Press in 1941. In early April she mailed the photograph to the State Department for exhibit in a prominent place in the U.S. embassy in Belgrade.

Nineteen sixty-six also marked the long-overdue introduction of an SPA newsletter. Sporadically produced, it replaced the former informational letters sent to the membership by the society presidents. The newsletter was titled *North Carolina Preservation News* until it was renamed *Antiquities* in September 1970. It contained a president's column, news on committee and board activities, and information about preservation projects throughout the state.

Membership and Money

The 1960s marked a turning point in the society's financial affairs as old policies were abandoned to assure long-term financial survival. Despite wealthy founders and leaders, almost all of the SPA budget depended on annual membership dues. Maude Moore Latham and the Kellenbergers earmarked their fortune for Tryon Palace. And while Ruth Cannon gave liberally of her purse and leadership, neither she nor her husband (nor any other of the society's founders and leaders) left an endowment for the future perpetuation of the society. Charles A. Cannon even discontinued sponsorship of the Cannon Cup award after the death of his wife. The award was continued only because the SPA chose to bear the cost, changing its name to the Ruth Coltrane Cannon Cup Award.

In 1968 SPA president Harry Gatton candidly assessed the society's financial position when he told the membership: "We must continue to substitute intelligent enthusiasm for money—because we are not an organization of wealth. We are, rather an organization of interest." By the mid-1960s the society's financial taproot was being strangled by non-income-producing life memberships that had been promiscuously sold in earlier years for fifty dollars (and termed "mighty cheap" in 1947 by an alarmed secretary-treasurer, Mary Emma Branch). By June 1966 nearly 60 percent of the approximately twelve hundred members of the society were life members.

At the December 1964 board meeting Christopher Crittenden, representing the SPA Committee for the Revision of the Constitution and Bylaws, recommended raising the dues structure. On the motion of Ruth Cannon, however, only the annual dues were increased—from two dollars to five dollars. At the society's annual meeting, held the following day, the membership adopted the increase in annual dues, and Cannon asked the members to "consider raising dues for life membership at next year's meeting."

By the next annual meeting in December 1965, Ruth Cannon was in her last illness and not present. Upon the motion of Gertrude Carraway (acting for the Committee for the Revision of the Constitution and Bylaws), the membership voted to amend the bylaws to raise life memberships from fifty dollars to one hundred dollars. At the same meeting, Lura Tally suggested that the SPA membership committee select two hundred people from lists of other cultural groups for membership solicitation. Her idea was unanimously adopted.

With the death of Ruth Cannon and the retirement of her colleague and friend, Mary Emma Branch, the way was clear for new strategies for reviving the SPA's unhealthy financial state. Branch's replacement, Jane A. Holliday, immediately went to work on a spring 1966 membership campaign that extended into 1967. Holliday, Crittenden, and Harry Gatton met in early April 1966 to plan "a most ambitious membership drive" to include new stationery, updated enclosures, and the selection of Dr. Robert Burton House as "a respected and beloved North Carolinian" to serve as campaign sponsor. House, former secretary of the North Carolina Historical Commission (1924-1926) and former chancellor of the University of North Carolina, agreed to allow mass mailings of membership invitations to be sent under his name to people on the rolls of other cultural and civic organizations, including arts councils, patriotic and historical societies, and the North Carolina Federation of Women's Clubs. The selection of House reflected Crittenden's view that the Antiquities Society needed a more visible masculine presence.

The mailings, which began on May 12, 1966, amounted to more than 4,500 a year later. Society leaders also made personal appearances at gatherings of other organizations. Elizabeth Stevenson Ives captivated a meeting of the Raleigh Fine Arts Society, gaining many members for the SPA. By the middle of May 1967, 451 new members, of which 354 were annual, had been recruited statewide, increasing the SPA membership to 1,290. At the same time, Jane Holliday pruned the files of 146 delinquent members. By the end of November 1967 the membership stood at 1,365 (of which 635 were annual).

An even more important milestone in the effort to attain long-term financial sufficiency was the board's decision to prohibit new hereditary life memberships after December 1, 1966. Moreover, in October 1966 Lillian Robinson wrote the life members, requesting voluntary contributions. She encouraged donations by saying that increased revenue would help the society raise the amount of its "token" two hundred-dollar grants, which were insufficient to meet the "restoration needs [that] are arising daily." The response to the membership drive was so favorable by the time of the 1966 annual meeting that Jane Holliday happily reported that 304 new members had been added, of which 246 were annual. She echoed Robinson's October appeal in expressing hope that the society would be able to give larger grants and provide more services.

Yet, the gains were not enough. Expectations of expanded programs gave way to continuing budget problems and, occasionally, insufficient money to pay Holliday's salary. After its December 1968 annual meeting, the society had to delay sending its two hundred-dollar check for its incentive grant to the Murfreesboro Historical Association by six months. Such strains led in 1969 to a critical Saint Valentine's Day emergency meeting of the state's preservation leadership. Archives and History staff member Mary Cornick felt that it "boiled down to the fact that Antiquities needs more members, more money, and a new program." Despite a wide-ranging discussion on possible new programs, President Gatton resolved that the organization had no choice but to give top priority to a corporate fund-raising drive. Without money, programs could not exist.

Therefore, Gatton, H. G. Jones, and Crittenden proceeded to gather corporate membership lists from other cultural organizations. With fund-raising letters drafted by Crittenden, they undertook a selective mailing in March, with Crittenden, Jones, and Charles Landt, senior vice-president of First Union National Bank (and president of Cameron Brown Company), signing the appeals. The letters varied but generally declared that on the thirtieth anniversary of its existence the SPA had a negligible amount (with sums such as $44.89 and $65.00 being quoted) in its checking account, that the SPA secretary could not be paid, and that the society's prospects would improve with an unspecified "new program which we are now launching." Christopher Crittenden informed the O. Max Gardner Foundation in Shelby that the SPA was "just about destitute." Despite Crittenden's reference to Fay Webb Gardner (who had just died in January 1969) and her love for the SPA, the foundation turned him down. Gardner's son, Ralph, apologetically explained that the foundation was "stretched to the limit" and could only offer hope of "assistance at some future date."

H. G. Jones had better luck with the Smith Richardson Foundation, which reluctantly authorized the Department of Archives and History to grant the ailing society two thousand dollars out of the remainder of a sixty thousand-dollar grant the foundation had made that year to the department for historic preservation challenge grants. In conveying the foundation's permission by letter in March 1969, G. C. Eichhorn, assistant to the president of the Smith Richardson Foundation, pointedly asked why, "after all these years and with approximately 1,400 members, the Society is suddenly 'just about destitute.'" Without equivocation, Jones replied the following day to Eichhorn's query: "Primarily there is one reason. Mrs. Charles A. Cannon, who as you know was president of the Society for many years, persuaded large numbers of her friends and associates to become Life Members and told them that these Life Memberships were 'hereditary.' By vote of the membership at their annual meeting in Raleigh in December, 1966, the Society stopped making Life Memberships hereditary. However, as a result of this practice, today nearly one-half the Society's membership consists of Life Members from whom it receives no annual revenue."

The much-needed two thousand dollars from the Smith Richardson Foundation arrived in early April, making the society, in the words of Holliday, "once again . . . solvent . . . through the interest and kindness of Dr. Crittenden and Dr. Jones." In informing Gatton of the donation, Holliday unburdened herself of her anxiety over the organization's lack of income: "While I am relieved to be able to pay a few bills, I find it difficult to accept this and forget it. Perhaps I shouldn't take the whole thing so seriously, but eventually, again, we are going to run out of money unless something of a very concrete nature is instigated. . . . I am sorry to be such a dreadful ole [sic] realist, but it does continue to bother me." Holliday submitted her resignation the following month, citing home responsibilities. Burnout resulting from three years of struggle with the society's seemingly intractable financial problems may have made her decision easier.

Yet, the corporate fund-raising campaign under Harry Gatton's presidency was modestly successful and, in combination with the more successful 1966-1967 membership drive, was enough to save the society from bankruptcy. Total receipts for the twelve months ended October 31, 1968, amounted to $3,702. The following year the 1969 receipts (exclusive of a cashed-in $8,000 savings bond left over from the revolving fund) increased about 75 percent to $5,077. The increase was most impressive among annual membership receipts, which climbed from $325 for the year ended October 1968 to $1,700 for the year ended October 1969. Except for the $2,000 from the Smith Richardson Foundation, other gifts and contributions remained the same.

At the December 1970 annual meeting, Secretary-Treasurer Sharon Sandling gained approval for a new billing system that included the mailing of yearly statements. Membership renewals apparently had been handled through meeting notices and other membership communications, which led to inconsistency and the loss of revenue and members. Membership was down to 1,014 from 1,365 in November 1967. Of that number, only 418 were annual, which was still 200 fewer than in 1959. The wolf had been kept from the door, but the society had not achieved lasting membership gains or financial stability.

The Old Guard Passes: "Kindly have the doctor double check to make sure that I am dead"

By the end of Harry Gatton's presidency in December 1970, the first-generation leadership of the North Carolina Society for the Preservation of Antiquities had passed from the scene. Archibald Henderson, who remained active in the society until the mid-1950s, died in 1963. Ruth Cannon followed in 1965; Gardner, Fletcher, and Crittenden, in 1969; and Edmund Harding, in 1970.

Throughout the SPA presidencies of the late 1950s and early 1960s, Cannon continued to play a dominant role in the society's deliberations and affairs. After her stroke, she improved remarkably between the 1956 and 1957 annual meetings and had been well enough to resume her annual tea at her beloved eighteenth-century home, "For Pity's Sake," in April 1958. Cannon's name and title as honorary president appeared on the society's letterhead until her death. At the 1964 annual meeting in December 1964, she shared the speaker's platform with Pres. Dan Paul and Vice-Pres. Lillian Moore Robinson.

The 1964 meeting was Ruth Cannon's last. By the 1965 annual meeting she was on her deathbed. At that meeting the membership rose as one to approve Gertrude Carraway's resolution (sent by telegram to Cannon) expressing "praise and gratitude for her inspiring leadership throughout the years." The indomitable Cannon, who had led the state's preservation efforts since the 1930s, died on December 22, 1965. Sadly and ironically, "For Pity's Sake" was allowed to deteriorate after her death. Cannon's husband, Charles, died in 1971, and four years later the house was consigned to the Kannapolis fire department for burning in a training exercise.

Christopher Crittenden died of a heart attack on October 13, 1969. Although he knew his health to be bad, he kept that information from his colleagues. In clearing out his desk, his staff found a one-page statement titled "Suggestions for My Funeral and Related Matters." Crittenden's first instruction was that his body be given to the Duke University anatomy department. Then, displaying his well-known penchant for humor, he wrote: "Kindly have the doctor double check to make sure that I am dead." He concluded with a thoughtful farewell: "Good luck to everybody."

Gov. Bob Scott observed that in death Christopher Crittenden became "a part of the history he loved so much." By resolution at its 1969 annual meeting, the SPA membership memorialized Crittenden's "gentle spirit and noble record." Crittenden's impact on the state's history program would not be forgotten, especially by McDaniel Lewis. By then Lewis had learned his lesson in unsuccessfully attempting to memorialize Joseph Hyde Pratt through the SPA. He tried a different strategy for honoring Crittenden. In 1974, as preparations for the celebration for the nation's bicentennial were developing in North Carolina, he wrote Grace J. Rohrer, secretary of the North Carolina Department of Cultural Resources, suggesting that as part of the bicentennial celebration a biography of Crittenden be written. In pressing his case, Lewis presented a fitting summation of the life of Christopher Crittenden: "For more than half of the existence of our state['s] official activities in the collection and preservation of our historical records, . . . Dr. Christopher Crittenden was in charge. . . . He was such a genius in this field our state owes him its very deepest gratitude. For many years he was the coordinator of our cultural resources and organizations, and became nationally famous for his professional leadership. . . . We honor ourselves by honoring this great man. . . ." The book was never written.

Boiling Down:
Changing Times and the Search for New Roles

By the end of the 1960s the SPA was at a crossroads. Its programs were faltering, and its old leadership was gone. A shrinking financial base caused by an ill-conceived emphasis on life memberships limited the society's flexibility and program options. Archives and History staff member Mary Cornick had precisely summarized the dilemma by saying that it "boiled down to the fact that Antiquities needs more members, more money, and a new program."

During the terms of Lillian Robinson and Harry Gatton, those factors led to greater introspection concerning existing programs and the future purpose and role of the society. At the 1967 annual meeting Robinson affirmed the society's function as an information exchange and morale booster: "One of the most important roles we play is that of furnishing a forum where restoration groups, big and small, can tell the world what they are doing—their hopes and their dreams, the progress they are making, problems they encounter, and their success in achieving their goals."

Earlier in the year, Jane Holliday had replied to a request for information from the North Carolina Arts Council. In describing the SPA's chief activities, she also cited its role as "a promoting organization and clearing house for other groups and individuals." Holliday identified the annual meeting as the means by which the society's "chief influence has been brought to bear." She also highlighted the society's fifty or more small grants and its revolving fund loans. As Holliday pointed out, such services helped to stimulate preservation activity within the state. Feeling, however, that the "aesthetics of preservation . . . [did] not appeal to the many," president Harry Gatton employed his appearances before public forums and civic clubs to emphasize the importance of historic preservation to the state's thriving tourism industry and to the quality of community life.

Yet, this was not enough to stem the tide of demolition, nor was it enough to bring historic preservation into the forefront of public concern. Under Gatton, society members began to search more earnestly for new programs and missions. In May 1968 Gatton and Holliday met with Crittenden, Sam Tarlton, and other Department of Archives and History staff in Crittenden's office to discuss the society's possible cosponsorship of regional preservation conferences to be conducted by Tarlton's Division of Historic Sites. Significantly, the conversation also presaged the creation of a future revolving fund. As reported by Jane Holliday in the meeting minutes: "the concept of the Society acting as a clearing house for individuals wishing to dispose of old houses or properties having historical and/or architectural significance was discussed. It was felt that this would be an excellent area for the Society to explore—being careful not to compete with real estate agencies."

At the December 1968 board meeting, the SPA directors continued to discuss ideas for expanding the society's services and endorsed the cosponsorship of regional preservation conferences and workshops. The first SPA newsletter, issued in November

1968, solicited the membership for ideas. The newsletter recited suggestions already offered, including SPA-sponsored restoration workshops and service as a clearinghouse for preservation information.

Yet, such hopes gave way to continuing budget problems. In a pessimistic mood, Gatton and Holliday had conferred on that fateful Saint Valentine's Day in 1969 in Crittenden's office with Crittenden, H. G. Jones, and Mary Cornick. In a wide-ranging discussion, the group again entertained new roles for the society and fund raising. Ideas ranged from merging the SPA with the Literary and Historical Association to having Prof. Robert Stipe of the Institute of Government lead an SPA-sponsored preservation workshop. In March 1968 Stipe had already offered a one-week "short course" on preservation planning for historic preservation professionals. The Institute of Government and the Department of Archives and History had cosponsored the enormously successful course, which helped to shape a new brand of preservationist who was able to see (in Stipe's words) "historic buildings in the context of neighborhood and community design and development . . . [and not] as disparate artifacts on the landscape." Nevertheless, Gatton resolved that the first order of need was for the society to embark on a corporate fund-raising drive, and the others concurred.

Thus, continuing money problems required deferral of new program initiatives. Energy and activity had to focus on fund raising in order to keep the society alive. Yet, that focus constituted a dilemma; ultimately, membership and successful fund raising depended on responsive new programs that saved historic buildings.

Chapter 6:
Forward to Renewal, 1970-1974

Leaders to the End

In December 1970 John Edward "Jack" Tyler II of Roxobel succeeded Harry Gatton as president of the SPA. Tyler, a fifty-two-year-old farmer and antiques dealer, had been active in preservation for more than twenty years. Known as a "quiet pusher," he was a founder of the Bertie County Historical Association in the 1950s, a founder of the Historic Hope Foundation in 1965, and the foundation's president in 1970. Tyler assumed office with a modest set of goals for his first year: improving the annual meeting, sponsoring tours of restorations in various parts of the state, and preparing a list and description of all the restoration projects in the state. In his second year, his objectives expanded to include more financial assistance to local preservation efforts.

In his two years as president, Tyler was able to make improvements in the annual meeting format and to oversee publication of a directory listing Tar Heel restoration projects. His proposal for a tour program generated discussion but not adoption by a cautious board fearful of overcommitment. Likewise, his proposal for a grants trust fund was stalled by reluctance from within the organization to increase its fund-raising burden. Like his predecessor, Harry Gatton, Jack Tyler sought to develop new programs and roles for the SPA while working with limited financial and staff resources. His most far-reaching act was to appoint a Constitution Committee in 1971.

By the time of Tyler's presidency, professionals and business people tended to hold the leadership and policy-making roles previously dominated by members of the social and financial elite. There is no ready explanation for that phenomenon. Years later, Tyler attributed it to the widening scope of historic preservation from being a "rich man's plaything," involving elegant mansions of important people, to being a movement involved with a wider range of resources. The professionalization of the field may have

John E. Tyler (*right*) SPA president, 1970-1972, looked on at the society's 1971 annual meeting as Gertrude Carraway presented a Cannon Cup Award to the Raleigh Historic Sites Commission, represented by its chairman, Dr. Banks C. Talley Jr.

been a factor, along with increasing competition from educational and social welfare organizations. Perhaps, too, expanding opportunities for women depleted the ready reserves of wealthy female volunteers and leaders.

Tyler was followed as president in December 1972 by his vice-president, Virginia Ford Zenke of Greensboro. The forty-eight-year-old Zenke was a native of Norfolk, Virginia. She operated a Greensboro-based interior decorating business with her husband, Henry Christian Zenke, and his brother, Otto. Virginia Zenke had restored a house dating from the 1830s and 1840s and had been a driving force in the restoration of Blandwood, the 1844 Italian Villa home of Gov. John Motley Morehead. Zenke had first become active in the SPA in the 1950s with the encouragement of Tempie Prince of Reidsville. She joined in hopes of receiving help for Blandwood and with a desire to stimulate greater preservation activity in the North Carolina Piedmont. Her work with Blandwood brought her statewide recognition. As a result, Nicholas Bragg, chairman of the nominations committee in 1969, had approached her "as just the 'live wire'" the society needed as vice-president.

Zenke's friend, William J. Moore, also of Greensboro, served as her vice-president. The thirty-four-year-old Moore was director of the Greensboro Historical Museum. He was a native of Asheboro and had been an actuary with the Jefferson-Pilot Insurance Company when he first became active with the Greensboro museum as a volunteer. Moore had served as an SPA district vice-president in 1970 and (having been nominated by McDaniel Lewis) as a member of the board since that year. He later had the distinction of rescuing and restoring the former home of Letitia Morehead Walker, who had helped Ann Pamela Cunningham save Mount Vernon.

The reformers in the SPA supported Virginia Zenke as president because she did not have many ties to the society's old guard and would not be afraid to back needed

Virginia Ford Zenke of Greensboro was elected president of the SPA in December 1972 and was its last president. When the society was rechartered and renamed in February 1974, she became the first president of the Historic Preservation Society of North Carolina. This photograph shows Mrs. Zenke with her husband, Henry Christian Zenke, in the library of their home after they had jointly received a Cannon Cup Award in November 1974.

changes. Both Zenke and Moore were eager to see the SPA shake the organizational torpor with which Gatton and Tyler had wrestled. Moore felt that in the mid-1960s the annual meeting had become boring and not "meaty," and Zenke thought that the SPA had "coasted" too long on Tryon Palace and Old Salem. During Zenke's term the constitutional revision committee appointed under Tyler presented amendments that eventually brought an end to the old SPA.

Beth M. Boxley, a clerk in the Department of Archives and History, replaced Sharon Sandling as secretary-treasurer in April 1972 when Sandling resigned because of her impending marriage and move from the state. Boxley had served as Sandling's assistant secretary-treasurer after Sandling accepted a professional position in the State Archives in September 1971. When Sandling finally left the SPA, Boxley also assumed her duties as editor of the society's quarterly newsletter *Antiquities*.

Beginning in 1970 the SPA and the North Carolina Literary and Historical Association shared the secretary-treasurer position and jointly paid the state for the salaries of Sandling and Boxley, who were state employees. John G. "Jack" Zehmer Jr., director of the Division of Historic Sites and Museums of the Office of Archives and History (a temporary new name of the former Department of Archives and History) replaced Boxley as secretary-treasurer in March 1973. At the same time, Frances Harmon Whitley was hired as a salaried assistant secretary-treasurer under Zehmer. She also served in the same capacity for "Lit and Hist" and was provided work space in H. G. Jones's outer office, for which, beginning in February 1974, "Lit and Hist" and the SPA each paid twenty-five dollars a year. Until her resignation in 1981, Whitley was the only paid employee of the society and its successor organization, the Historic Preservation Society of North Carolina.

Whitley was a native of Statesville and a graduate of Furman University in Greenville, South Carolina, where she studied history and political science. She had worked for the Department of Archives and History from 1946 to 1956, when she left to be at home with her children. While employed with Archives and History, Whitley set up the agency's laboratories for laminating documents and developing photographs. She reentered the job market in 1973 and signed on with the SPA for $2.75 an hour. The competent part-time services of Frances Whitley served the SPA well in its concluding days. The SPA leadership hoped someday to hire a full-time executive director, but the society lacked the financial means to do so.

In early 1974 both the Division of Archives and History and the SPA suffered the loss of two important leaders. At the January board meeting, Jack Zehmer submitted

From 1973 to 1981 Frances Harmon Whitley of Raleigh was the only paid employee of the SPA and its successor organization, the Historic Preservation Society of North Carolina. This photograph was taken at her retirement from the Preservation Society in November 1981. Photograph courtesy Mrs. Whitley.

his resignation as secretary-treasurer. A Virginian, he returned to his native state, where he eventually became director of the Valentine Museum in Richmond and executive director of the Historic Richmond Foundation. The board appointed, as acting secretary-treasurer, Elizabeth Wall "Libb" Wilborn, who was research supervisor in the newly renamed Division of Archives and History.

At the same meeting in which Zehmer submitted his resignation, H. G. Jones, director of the Division of Archives and History, announced that he, too, would soon be leaving the SPA board because he was resigning as director of the division. Jones had accepted the position of curator of the North Carolina Collection, University of North Carolina, Chapel Hill. He had given the society six years of valuable service and had admirably assumed the leadership and advisory role of his predecessor, Christopher Crittenden.

Although he had supported a constitutional amendment directing the reduction in the number of departments in state government and had worked closely with the reorganization staff, Jones was disappointed with the details of subsequent legislation that took away the direct access of the director to the governor. In 1972 the former Department of Archives and History, an independent agency for nearly seventy years, had been made a division and absorbed into the new Department of Art, Culture and History (renamed the Department of Cultural Resources in 1973). Jones feared that the professionalism and scholarly standing of the new division would be vulnerable to political pressure and believed he could better protect the agency's interests from the outside. The SPA board regretted his leaving and lauded his "outstanding leadership."

Grants—and Revolving Thoughts about Revolving Funds

In the late 1960s and early 1970s, SPA leaders realized that in addition to governmental assistance and protection programs, a comprehensive state preservation effort depended on the expansion of society programs. In April 1971 the SPA board sought to adjust for the inflationary erosion of its traditional $200 incentive grant. It decided that if one annual grant were awarded, it would be $500 and if two were awarded, they would be limited to $300 each.

The system worked until 1973, when the incentives grant committee, chaired by Gertrude Carraway, could not choose among three grant applicants even "after lengthy studies, comparisons and discussions, with an opinion from an outside authority. . . ." Therefore, Carraway and her committee (Al Honeycutt of the Division of Archives and History and William J. Moore) reluctantly recommended approval of grants in the amount of two hundred dollars each for the Dolley Madison Birthplace Memorial, Guilford County; the Latimer House, Wilmington; and the William Gaston House, New Bern.

Despite the small size of the awards, the SPA grants program had been greatly improved. In 1970 Nicholas Bragg assumed charge of a committee to put the grants on a more businesslike basis. Bragg's only committee member was Al Honeycutt. By the April 1971 board meeting, Bragg and Honeycutt had prepared draft criteria and an application form. After Bragg resigned from the board, Honeycutt and Sally Labouisse continued through the year to refine further the criteria and application form for use in the fall. The grants committee also assumed responsibility for recommending grant recipients to the SPA board.

In December 1971 society president Jack Tyler called for the establishment of a fifty thousand-dollar trust fund, with interest reserved for incentive grants. Tyler felt that the society would have greater impact on local organizations if its grants were expanded to amounts between one thousand and two thousand dollars. At the same time, Robert E. Stipe of the Institute of Government of the University of North Carolina called for a revolving fund capitalized at one million dollars—the minimum needed, in his view, to "make much of a dent." In a proposal conveyed to Tyler by Ray Pisney of the Department of Archives and History, Stipe further asserted that the fund required "a new and separate organization."

Robert Stipe thought expansively, influenced by his overseas experience in the late 1960s as a senior Fulbright research fellow studying British planning and preservation law. Such thinking was reflected in his conception of a North Carolina Civic Trust, loosely modeled on Britain's Civic Trust, founded in 1957. Consulting with like-minded people such as Lindsay Cox, then Guilford County planning director, Stipe (in his later words) envisioned a "revolving fund not just for preservation but for low-income housing, scenic character, and a bunch of other then-modernist ideas."

Seizing the initiative, Tyler in May 1972 spearheaded an SPA application to the National Trust for Historic Preservation for a feasibility study of a "North Carolina Historic Preservation Fund" to make grants and loans to assist local preservation projects. Although the SPA pledged to organize its membership for a statewide effort to finance the proposed fund, the application did not specifically tie the fund to the society. H. G. Jones believed that such a study could result in a state-chartered corporation administered through the Department of Archives and History.

The National Trust initially rejected the application, citing budget cuts; at the same time, its staff praised the proposal. Soon afterward, however, that body reappraised its position and in February 1973 awarded the SPA a consultant services grant in the amount of six hundred dollars. Realizing the need to establish a set of priorities before using the grant money, the elated SPA leaders embarked on a new study of plans and goals, which they assumed would include creation of a preservation fund. Nevertheless, progress slowed throughout the remainder of 1973. The National Trust unaccountably failed to communicate further with the SPA, despite repeated inquiries by President Zenke and Frank Stephenson, chairman of the society's Finance Committee. In addition, at the society's March 1973 board meeting, some board members expressed skepticism about prospective fund-raising goals for district vice-presidents and fretted over possible competition with local historical societies for grant moneys. Whether those misgivings were specifically directed toward fund raising for a revolving fund is not clear, but in any case they did not augur well for any new enterprise requiring large infusions of fresh capital. Prospects appear to have brightened, however, when Frank Stephenson announced at the January 1974 board meeting that the National Trust had finally sent the documents and instructions necessary in applying for the grant. The board immediately decided to seek the assistance of Robert Stipe in developing the grant proposal and selecting a consultant. Thus was set in motion what would eventually become the most successful revolving preservation fund in the nation.

The SPA's annual fifty-dollar grant to the North Carolina Federation of Women's Clubs was continued, but that program, in operation since 1961, was almost terminated in 1973 because the federation neither cashed the check for the last award nor bothered to communicate with the SPA. SPA vice-president William Moore called for with-holding the grant for 1974, but at the request of Lura Tally no action was taken, pending an investigation by her. In response to Tally's inquiry, the check was returned in December, along with the embarrassed explanation that the federation's judges found no local club with a project worthy of the award. Urged by Ann Brown of Wilmington, chair of the federation's awards committee, to continue the program, the SPA did so, at least for 1974, its last year of existence under its original charter.

In 1971 the North Carolina General Assembly made matching grants to eleven non-state-owned historic properties, some of which had long been the object of SPA interest, including Richmond Hill, the Hezekiah Alexander House, Blandwood, and Hope Plantation. In 1972 the Smith Richardson Foundation made ten grants through the Department of Archives and History. Principal landmarks such as Richmond Hill and Hope Plantation were again assisted. H. G. Jones announced that Smith Richardson grants made through the department since 1960 amounted to $344,616, with $450,000 raised as matching funds.

Culture Week

Reports differ on whether attendance at Culture Week and the SPA annual meeting was in decline in the early 1970s. First District vice-president Frank Stephenson remembered there being strong turnouts in the late 1960s and early 1970s, with "all the rooms packed." But Al Honeycutt recalled that turnout for both the SPA and "Lit and Hist" meetings was in decline compared to the 1950s and 1960s. Giving yet another perspective, Virginia Zenke and William Moore, officers in 1973 and 1974, remembered SPA attendance at that time as good but attendance for Culture Week as declining. Zenke also noted the sport that was made of the name "Culture Week" and of its participants, who were termed "Culture Vultures." She recalled that an out-of-state newspaper found humor in saying that North Carolinians "took one week out to do culture." And Frances Whitley later observed that it was hard for Culture Week to thrive in the age of television and a growing number of competing events.

Annual SPA meetings of the early 1970s still presented prominent speakers such as Frances Edmunds, director of the Historic Charleston Foundation, Charleston, S.C., who titled her 1971 lecture "Preserving the Cityscape." In the same year, Jack Tyler's goal of improving the annual meeting resulted in a display of exhibits by historical and preservation organizations. The lack of media coverage of the annual meeting spurred the SPA in 1972 to create a publicity committee, chaired by William Moore of Greensboro. Suggestions for action included writing news releases, inviting reporters to meetings, and working to obtain television coverage.

Frances Edmunds, director of the Historic Charleston Foundation, spoke on the topic "Preserving the Cityscape" at the 1971 SPA annual meeting. She is shown flanked by SPA president Jack Tyler and board member Gertrude Carraway.

Those attending annual meetings continued to be predominantly female and middle-aged or older. But with the growing public interest in historic preservation in the late 1960s and early 1970s, more business people and professionals joined and began to assume SPA leadership positions. Representative of the new officers and board members were college administrators E. Frank Stephenson Jr. and Dr. Banks C. Talley Jr. and museum director William J. Moore. Others, such as Jack Tyler and Virginia Zenke, had been members for many years. The new leadership tended to include more men and to be young or middle-aged.

Awards

The Cannon Cup remained the society's principal award, but the limited number of cups that were awarded each year left many important projects and preservationists unrecognized. During Tyler's presidency, Al Honeycutt of the Archives and History staff suggested to him that a new merit award program be established and that district vice-presidents nominate the candidates. Other ideas followed. At the April 1972 board

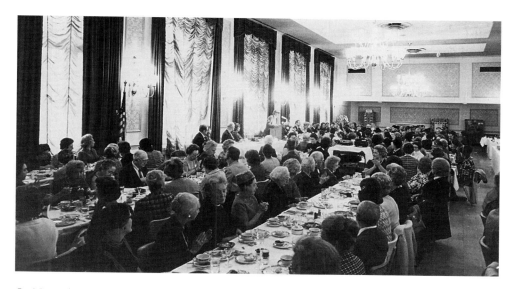

On November 30, 1972, John E. Tyler presided at this SPA luncheon, which took place in the Virginia Dare Ballroom of the Sir Walter Hotel in Raleigh.

meeting, Virginia Zenke suggested that the society identify and recognize people who privately restored their homes. In February 1973 Fourth District vice-president (and vice-chancellor for student affairs at North Carolina State University) Banks C. Talley Jr. recommended to then president Zenke that the society honor those who restored their homes (to be identified by district vice-presidents) by awarding them certificates at regional luncheons. Talley viewed the proposal as a membership builder. The following month Dr. Harley E. Jolley of Mars Hill, vice-president for the Eleventh District, suggested that the board sponsor achievement awards similar to those of the United States Forest Service. A ground swell developed for a new award with criteria separate from the Cannon Cup Awards. At Jack Tyler's urging, the board resolved in January 1974 to "inaugurate a program whereby worthy individuals and groups would be recognized for their efforts in preservation and restoration and that the program

Cannon Cup Award winners of 1973 were (*left to right*): Dr. Robert E. Stipe, Chapel Hill; A. L. Honeycutt Jr., Raleigh; and Dr. Henry C. Landon III, North Wilkesboro.

be instrumented through the congressional vice presidents who would make the recommendations from their areas."

At the same time the SPA was developing a new awards program, Secretary-Treasurer Jack Zehmer sought to instill a greater sense of occasion in the awarding of Cannon Cups. He convinced the board to have the 1973 awards banquet be black tie. Thus, as the Antiquities Society began a metamorphosis into a new organization better suited to the late twentieth century, it maintained continuity with its earlier history and traditions.

Advocacy: The State and Its Buildings

In the early 1970s the SPA vigorously advocated good state stewardship of historic resources under state control. In 1972 the SPA strongly opposed the proposed abandonment of the North Carolina Executive Mansion by the state. The mansion, completed in 1891, was designed by Samuel Sloan of Philadelphia and his assistant, Adolphus Gustavus Bauer. It was a pioneering example of the Queen Anne style of architecture in North Carolina. Though advanced for its day, it had not been upgraded to meet modern standards of comfort and convenience. The house lacked central temperature and humidity controls and a fire-suppression system.

Those deficiencies led to a proposal to build a new executive mansion at a different location. North Carolina preservationists became especially alarmed when the state legislature ordered the North Carolina Executive Residence Building Commission to develop plans for a modern residence by April 1973. In response to the threat, at its April 1972 meeting the SPA board adopted a resolution by Gertrude Carraway calling upon the North Carolina Department of Administration to "investigate the cost of restoring the Executive Mansion to a safe, reusable condition, keeping to the original character as much as possible, so that this significant building may continue in the future as the official residence of North Carolina's governors."

In January 1973 SPA president Virginia Zenke appealed directly to Patricia Hollingsworth Holshouser, wife of Gov. James E. Holshouser Jr. The Tar Heel first lady had expressed a willingness to accept residence in what even Zenke felt was "certainly an architectural curiosity." Zenke strove to reinforce Mrs. Holshouser's inclination by extolling the importance of the Victorian mansion in North Carolina's history as home to the state's first families. The executive quarters remained in the 1891 mansion.

In 1972 and 1973 the society appealed to the state legislature and the Raleigh Historic Sites Commission to save from demolition the antebellum Lewis-Smith House of Raleigh. The majestic Greek Revival mansion was in the path of development of the state's governmental mall and was the home of Cora Vaughan Smith. Smith, a lifelong friend of Ruth Cannon, had served as SPA district vice-president from 1943 to 1969. It was in the Lewis-Smith House in 1938 that Smith and her husband, Charles Lee Smith, had hosted Margaret Wilmer, president of the Association for the Preservation of Virginia Antiquities, when Wilmer visited Raleigh to spur the formation of the SPA. Thus the house was a landmark in the early history of the society.

The Smiths' daughter-in-law, Virginia Camp Smith, had alerted the society to the threat. Past SPA president Lura Tally, a newly elected state representative, was enlisted to help save the house, which by July 1, 1974, had been moved one block to Blount Street, where it was eventually occupied by the historic preservation staff of the Division of Archives and History.

Policies of the Times: Limiting Entanglements

Eager to rid the society of the Caldwell log college property, which had generated so much adverse publicity in 1969, the board of directors happily transferred it in 1971 to the city of Greensboro with the proviso that the city assume the society's liabilities for street assessment. The SPA had delayed its action from December 1970 to allow James MacLamroc time to interest Burlington Industries in developing the Caldwell property as a historic site. But no word had been received from MacLamroc by the time of the board's April 1971 meeting. Therefore, Harry Gatton made the motion to proceed. The land was incorporated into Greensboro's city park system. Thus, with seeming finality the SPA once more shed the burdens of property ownership.

The society also avoided involvement in other projects because of its limited operational capacity and because of a desire to adhere to its basic mission to preserve historic properties. In April 1971 the SPA board rejected Jack Tyler's proposal for a tour program even though it was bolstered by an offer from the North Carolina Society of County and Local Historians to serve as cosponsor of such an undertaking. The board felt that the SPA lacked the requisite "facilities and manpower." At the same meeting the SPA board also refused to serve as a depository for documentary materials. It declined to accept from Dr. Lenox D. Baker files relating to the restoration of Bennett Place State Historic Site. Nevertheless, the board softened its rejection with an expression of willingness to assume an advisory role for individuals wishing to make such donations.

The policy of staying out of controversies that did not directly involve the society continued into 1973. Intense debate then raged on where to locate the North Carolina Museum of Art—in downtown Raleigh or west of the city limits. The outspoken McDaniel Lewis was the chief advocate for the downtown site, but in March the SPA board declined to take a stand on the issue and left it up to each board member and vice-president to write his or her own legislator. The General Assembly eventually chose the suburban location.

Other Projects: Neither Tours nor History Be

Efforts in the realm of public education expanded according to the plans of society president Jack Tyler with the publication in 1971 of the *North Carolina Historic Preservation Directory*. The directory listed restoration projects, consultants, and sources of aid. It was prepared with the assistance of the staff of the Division of Historic Sites and Museums of the Department of Archives and History. At the same time, the SPA produced a new promotional brochure.

In contrast (and as indicated previously), Tyler's hope of developing an SPA tour program was not realized during his term as president. Even though the SPA board in 1971 rejected the tour program proposed by Tyler and the county and local historians, it continued to be intrigued by the possibility of a tour operation. During Zenke's presidency tours received an inordinate amount of discussion at the March and May 1973 board meetings. Ideas included cosponsoring tours with local garden clubs; preparing maps of tours, "as in the state of Virginia"; and conducting small-scale house tours, with Virginia examples again being cited. Those discussions likely arose from a January 1973 proposal by Junius W. Davis, president of the New Bern Historical Society, that the SPA organize a statewide "Garden Week" modeled on Virginia and Maryland examples. But, again, concerns over logistics and expenses dampened enthusiasm. Too, Gertrude Carraway questioned the appeal of tours among North Carolinians, most of whom, she felt, "have already visited local places of interest." The subject died, and it was not resurrected at the 1973 annual meeting.

The society made an unusual gift in the spring of 1971 to the eighteenth-century Cupola House in Edenton. Dr. Charles S. Norburn of Asheville had donated to the SPA in 1969 a seventeenth-century cast iron fireback bearing the royal insignia of Charles II of England. After determining that the fireback was not appropriate to the period for Tryon Palace, the society donated it to the Cupola House.

Under Tyler, the SPA produced a new promotional brochure, which soon faced obsolescence in light of growing sentiment for changing the organizational name—a name characterized by Tenth District vice-president Frances Moody of Hickory as "most unwieldy and tongue twisting." The SPA had the good fortune of having as chairman of its Promotion Committee John Harden, Seventh District vice-president and principal in a Greensboro public relations firm. In 1973 Harden's design staff began to lay out an all-purpose brochure for the society, only to have the SPA board scuttle the project at the end of the year for lack of funds.

Descending prospects likewise characterized most other society publications in the early 1970s. In 1973 SPA leaders indefinitely suspended the society's membership publication (printed at bargain rates by the State Department of Correction), formerly titled *Antiquities* and renamed the *Newsletter.* Jack Zehmer and Frances Whitley had suggested the suspension with the rationale that the content of the *Newsletter* was usually stale by the time that it was printed and that the time devoted to its preparation would be better spent on membership development. In place of the *Newsletter*, the membership received *Carolina Comments*, the bimonthly newsletter of the North Carolina Department of Archives and History. Although the change may have saved staff time and possibly money, the loss of public identity and goodwill could not have helped the society's long-term prospects. The move was an indication of a continuing sacrifice of programs caused by a shortage of staff and money.

In 1971 SPA leaders finally decided that a history of the organization was long overdue. Eleven years earlier, McDaniel Lewis had written a very brief account of the founding, and at the December 1964 board meeting Christopher Crittenden suggested a history as a good project for the society's twenty-fifth anniversary. At last in 1972, upon the suggestion of Gertrude Carraway, the society hired writer Lee Wilder to prepare the history.

In 1971 Ms. Wilder had edited a handsomely illustrated public education booklet titled *A Lonesome Place Against the Sky*, published by the Department of Archives and History. *Lonesome Place* had been so successful that the U.S. Department of the Interior adopted it as a model for other states to follow. For Wilder's history of the society, Gertrude Carraway and Elizabeth Wilborn agreed to serve as editorial advisers. In

March 1973 Wilder gave the board a progress report on the history, saying that there were gaps in the records. She therefore made a general call for information about the society. Although her work appeared to be on track in 1973, the history was never written.

Money and Membership

Money problems continued to plague the SPA. In 1971 Jack Tyler urged the raising of fifty thousand dollars for a grants endowment. In March 1973 the board discussed the possibility of asking each district vice-president to raise one thousand dollars in each county of his or her district. John Newton of Beaufort, vice-president of the Third District, cautioned against competing against local historical societies in fund raising and argued that one thousand dollars was too much to ask of the smaller, less-prosperous counties. The idea was dropped.

Through the first few years of the 1970s, membership hovered between 1,000 and 1,200, which compared unfavorably to the membership of 1,365 at the end of the 1966-1967 membership drive. Despite reforms in the 1960s ending hereditary life memberships and raising the cost of new life memberships from fifty dollars to one hundred dollars, life members continued to outnumber revenue-producing annual members. A large proportion of the life members had been nonactive for many years. In an attempt to boost membership early in her term as president, Virginia Zenke requested each district vice-president to submit a list of ten to twenty prospects. Only about one-third of the eleven vice-presidents complied.

Assistant Secretary-Treasurer Frances Whitley undertook another overhaul of membership record keeping and billing. In May 1973 she reported to the board that, alarmingly, only half the annual members were renewing their memberships; therefore, with the board's approval, she implemented a billing practice similar to that of the North Carolina Literary and Historical Association, by which second notices were mailed to members who failed to renew within a given time. Initial SPA notices (sent to all members listed since 1970) highlighted the grants program and appealed for support against rampant "bulldozeritis."

Once Whitley had finished pruning the membership rolls of delinquents, she reported to the board in November that the society had a total enrollment of 993, including 491 life members and 394 annual members. That figure was the lowest overall count since 1956 and the lowest number of annual members since 1946. Attempting to halt the slide in membership, the board in September 1973 inaugurated a policy of holding regional board meetings throughout the state in order to generate more interest. Discouragingly, after so many years of trying to raise membership and funds, the society was losing ground and entered 1974 operating at a deficit. It was clear that more had to be done.

Plans and Goals: Striving for New Purpose

The introspective discussions on the future activities and role of the society that had begun under the presidency of Harry Gatton continued under Jack Tyler and

Virginia Zenke. The board conducted a particularly expansive discussion at its April 1972 meeting. Suggestions ranged from developing new award programs to instituting a revolving fund in lieu of grants. Upon the motion of Dr. Banks C. Talley Jr., the board resolved to apply for a study grant from the National Trust. Accordingly (and as mentioned above), the SPA in May 1972 applied for funds to study the possibility of establishing a statewide fund for preservation grants and loans.

Once word was received from the National Trust in early 1973 that the grant had been approved, society members weighed their options on how the funds should be used. The trust awarded the grant for consultant services only, although at first that limitation was not clear to SPA leaders, who thought they had greater latitude in applying the money. At its March meeting the board considered using the grant to prepare materials for soliciting new members, but Frank Stephenson argued that the society needed a statement of purpose before taking action on the grant. (Years later Stephenson remembered that with the old leadership "aging out," he felt the society was drifting, with no agenda for the future.) The board responded (upon a motion by Harry Gatton) by authorizing President Zenke to "appoint a committee to develop a specific plan . . . to implement the goals of the society . . . and to receive funds to achieve these goals, including the establishment of a trust fund."

With the board committed to rejuvenating the society, at least one SPA leader recognized that the capability of the existing all-volunteer board with a part-time staff member was already stretched to the limit. Within a week of the free-ranging March discussion, Frank Stephenson wrote Virginia Zenke to urge that the society "shoot for" a full-time executive director to take the organizational "bull by the horns." He warned that otherwise the board would continue to face many problems that it could not solve.

With the help of Robert Stipe, who in September 1974 would assume the directorship of the North Carolina Division of Archives and History (and thereby also become a member of the society's board), the search for new goals extended through and beyond 1974, the last year in which the society existed under its original charter. Therefore, although frequently discussed, no comprehensive revisions of SPA goals were adopted during its waning years. This is not to say, however, that the society was then without any sense of direction. Through the final years of the SPA, all agreed that principal purposes included raising public awareness of historic preservation and assisting Tar Heels in their local preservation projects. The society also recognized the state's heritage as worth saving for what it was. As Virginia Zenke later recalled, "North Carolina was finally waking up to the fact that we did not have to look like Williamsburg in order to be important."

Constitutional Change

The SPA leadership saw the need to make the image of the society more acceptable to the broad mass of North Carolinians and to speed the change of focus from "the social side" to new goals and programs. Harry Gatton remembered well the self-depreciating joke of his old boss, Sen. Sam Ervin, that Ervin qualified as a member of SPA because he was an "antique." Memories of the difficulties in managing gifts of real estate were also fresh. Finally, non-income-producing life memberships continued to sap the financial strength of the society. For those reasons the new generation of SPA leaders established a constitutional study committee that eventually achieved the renaming and rechartering of the society in 1974.

Upon the motion of John G. Newton at its April 1971 meeting, the board directed President Tyler to establish a committee of three to study the society's constitution and report its findings to the board. Tyler appointed a Constitution Committee the following December. Originally the committee was composed of Virginia Ford Zenke, H. G. Jones, and Newton. Citing business demands, Newton stepped down and was replaced in April 1972 by Frank Stephenson, who was made chairman. In 1973 committee membership again changed under the presidency of Virginia Zenke. Stephenson remained as chairman and H. G. Jones as a member; joining the two men were past presidents Harry Gatton and Jack Tyler.

The thirty-year-old Stephenson was director of admissions at Chowan College. He was also executive director of the Murfreesboro Historical Association, which planned to restore a twelve-block historic district. Stephenson's group had raised $225,000 and owned a number of historic properties, two of which it was developing as a museum and a village center. As a leader of those efforts, Stephenson received a Cannon Cup Award in 1970. He had also taken his "show on the road" and, with before-and-after slides of the Murfreesboro restorations, inspired others in North Carolina to do the same. As an example of the growing inclusiveness of the preservation movement, Stephenson helped an African American group in Winton save the historic C. S. Brown School for reuse as a cultural arts center.

Among its duties to review and propose updates to the constitution, Stephenson's committee was directed to deal with the continuing problem of life members, a large proportion of whom were inactive. Stephenson presented a draft for a new constitution to the board in March 1973. Principal changes included: adopting as a new name "The North Carolina Preservation Society"; making the district vice-presidents members of the board of directors; deleting Section (a) of Article II, which authorized the society's ownership and restoration of historic properties; and deleting Section (c) of Article II, which provided for the establishment of branch societies.

E. Frank Stephenson Jr. of Murfreesboro chaired the SPA's Constitution Committee in 1972 and 1973. Photograph (1967) courtesy Mr. Stephenson.

A generic all-purpose clause was substituted for the deleted property ownership section: "To encourage the preservation and restoration of early North Carolina structures of local, regional, state and national significance." Despite a directive to address the thorny issue of nonproductive life memberships, no amendment was offered except for raising their cost from one hundred to five hundred dollars.

In its meetings of March and May 1973, the SPA board discussed and debated the new constitution. All agreed that the old name was too long and that the term "antiquities" reflected a negative image for historic preservation. Virginia Zenke recalled that they "wanted more of an architectural image" in the name. But Newton and Tyler felt that the name "North Carolina Preservation Society" was not descriptive enough. The issue was resolved when H. G. Jones suggested the name "The Historic Preservation Society of North Carolina, Inc." Nonetheless, at the 1973 annual meeting Jones's compromise had to weather a final riposte from sixty-five-year-old artist Henry Jay MacMillan of Wilmington. Arguing against use of the word "historic" as part of the society's name, the former SPA vice-president brought down the house when he declared in a rich drawl, "Everyone knows that we're not preserving fruit for the winter!"

Jack Zehmer, attending his first SPA meeting as an officer, questioned dropping the property ownership section. But Tyler informed him that it was to protect the SPA from having properties donated to it "only when there is nothing else to do with them." Of course, Tyler spoke for the rest of the board, and striking the ownership clause would be an effective shield against pressures to accept properties. Yet, the deletion of the clause deprived the society of future flexibility in devising ways to save historic properties. There had never been any compulsion for the SPA to accept properties merely because they were offered.

Upon the motion of Banks Talley, the SPA membership approved the constitutional changes at the November 1973 annual meeting. Stephenson and Frances Whitley handled the paperwork necessary to change the corporate name and to amend the constitution. Whitley hit a temporary roadblock when she was shocked to learn that the original charter of the society had been suspended since 1963, because of (in the words of the society's minutes) a "lack of communication with the North Carolina Department of Revenue." She moved quickly to reinstate the old charter as a necessary step for its amendment. Finally, on February 4, 1974, the articles of amendment were filed with the office of the North Carolina Secretary of State, and the name of the old society was officially changed to the Historic Preservation Society of North Carolina.

Sunrise on the Eno

Virginia Ford Zenke was the last president of the North Carolina Society for the Preservation of Antiquities. She was also the first president of the Historic Preservation Society of North Carolina. In April 1994 she recalled her years as president, when she drove from Greensboro to Raleigh for the society's meetings. To arrive on time, Zenke would leave in the pitch-darkness of night. At about the time she crested a hill near the Eno River, she would see the sunrise, which gave her a feeling of hope and encouragement for the day to come.

Preservation North Carolina (the Historic Preservation Foundation of North Carolina) owns and operates the Bellamy Mansion Museum of History and Design Arts (*top*) in Wilmington. Ayr Mount in Hillsborough (*bottom*), an important 1817 Federal-style house restored and magnificently furnished by Richard H. Jenrette, is open to the public through the stewardship program of Preservation North Carolina. The SPA attempted to acquire the property in the early 1940s. Both photographs by Tim Buchman from Bisher, *North Carolina Architecture*; reproduced courtesy Preservation North Carolina.

The society's fortunes rose with its rechartering in February 1974. It could move ahead to fulfill its role as the private-sector leader in North Carolina's historic preservation movement. Many challenges lay ahead. The development of goals and programs continued, and in January 1984 the society again restructured itself to become the Historic Preservation Foundation of North Carolina, also known as Preservation North Carolina.

Eventually the organization discontinued life memberships; hired full-time professional staff; fielded regional offices; established an endowment; increased its advocacy; quadrupled its membership; and resumed its revolving fund, which by 1997 had saved more than 275 buildings and generated an estimated seventy million dollars in private investment. The foundation also achieved national fame for its new award-winning programs, including educational materials for schools, books, films, exhibits, conferences, and workshops. Finally, in coming full circle as a property owner, it would successfully undertake the stewardship of North Carolina's greatest historic houses, including the Bellamy Mansion in Wilmington, Ayr Mount in Hillsborough, Coolmore in Tarboro, and the Banker's House in Shelby. Today it stands, in the words of the National Park Service, "as the premier statewide preservation organization of the South, if not the Nation. . . ."

Conclusion

At the beginning of the twentieth century, no organized historic preservation movement existed in North Carolina. Isolated private-sector attempts to preserve some of the state's most significant local landmarks occurred in the first three decades of the century, as in the case of the Cupola House in Edenton and the Joel Lane House in Raleigh. Much of the early preservation work was performed by women's patriotic and civic groups.

History-minded North Carolinians took notice of the visible and effective preservation organizations that existed outside the state; one notable example was the Association for the Preservation of Virginia Antiquities, founded in 1889. A sense of state pride generated a desire in socially elite North Carolinians to emulate the Virginians. The establishment in 1903 and the subsequent growth of the North Carolina Historical Commission, which became the Department of Archives and History in 1943, likewise stimulated interest in historic preservation in North Carolina. The restoration of Williamsburg fueled a desire to reconstruct Tryon Palace in the old colonial capital of New Bern.

In 1939, energized by the publication of the state garden club's *Old Homes and Gardens of North Carolina*, Tar Heels followed the Virginia example by forming a statewide organization dedicated to the preservation of historic buildings and sites. A combination of socially prominent women, academicians, and the state's foremost public historian, Dr. Christopher Crittenden, secretary of the North Carolina Historical Commission, initially dominated the resulting North Carolina Society for the Preservation of Antiquities (SPA).

The SPA originally sought to follow the Virginia model of property holding through local chapters. That policy failed because of a lack of local enthusiasm and the effect of World War II in creating scarcities in construction materials and manpower and in cutting off hoped-for federal public works funding. The untimely death in 1942 of the SPA's capable first president, Col. Joseph Hyde Pratt, slowed the society's initial momentum.

Following the war, a circle of wealthy and socially prominent women, headed by Ruth Coltrane Cannon, dominated the SPA. Cannon's preservation oligarchy abandoned efforts to create a statewide organizational structure based on branches and in 1951 disavowed property ownership by the society as being beyond its operational and financial capabilities. Under Cannon the SPA developed small but innovative financial assistance programs of direct grants and revolving-fund loans to local groups seeking to acquire and restore historic properties. The precedent-setting revolving fund was probably the first of its kind in the nation.

The society also responded to local needs with advice and encouragement and provided a growing number of the state's preservationists with a centralized information

The Banker's House in Shelby, an 1875 French Second Empire house, is a stewardship property of Preservation North Carolina. Photograph by Tim Buchman from Bisher, *North Carolina Architecture*, reproduced courtesy Preservation North Carolina.

exchange and educational forum through an annual meeting during Culture Week, North Carolina's unique fall convocation of organizations devoted to promoting the arts, history, and literature. The society also conferred encouragement and recognition for achievement through the Cannon Cup Awards, initiated in 1948. At the same time, Cannon and her colleagues unwittingly undermined the future financial stability of the SPA by promoting the growth of life memberships, which deprived the society of annual revenue.

Although the society's leaders were wealthy and conservative, they were pragmatic enough to see that in the booming post-World War II era North Carolina's historic properties could not be saved by private philanthropy alone. Beginning in the late 1940s the SPA began a gradual change from emphasizing single-landmark preservation by nonprofit groups to preservation on a larger scale through governmental planning and controls. Advocacy by the society for comprehensive state preservation legislation helped to set the stage for the passage of preservation planning and protection laws in the early 1970s.

By the end of the 1960s, the success of the old society elites in educating the public in the values of historic preservation helped to generate the involvement of a greater number of North Carolinians from various walks and stations of life. More middle-class professionals and business people assumed the leadership and policy-making roles previously dominated by Ruth Cannon and her circle. As a group, people of great wealth and social prominence tended to fade from positions of leadership. Reasons for that change may lie in part in the greater democratization of the movement, the professionalization of the field, competition from charitable organizations, and changes in emphasis from high-style domestic architecture to a wider range of resources. Such questions offer potential for future study.

The passing of the founding generation of the SPA resulted in fresh ways of looking at the programs and mission of the society. Nevertheless, in their day Ruth Cannon and her colleagues had shown great resourcefulness in fitting the society into the much-changed post-World War II era. The shift from the Virginia model of property holding to advisory and financial-assistance services gave the organization a mission that it could fulfill with limited staff and operational resources. The innovative revolving fund was undercapitalized but, along with the society's two hundred-dollar grants, directly addressed critical preservation needs. The educational aspects of Culture Week and the advice and moral support that the leaders of the SPA gave to fledgling groups helped to build a grass-roots preservation movement throughout the state.

Yet, just as the society had adapted to new circumstances in the postwar era, a combination of external factors brought new stresses and by the late 1960s elicited the widespread belief that the society needed to change. Culture Week was quickly losing its place and prominence, and the SPA grants, now overshadowed by state and federal financial assistance programs, had lost half of their purchasing power through inflation since the 1940s. Although characterized by amicable relations and mutual support, the development of a professional historic preservation staff within the Department of Archives and History required new consideration of the place of the SPA in the division of public and private sector service responsibilities.

Perhaps of all the SPA programs, the revolving fund offered the greatest potential for valuable service in the future; but its undercapitalization, its conservative management, and its dissolution after the death of Ruth Cannon eliminated it as a program to build upon. Probably more than anything else, the disastrous excursions into property ownership with Richmond Hill and the Caldwell log school site underscored the limited operational capacity of the society as a volunteer organization.

Coolmore in Edgecombe County, an 1858-1860 Italian Villa house, is also a stewardship property of Preservation North Carolina. Photograph by Tim Buchman from Bisher, *North Carolina Architecture*; reproduced courtesy Preservation North Carolina.

All of those factors caused the society's leaders in the late 1960s and early 1970s to consider the development of new programs pertinent to the times. Nevertheless, the accumulated growth of underpriced life memberships over the years left the society financially prostrate. From outside appearances, it was an almost bankrupt association whose organizational energies were spent. Staff was limited to a part-time secretary, for whom office space was supplied by the Department of Archives and History. It was a time of crisis for the SPA. It could continue to stagnate (and at best evolve into being only a support group for the state preservation agency); it could merge with another organization and lose its essential identity and purpose; it could disband; or it could move forward.

The SPA moved forward. In order to regenerate vigor and to find a role for the organization in the remaining decades of the twentieth century, the society's leaders knew that its name had to be changed, that its membership and annual income had to be increased, and that new programs had to be developed. Thus, the Antiquities Society came to be renamed, rechartered, and reborn in 1974—and yet, the metamorphosis was incomplete. Life memberships should have been discontinued, and the old constitution's property-holding and development clause should have been retained to allow organizational flexibility in saving historic properties.

Still, the constitutional revisions of 1974 were less important in saving the society than that they were emblematic of the resolve of SPA leaders to keep striving for organizational improvement—a process that eventually resulted in the dropping of life memberships, the hiring of a full-time professional staff, the establishment of an independent headquarters, the development of new and innovative technical assistance and educational programs (such as supplementary materials for the public schools), and, most important of all, the operation of an aggressive revolving fund.

Because elite women played a prominent role in the SPA's history, it would be easy to conclude that their emphasis on high-style buildings left a unique imprint on the state's preservation movement. To a limited degree that may be true. Yet, in the nineteenth and early twentieth centuries men and women of all social classes believed that historic buildings were by definition rare, high style, and associated with prominent people.

Rather than being remembered for orienting the preservation movement toward a particular view of what was historic, the women of Cannon's circle should be credited for giving the movement respectability and entrée to the state's highest social and political circles. Fay Webb Gardner and Lillian Moore Robinson were businesswomen; Gardner and Elizabeth Stevenson Ives had powerful political connections; Ives had lived abroad, and like Inglis Fletcher had traveled extensively, gaining a world view of historic preservation. That unusual combination of talent, experience, and power gave the society benefits in innovative and pragmatic programs that shed the society of its house-museum mentality and stressed advisory and financial services at the local level. At a formative time in the national preservation movement, those women also had the courage and insight to recognize the limitations of private-sector preservation efforts and to call for comprehensive governmental planning and protection of the state's historical resources.

Although female leaders of the SPA enjoyed power and prestige as members of North Carolina's elite, they still shared the disadvantages of their gender. Their effectiveness as preservation advocates too often was undercut by relegation to the

142

Working with a private owner, Preservation North Carolina is rehabilitating the 1929-1930 Shell Station in Winston-Salem for use as a PNC satellite office. The station is a rare surviving example of "roadside architecture." Photograph by Tim Buchman from Bisher, *North Carolina Architecture*; reproduced courtesy Preservation North Carolina.

society pages. Until the final few years of the SPA's existence, a constant anxiety (especially expressed by Christopher Crittenden) was that the society might be viewed as a "woman's organization."

The obvious reason for the concern was that female endeavors were too often viewed as inconsequential. Therefore, a movement dominated by women had a built-in credibility problem. Of course, time and time again, the female leaders of the SPA proved themselves to be just as practical, creative, and decisive as the men, if not more so, and it was Lura Tally, an SPA president, who went on to the legislature—not one of the male leaders.

Furthermore, outside observers of the SPA and its sister organizations viewed older people, male and female, as secondary players. The predominance of older members may have raised legitimate questions about the future of the organization. Yet, older people themselves were unfavorably and unfairly stigmatized, as in the Raleigh *News and Observer* editorial that ridiculed participants in Culture Week as "inbred . . . and unexciting," with their "dilapidated circus of culture." Little acknowledgment was made of the wisdom and leadership that older men and women provided such organizations. Both Pratt and Cannon, among the strongest of the SPA presidents, remained vigorously involved into their seventies.

As endemic and serious as those prejudices may have been, they dissipated in the final years of the SPA. The sex or age of the leaders and members ceased to be an issue. The new leadership and society activists were more evenly apportioned between men and women and among the young, middle-aged, and old. The appeal of historic preservation had stretched across class, age, and gender lines. By 1974 the society had forged a statewide citizens' movement. It had also given historic preservation public visibility and assisted almost every significant preservation project in the state. Led by twelve presidents, from Col. Joseph Hyde Pratt to Virginia Ford Zenke, the North Carolina Society for the Preservation of Antiquities gave the citizens of North Carolina a lasting gift of heritage.

Appendix A

Charter Members of the SPA and Names of Persons Who Attended the Organization's First Meeting

(All names are shown exactly as they appear in the society's records, with corrections or possible alternate spellings shown in brackets. Some names have also been placed in proper alphabetical order.)

Charter Members

Adickes, Mrs. Thomas W., 2212 Circle, Raleigh

Akers, Miss Susan Grey, Box 766, Chapel Hill

Albertson, Catherine, Elizabeth City

Allen, Ada H., 730 Church St., Winston-Salem

Anderson, Mrs. John H., 617 N. Blount St., Raleigh

Andrews, Graham H., 1906 Park Drive, Raleigh

Andrews, Miss Jane Virginia, 105 E. North St., Raleigh

Andrews, Miss Martha Bailey, 105 E. North St., Raleigh

Armfield, C. C., Winston-Salem

Arrington, Mrs. Katherine Pendleton, Warrenton

Bahnson, A. H., 702 W. 5th St., Winston-Salem

Bahnson, Mrs. A. H., 702 W. 5th St., Winston-Salem

Bahnson, Fred, 28 Cascade Ave., Winston-Salem

Bahnson, Mrs. Fred, 28 Cascade Ave., Winston-Salem

Ballou, Mrs. James W., Linden Ave., Oxford

Battle, George Gordon, 70 Pine St., New York, N.Y.

Battle, K. D., Rocky Mount

Battle, Mrs. S. Westray, Asheville

Bedinger, Henry G., Flora MacDonald College, Red Springs

Bell, Mrs. Hiram, 601 Summit Ave., Greensboro

Bellamy, Mrs. Hargrove, 1417 Market St., Wilmington

Bellamy, Mrs. William McKoy, 203 N. 15th St., Wilmington

Berg, Mrs. T. A., Brevard

Bernhardt, Mrs. R. L., 202 W. Banks [Bank] St., Salisbury

Biggs, Miss Jeannette E., Oxford

Blair, William A., 210 S. Cherry St., Winston-Salem

Bluethenthal, Mrs. Herbert, 1704 Market St., Wilmington

Bond, Mrs. Lyn, 1307 St. Andrew St., Tarboro

Boone, Mrs. W. D., Winton

Borden, Mrs. Paul L., 305 W. Mulberry St., Goldsboro

Bowling, Edgar S., Lawrence Park, Bronxville, N.Y.

Boyd, James, Southern Pines

Boyd, Mrs. William Norwood, Warrenton

Bridgers, Miss Ann Preston, 1306 Hillsboro St., Raleigh

Briggs, Willis G., Capital Club Bldg., Raleigh

Brinkley, Dr. John R., 1929 Wright Ave., Little Rock, Ark.

Brooks, A. L., Irving Park, Greensboro

Brooks, Mrs. A. L., Irving Park, Greensboro

Brooks, Mrs. T. A., Bath

Brown, Miss Ettie, Flora MacDonald College, Red Springs

Burt, Miss Clare Louise, Mystic, Pinehurst

Cannon, Charles A., Box 416, Concord

Cannon, Mrs. Charles A., Box 416, Concord

Carlson, Mrs. C. I., 705 Sunset Drive, Greensboro

Carr, Mrs. Elias, Bracebridge Hall, Macclesfield

Carr, George Watts, Durham

Carraway, Miss Gertrude S., New Bern

Caviness, Mrs. Vern [Verne] S., 913 Vance St., Raleigh

Chaffin, Miss Nora C., 285 College Station, Durham

Chamberlain, Miss Helen B., Kinston

Cheatham, Mrs. W. T., 903 W. Davis St., Burlington

Cheshire, James W., Hillsboro

Clark, Miss Nan G., Tarboro

Clark, Miss Rena H., Tarboro

Clarkson, Francis, Charlotte

Clarkson, Judge Heriot, Raleigh

Clarkson, Mrs. Heriot, 215 E. Lane St., Raleigh

Claypoole, Mrs. J. S., New Bern

Clonts, Mrs. F. W., Wake Forest

Cobb, Miss Lucy, Raleigh

Coffman, George R., Chapel Hill

Combs, A. B., 2238 Circle Drive, Raleigh

Conner [Connor] , Mrs. R. D. W., The Kennedy-Warren, Washington, D.C.

Cooper, Mrs. Alex, Henderson

Cooper [Cowper], [Judge] G. V., Kinston

Cooper, Mrs. John D., Jr., Stoneridge, Henderson

Cotten, Bruce, 4915 Greenspring Ave., Baltimore, Md.

Cotten, Mrs. Lynn [Lyman] A., Hooper Lane, Chapel Hill

Cox, Albert L., Shoreham Bldg., Washington, D.C.

Craig [Craige], Burton, Winston-Salem

Cramer, Mrs. Rebecca Warren, Maymont, Cramerton

Crittenden, Dr. C. C., Raleigh

Crittenden, Miss [Mrs.] Ethel, Wake Forest

Crowder, Miss Ethel S., Henderson

Curl, Mrs. N. W., 203 N. Cherry St., Winston-Salem

Currie, Mrs. Neill A., 1305 Morganton Rd., Fayetteville

Daniels, Josephus, Raleigh

Davidson, Mrs. Baxter Craighead, "Rosedale," Salisbury Rd., Charlotte

Davis, Harry T., N.C. State Museum, Raleigh

Deitrick, Wm. Henley, 115 W. Morgan St., Raleigh

Deitrick, Mrs. Wm. Henley, Country Club Dr., Raleigh

Delemar [Delamar] , Miss Marybelle, 100 N. Bloodworth St., Raleigh

DeVane, Miss Annie Belle, Red Springs

Dixon, Richard Dillard, Beverly Hall, Edenton

Dodge, J. P., Marion

Dortch, Miss Sally, 220 N. Wilmington St., Raleigh

Douglas, Martin F., Greensboro

Dunavant, Mrs. H. J., 1040 Queens Rd., Charlotte

Dwelle, Mr. & Mrs. Harold C., 812 E. Trade St., Charlotte

Edwards, Miss Mattie Erma, Box 1881, Raleigh

Elliott, Mrs. George B., Wilmington

Evans, Mrs. M. H., Hertford

Evans, Mrs. R. Bailey, Summertime Place, Fayetteville

Farrell, Chas. A., The Art Shop, Greensboro

Fenner, Mrs. Anna Baker, Tarboro

Fisher, Mrs. L. E., 308 Cumberland Ave., Asheville

Fleming, Mrs. Loula W., 302 Green St., Greenville

Fore, Mrs. James A., 821 N. College St., Charlotte

Foust, Mrs. Julius I., Greensboro

Fries, Dr. Adelaide L., 224 S. Cherry St., Winston-Salem

Fry, Fielding L., Greensboro

Gary, Mrs. Sterling M., Halifax

Goode, Mrs. J. B., Box 168, Rocky Mount

Gosney, Mrs. C. A., 2205 Circle Drive, Raleigh

Graham, Dr. Frank P., Chapel Hill

Gray, Gordon, Winston-Salem

Gray, Mrs. Gordon, Reynolda, Winston-Salem

Gray, Mrs. James A., Winston-Salem

Green, Ernest M., Box 941, Raleigh

Green, Mrs. Ernest M., Wendell Road, Raleigh

Green, Walter G., Jr., 28 West Grove Ave.,
Alexandria, Va.

Greenlee, Miss Mary M., Old Fort

Grier, Harry P., Jr., 939 Davie Ave., Statesville

Grier, Mrs. Harry P., Sr., 923 Davie Ave.,
Statesville

Griffin, Clarence, Forest City

Grimes, Miss Olivia Blount, 501 New Bern
Ave., Raleigh

Haberkern, Mrs. R. C., 833 Oaklawn Ave.,
Winston-Salem

Hale, Dr. Fred, Raleigh

Hall, Dr. J. K., Westbrook Sanatorium,
Richmond, Va.

Hanes, Pleasant Huber, 2000 Georgia Ave.,
Winston-Salem

Hanes, Ralph P., Box 202, Winston-Salem

Harrison, Mrs. Jno. W., 815 Holt Dr., Raleigh

Haywood, Mrs. Marshall Delancey [De
Lancey], 127 E. Edenton St., Raleigh

Haywood, Miss Martha H., 204 S. Boylan Ave.,
Raleigh

Haywood, Mrs. T. Holt, 106 Cherry St.,
Winston-Salem

Henderson, Dr. Archibald, Chapel Hill

Henderson, Miss Mary F., Hooper Lane,
Chapel Hill

Highsmith, Mrs. J. Henry, 832 W. [Wake]
Forest Road, Raleigh

Hill, John Sprunt, Durham

Hines, Chas. A., Greensboro

Hinton, Miss Mary Hilliard,
Midway Plantation, Raleigh

Hoey, Mrs. C. R., Governors Mansion, Raleigh

Hoge, James Fulton, 850 Park Ave.,
New York, N.Y.

Hoge, Mrs. James Fulton, 850 Park Ave.,
New York, N.Y.

Hollister, Mrs. John H., New Bern

Hollowell, Miss Margaret, Bay Side,
Elizabeth City

Holmes, J. S., 302 Forest Road, Raleigh

Holt, Mrs. Thomas J., Warrenton

Horne, Josh L., The Evening Telegram,
Rocky Mount

Horn [Horne], Miss Virginia, Wadesboro

Hudson, K. G., Raleigh

Humber, Robert Lee, 44 Ave.
des Champs Elipees [Elysees], Paris, France

Hunter, H. T., Cullowhee

Hyatt, Miss Sybil, Kinston

Idol, Mrs. Virgil, 1355 Peachtree St., N.E.,
Atlanta, Ga.

Jackson, Mrs. Herbert W., 1024 W. Franklin St.,
Richmond, Va.

James, Mrs. J. B., Fifth St. & Holly Lane,
Greenville

Jerman, Mrs. T. Palmer, 109 E. Lane St.,
Raleigh

Johnson, Julian, Greensboro

Johnson, Dr. Wingate M., Winston-Salem

Johnston, Hugh B., Jr., Wilson

Jones, Mrs. Cecil, Public Library, Greensboro

Jones, Mrs. H. C., 201 Cherokee Rd.,
Charlotte

Kellenberger, John A., Box 263, Rt. #4,
Greensboro

Kellenberger, Mrs. John A., Box 263, Rt. #4,
Greensboro

Kenan, Miss Emily Howard, Wilmingon

Kenan, Mrs. Graham, St. Augustine, Fl.;
Wilmington

Killian, J. Y., Newton

King, Mrs. W. J., 107 S. Deans St., Wilson

Knapp, Mrs. Jos. P., 435 E. 52nd St.,
New York, N.Y.

Koch, Frederick H., Chapel Hill

Koonce, Mrs. Marvin Burke, 2203 Byrd St.,
Raleigh

LaBouice [Labouisse], Mrs. John W.,
232 Cherokee Rd., Charlotte

Langston, Mrs. Arthur E., 110 E. North St.,
Raleigh

Latham, Mrs. J. E., Hood Place, Greensboro

Lewis, K. P., Durham

Lewis, McDaniel, Greensboro

London, Mrs. Henry M., 301 N. Blount St.,
Raleigh

Long, Mrs. Glenn, Newton

Long, Dr. T. W. M., Roanoke Rapids

Long, Mrs. T. W. M., Roanoke Rapids

Lucas, Mrs. William A., 1407 Nash St., Wilson

MacClamroch [MacLamroc], James G. W.,
Greensboro

MacClamroch [MacLamroc], Mrs. James G. W.,
Greensboro

McClamroch, Mrs. James Robbins,
Greensboro

McClamroch, Julian Westwarren, Greensboro

McClamroch, Dr. Roland, Chapel Hill

MacClure, Mrs. J. G. K., Fairview

McGirt, Mrs. Harry S., Wilmington

McIven, Brig. Gen. George, Washington, D.C.

McKie, George, Chapel Hill

McKimmon, Dr. Jane S., State College,
Raleigh

MacLean, Mrs. Neill Archibald,
1103 N. Elm St., Lumberton

MacMillan, Mrs. C. S., Red Springs

MacMillan, Henry Jay, 118 S. 4th St.,
Wilmington

McMillan, Mrs. R. L., 1810 Park Drive,
Raleigh

McNatt, Mrs. J. C. D., Barium Springs

McNeill, Mrs. George, 325 Green St.,
Fayetteville

McPhetters [McPheeters], Miss Susan,
114 S. Dawson St., Raleigh

MacRae, Miss Monina F., 75 S. 3rd St.,
Wilmington

Mahler, Mrs. L. A., 802 N. Person St., Raleigh

Mann, Mrs. Carroll, 1702 Hillsboro St.,
Raleigh

Matthis, Mrs. George M., 1107 Watts St.,
Durham

Maurice, George H., Eagle Springs

Maxwell, A. J., Raleigh

Mebane, Mrs. Frank, Spray

Michie, Mrs. J. C., 108 Jackson St., Durham

Montague, Mrs. B. F., 313 New Bern Ave.,
Raleigh

Moore, Mrs. Margaret Fetner, Bentley Hotel,
Alexandria, La.

Newbold, N. C., Raleigh

Noe, Alex C. D., Bath

O'Berry, Annie L. (Mrs. Thomas), Goldsboro

Olsen, Mrs. William C., 806 Glenn Ave.,
Raleigh

Odum, Dr. Howard W., Chapel Hill

Outlaw, A. T., Kenansville

Owen, Mrs. Louis F., Kent Road, East,
Winston-Salem

Parker, J. Ray, Ahoskie

Parks [Park], John A., Raleigh Times, Raleigh

Parks [Park], Mrs. P. B., 1715 W. Pettigrew St.,
W. Durham

Parrish, Fred M., Winston-Salem

Parrott, Mrs. Dan W., Kinston

Patton, Mrs. Sadie L., Henderson
[Hendersonville]

Paylor, I. Irvin, 105 Brantley Circle,
Roland Park, High Point

Peace, Mrs. S. T., Henderson

Pell, Mrs. George P., 111 E. North St., Raleigh

Perry, Mrs. Emily Braswell, 1 Cornwallis Rd.,
Chapel Hill

Person, Mrs. T. A., 801 Evans St., Greenville

Plummer, James, 301 53rd St.,
Newport News, Va.

Poe, Dr. Clarence, Raleigh

Pratt, Dr. Joseph Hyde, Chapel Hill

Pratt, Mrs. Joseph Hyde, Chapel Hill

Pratt, Mrs. Stewart C., 205 Cascade Ave.,
Winston-Salem

Preter [Preyer], Mrs. William Y.,
122 E. 42nd St., New York, N.Y.

Preyer, William Y., 122 E. 42nd St.,
New York, N.Y.

Proctor, Mrs. Ivan M., 800 New Bern Ave.,
Raleigh

Proctor, Miss Jennie, 800 New Bern Ave.,
Raleigh

Pruden, Mrs. I. N., Edenton

Pruden, W. D., Edenton

Puett, Mrs. W. B., Belmont

Rankin, Mrs. P. R., Mount Gilead

Rhyne, Miss Alice H., Mount Holly

Rights, Rev. Douglas, Winston-Salem

Ritchardson [Richardson], Mrs. J. T.,
1715 Hillsboro St., Raleigh

Roberts, Coleman W., Charlotte

Robertson, Mrs. C. H., Hillsboro

Robertson, Miss Julia Johnston, Addison Apts.,
Charlotte

Rodman, Mrs. W. B. Jr., 520 W. Main St.,
Washington, N.C.

Rood, Henry Jr., 214 N. Cedar St., Greensboro

Ruffin, Peter B., Wilmington

Russell, Lindsay, Wilmington

Sanders [Saunders], W. O., Elizabeth City

Seagle, Rev. Nathan A.[,] D.D.,
120 W. 69th St., New York, N.Y.

Shaffner, Miss C. L., 147 S. Cherry St.,
Winston-Salem

Shaffner, H. F., Winston-Salem

Shaffner, William F., Winston-Salem

Shepherd, Mrs. S. Brown,
2411 Country Club Dr., Raleigh

Sidbury, Dr. J. Buren, Wilmington

Sidbury, Mrs. J. Buren, Wilmington

Smethurst, Mrs. Frank, 1605 St. Mary's St.,
Raleigh

Smith, Mrs. Charles Lee,
515 N. Wilmington St., Raleigh

Smith, Miss Pauline, Washington, N.C.
Smith, Mrs. Seth L., 401 N. Madison Ave.,
    Whiteville
Smith, Willis, Raleigh
Smithwick, D. T., Louisburg
Smoot, Dr. J. Edward, Concord
Soencer [Spencer], Mrs. C. Wayne,
    514 Princess St., Wilmington
Somers, Mrs. J. F., Mansion Park Hotel,
    Raleigh
Sparger, Mrs. S. Gilmer, 2214 Fairview Road,
    Raleigh
Spaugh, Mrs. R. Arthur, 745 Arbor Road,
    Winston-Salem
Spruill, Mrs. F. S., Rocky Mount
Sprunt, Mrs. Lawrence [Laurence],
    Wilmington
Stallings, Mrs. Poteat, Yanceyville
Staples, John N., 745 Fifth Ave.,
    New York, N.Y.
Stewart, Mrs. Mattie H., 917 N. College St.,
    Charlotte
Stone, Mrs. R. R., Wilmington
Street, Mrs. Robert B., 1522 Park Drive,
    Charlotte
Swindell, Mrs. J. E., 2109 Fairview Road,
    Raleigh
Syme, Mrs. George F., 226 E. North St.,
    Raleigh
Taylor, C. Ed., Southport
Thompson, Miss Elizabeth Warren,
    1117 Hillsboro St., Raleigh

Thompson, Miss Lillian Macon,
    1117 Hillsboro St., Raleigh
Tillett, C. W., Charlotte
Townsend, Dallas S., 120 Broadway,
    New York, N.Y.
Tucker, Mrs. Garland S., 420 N. Blount St.,
    Raleigh
Vail, Mrs. J. M., Edenton
Vass, Miss Eleanor M., E. Edenton St., Raleigh
Ward, Miss Mary Pickett, New Bern
Watkins, Dr. J. C., Winston-Salem
Weddell, Mrs. Louie M., 142 N. Church St.,
    Rocky Mount
Weil, Leslie, Goldsboro
Welborn, Mrs. John Scott, High Point
White, Mrs. Lorentz, 404 Whitaker Mill Rd.,
    Raleigh
Wicker, Rassie, Pinehurst
Williamson, Mrs. J. Walter, 602 Market St.,
    Wilmington
Willis, Mrs. W. R., Farmville
Winfree, Mrs. John N. [M.], 330 Hillsboro,
    Raleigh
Winslow, Francis E., Rocky Mount
Winston, Mrs. Robert W., Jr., Oxford Road,
    Raleigh
Woodard, Mrs. P. L., Wilson
Worthington, Samuel Wheeler, Wilson
Wright, Mrs. R. Lee, 302 S. Fulton St.,
    Salisbury
Wyche, Mrs. Benjamin, 1943 Queens Road,
    Charlotte
Zoeller, E. V., Tarboro

Names of Persons Who Attended the First Meeting of the SPA (Raleigh, October 20, 1939)

Mrs. Katherine Pendleton Arrington,
    Warrenton
Mrs. Willis G. Briggs, Raleigh
Mr. DeWitt Carroll, Raleigh Times, Raleigh
Mrs. Vern [Verne] Caviness, Raleigh
Miss Helen Bryan Chamberlain, Kinston
Judge Heriot Clarkson, Raleigh
Miss Lucy M. Cobb, Raleigh
Dr. C. C. Crittenden, Raleigh
Mrs. Christopher Crittenden, Raleigh
Miss [Mrs.] Ethel Taylor Crittenden,
    Wake Forest
Mr. & Mrs. Wm. H. Deitrick, Raleigh

Miss Sally Dortch, Raleigh
Miss [Mattie] Erma Edwards, Raleigh
Mr. Chas. A. Farrell, Greensboro
Dr. Adelaide Fries, Winston-Salem
Mrs. Sterling M. Gary, Halifax
Mr. and Mrs. C. A. Gosney, Raleigh
Mr. Ernest M. Green, Raleigh
Mrs. Harry P. Grier Sr., Statesville
Miss Olivia Blount Grimes, Raleigh
Mrs. Marshall DeLancey [De Lancey]
    Haywood, Raleigh
Dr. Archibald Henderson, Chapel Hill
Mrs. J. Henry Highsmith, Raleigh

Mr. J. S. Holmes, Raleigh
Mr. & Mrs. J. A. Kellenberger, Greensboro
Mr. Paul Kelly, Raleigh
Mrs. Marvin Burke Koonce, Raleigh
Mrs. J. E. Latham, Greensboro
Mr. McDaniel Lewis, Greensboro
Mrs. Henry M. London, Raleigh
Mr. James G. W. MacClamrock [MacLamroc], Greensboro
Dr. Jane S. McKimmon, Raleigh
Mrs. R. L. McMillan, Raleigh
Miss Suan [Susan] McPheeters, Raleigh
Mr. George H. Maurice, Eagle Springs
Mr. Walter Murphy, Salisbury

Mrs. Annie L. O'Berry (Mrs. Thomas), Goldsboro
Mrs. Dan W. Parrott, Kinston
Dr. Joseph Hyde Pratt, Chapel Hill
Mrs. William B. Rodman Jr., Washington, N.C.
Mr. Henry Rood Jr., Greensboro
Miss C. S. [L.] Shaffner, Winston-Salem
Mrs. Sprague Silver, Raleigh
Mrs. Frank Smethurst, Raleigh
Mrs. Charles Lee Smith, Raleigh
Mrs. J. F. Somers, Raleigh
Mrs. J. E. Swindell, Raleigh
Miss Elizabeth Warren Thompson, Raleigh
Mrs. Elizabeth H. Winfree, Raleigh

Appendix B

Officers, Directors, and District Vice-Presidents of the SPA, 1939-1974

October 20, 1939-December 5, 1940

Officers

President: Dr. Joseph Hyde Pratt, Chapel Hill
Vice-President: James Boyd, Southern Pines
Secretary-Treasurer: Janie Fetner Gosney
(Mrs. C. A. Gosney), Raleigh

Directors

Ruth Coltrane Cannon
(Mrs. Charles A. Cannon), Concord
Judge Richard Dillard Dixon, Edenton
Adelaide Lisetta Fries, Winston-Salem
Emily Gregory Gilliam Gary
(Mrs. Sterling Gary), Halifax
Dr. Archibald Henderson, Chapel Hill

District Vice-Presidents

First: Mrs. W. B. Rodman Jr., Washington, N.C.
Second: Anna Baker Fenner, Tarboro
Third: Gertrude S. Carraway, New Bern
Fourth: Willis Briggs, Raleigh
Fifth: Rev. Douglas L. Rights, Winston-Salem
Sixth: McDaniel Lewis, Greensboro
Seventh: Eliza Bellamy Williamson
(Mrs. J. Walter Williamson), Wilmington
Eighth: George H. Maurice, Eagle Springs
Ninth: Marietta Grier
(Mrs. Harry P. Grier), Statesville
Tenth: C. W. Tillett, Charlotte
Eleventh: Mrs. S. Westray Battle, Asheville

December 5, 1940-December 4, 1941

Officers

President: Dr. Joseph Hyde Pratt, Chapel Hill
Vice-President: McDaniel Lewis, Greensboro
Secretary-Treasurer: Janie Fetner Gosney,
Raleigh

Directors

Ruth Coltrane Cannon, Concord
Adelaide Lisetta Fries, Winston-Salem
Emily Gregory Gilliam Gary, Halifax
Dr. Archibald Henderson, Chapel Hill
Maude Moore Latham
(Mrs. James Edwin Latham), Greensboro

District Vice-Presidents

First: Mrs. M. H. Evans, Hertford
Second: Katherine Pendleton Arrington,
Warrenton
Third: Gertrude S. Carraway, New Bern
Fourth: Mrs. Verne S. Caviness, Raleigh
Fifth: Rev. Douglas L. Rights, Winston-Salem
Sixth: James G. W. MacLamroc
(McClamroc, MacClamroch), Greensboro
Seventh: Erla Stone, Wilmington
Eighth: George H. Maurice, Eagle Springs
Ninth: Marietta Grier, Statesville
Tenth: Alice H. Rhyne, Mount Holly
Eleventh: Mrs. R. N. Barber, Waynesville

December 4, 1941-December 2, 1942

Officers

President: Dr. Joseph Hyde Pratt
(died June 3, 1942)
Vice-President: McDaniel Lewis, Greensboro
(became president June 1941)
Secretary-Treasurer: Janie Fetner Gosney,
Raleigh

Directors

Ruth Coltrane Cannon, Concord
Adelaide Lisetta Fries, Winston-Salem
Emily Gregory Gilliam Gary, Halifax
Dr. Archibald Henderson, Chapel Hill
Maude Moore Latham, Greensboro

District Vice-Presidents

First: Judge Richard Dillard Dixon, Edenton
Second: Katherine Pendleton Arrington,
Warrenton
Third: Gertrude S. Carraway, New Bern
Fourth: Mrs. Verne S. Caviness, Raleigh
Fifth: Rev. Douglas L. Rights, Winston-Salem
Sixth: James G. W. MacLamroc, Greensboro
Seventh: Erla Stone, Wilmington
Eighth: George Maurice, Eagle Springs
Ninth: Mrs. Robert L. Bernhardt, Salisbury
Tenth: Alice Rhyne, Mount Holly
Eleventh: Mrs. R. N. Barber, Waynesville

December 2, 1942-December 6, 1943

Officers

President: McDaniel Lewis, Greensboro
Vice-President: Gertrude S. Carraway,
New Bern
Secretary-Treasurer: Janie Fetner Gosney,
Raleigh

Directors

Ruth Coltrane Cannon, Concord
Adelaide Lisetta Fries, Winston-Salem
Emily Gregory Gilliam Gary, Halifax
Dr. Archibald Henderson, Chapel Hill
Maude Moore Latham, Greensboro

District Vice-Presidents

First: Judge Richard Dillard Dixon, Edenton
Second: Katherine Pendleton Arrington,
Warrenton,
Third: Alice Parrott
(Mrs. Daniel Worth Parrott), Kinston
Fourth: Mrs. Verne S. Caviness, Raleigh
Fifth: Rev. Douglas L. Rights, Winston-Salem
Sixth: James G. W. MacLamroc, Greensboro
Seventh: Erla Stone, Wilmington
Eighth: George H. Maurice, Eagle Springs
Ninth: Mrs. Robert L. Bernhardt, Salisbury
Tenth: Alice H. Rhyne, Mount Holly
Eleventh: Mrs. R. N. Barber, Waynesville

December 6, 1943-December 11, 1944

Officers

President: McDaniel Lewis, Greensboro
Vice-President: Gertrude S. Carraway,
New Bern
Secretary-Treasurer: Janie Fetner Gosney,
Raleigh

Directors

Ruth Coltrane Cannon, Concord
Adelaide Lisetta Fries, Winston-Salem
Emily Gregory Gilliam Gary, Halifax
Dr. Archibald Henderson, Chapel Hill
Maude Moore Latham, Greensboro

District Vice-Presidents

First: Judge Richard Dillard Dixon, Edenton
Second: Katherine Pendleton Arrington,
Warrenton
Third: Alice Parrott, Kinston
Fourth: Mrs. Verne S. Caviness, Raleigh
Fifth: Rev. Douglas L. Rights, Winston-Salem
Sixth: James G. W. MacLamroc, Greensboro
Seventh: Erla Stone, Wilmington
Eighth: George H. Maurice, Eagle Springs
Ninth: Mrs. Robert L. Bernhardt, Salisbury
Tenth: Alice H. Rhyne, Mount Holly
Eleventh: Mrs. R. N. Barber, Waynesville

December 11, 1944-December 13, 1945

Officers

President: Ruth Coltrane Cannon, Concord
Vice-President: Gertrude S. Carraway,
New Bern
Secretary-Treasurer: Janie Fetner Gosney,
Raleigh, to November 1945;
Charlie Huss Lovejoy
(Mrs. Gordon Lovejoy), Raleigh, from
November 1945

Directors

Adelaide Lisetta Fries, Winston-Salem
Maude Moore Latham, Greensboro
McDaniel Lewis, Greensboro
Mary Lee McMillan (Mrs. R. L. McMillan),
Raleigh

District Vice-Presidents

First: Judge Richard Dillard Dixon, Edenton
Second: Katherine Pendleton Arrington,
Warrenton
Third: Minnette Chapman Duffy
(Mrs. Richard Nixon Duffy), New Bern
Fourth: Cora Vaughan Smith
(Mrs. Charles Lee Smith), Raleigh
Fifth: Rev. Douglas L. Rights, Winston-Salem
Sixth: May Gordon Latham Kellenberger (Mrs.
John A. Kellenberger), Greensboro
Seventh: Erla Stone, Wilmington
Eighth: George H. Maurice, Eagle Springs
Ninth: Mrs. J. C. D. McNatt,
Barium Springs
Tenth: Julia J. Robertson, Charlotte
Eleventh: Mrs. S. Westray Battle, Asheville

December 13, 1945-December 5, 1946

Officers

President: Ruth Coltrane Cannon, Concord
Vice-President: Judge Richard Dillard Dixon,
Edenton
Secretary-Treasurer: Charlie Huss Lovejoy
(Mrs. Gordon Lovejoy), Raleigh, to April
1946; Joye Esch Jordan (Mrs. Coy Jordan),
Raleigh, May 1946; Christopher Crittenden,
Raleigh, acting, spring 1946 to September
1946; Mary Emma Parker Branch
(Mrs. Ernest Branch), Raleigh, from
September 1946

Directors

Gertrude S. Carraway, New Bern
Adelaide Lisetta Fries, Winston-Salem
Dr. Archibald Henderson, Chapel Hill
Maude Moore Latham, Greensboro
Mary Lee McMillan, Raleigh

District Vice-Presidents

First: Inglis Fletcher, Edenton
Second: Katherine Pendleton Arrington,
Warrenton
Third: Minnette Chapman Duffy, New Bern
Fourth: Cora Vaughan Smith, Raleigh
Fifth: Jane Henderson Boyden Craige Gray
(Mrs. Gordon Gray), Winston-Salem
Sixth: May Gordon Latham Kellenberger,
Greensboro
Seventh: Eliza Bellamy Williamson,
Wilmington
Eighth: George H. Maurice, Eagle Springs
Ninth: Mrs. Henkel Spillman, Statesville
Tenth: Julia J. Robertson, Charlotte
Eleventh: Ralph Erskine, Tryon
Twelfth: Mrs. Robert T. Cecil, Asheville

December 5, 1946-December 4, 1947

Officers
President: Ruth Coltrane Cannon, Concord
Vice-President: Judge Richard Dillard Dixon, Edenton
Secretary-Treasurer:
  Mary Emma Parker Branch, Raleigh

Directors
Gertrude S. Carraway, New Bern
Adelaide Lisetta Fries, Winston-Salem
Dr. Archibald Henderson, Chapel Hill
Maude Moore Latham, Greensboro
Mary Lee McMillan, Raleigh

District Vice-Presidents
First: Inglis Fletcher, Edenton

Second: Katherine Pendleton Arrington, Warrenton
Third: Minnette Chapman Duffy, New Bern
Fourth: Cora Vaughan Smith, Raleigh
Fifth: Jane Gray, Winston-Salem
Sixth: May Gordon Latham Kellenberger, Greensboro
Seventh: Eliza Bellamy Williamson, Wilmington
Eighth: George H. Maurice, Eagle Springs
Ninth: Mrs. Henkel Spillman, Statesville
Tenth: Julia J. Robertson, Charlotte
Eleventh: Ralph Erskine, Tryon
Twelfth: Mrs. Robert T. Cecil, Asheville

December 4, 1947-December 2, 1948

Officers
President: Ruth Coltrane Cannon, Concord
Vice-President: Inglis Fletcher, Edenton
Secretary-Treasurer:
  Mary Emma Parker Branch, Raleigh

Directors
Gertrude S. Carraway, New Bern
Adelaide Lisetta Fries, Winston-Salem
Dr. Archibald Henderson, Chapel Hill
Maude Moore Latham, Greensboro
Mary Lee McMillan, Raleigh

District Vice-Presidents
First: Mrs. Samuel N. Clark, Tarboro

Second: Katherine Pendleton Arrington, Warrenton
Third: Minnette Chapman Duffy, New Bern
Fourth: Cora Vaughan Smith, Raleigh
Fifth: Jane Gray, Winston-Salem
Sixth: May Gordon Latham Kellenberger, Greensboro
Seventh: Mrs. Henry J. MacMillan, Wilmington
Eighth: George H. Maurice, Eagle Springs
Ninth: Mrs. Henkel Spillman, Statesville
Tenth: Julia J. Robertson, Charlotte
Eleventh: Ralph Erskine, Tryon
Twelfth: Mrs. Robert T. Cecil, Asheville

December 2, 1948-December 1, 1949

Officers
President: Ruth Coltrane Cannon, Concord
Vice-President: Inglis Fletcher, Edenton
Secretary-Treasurer:
  Mary Emma Parker Branch, Raleigh

Directors
Gertrude S. Carraway, New Bern
Mrs. James A. Gray, Winston-Salem
Dr. Archibald Henderson, Chapel Hill
Maude Moore Latham, Greensboro
Mrs. P. R. Rankin, Mount Gilead

District Vice-Presidents
First: Mrs. Samuel N. Clark, Tarboro
Second: Katherine Pendleton Arrington, Warrenton

Third: Minnette Chapman Duffy, New Bern
Fourth: Cora Vaughan Smith, Raleigh
Fifth: Jane Gray, Winston-Salem
Sixth: May Gordon Latham Kellenberger, Greensboro
Seventh: Mrs. Henry J. McMillan, Wilmington
Eighth: George H. Maurice, Eagle Springs
Ninth: Mrs. Henkel Spillman, Statesville
Tenth: Fay Webb Gardner
  (Mrs. O. Max Gardner), Shelby
Eleventh: Ralph Erskine, Tryon
Twelfth: Mrs. Robert T. Cecil, Asheville

December 1, 1949-November 30, 1950

Officers
President: Ruth Coltrane Cannon, Concord
Vice-President: Inglis Fletcher, Edenton
Secretary-Treasurer: Mary Emma Parker
  Branch, Raleigh

Directors
Gertrude S. Carraway, New Bern
Mrs. James A. Gray, Winston-Salem
Dr. Archibald Henderson, Chapel Hill
Maude Moore Latham, Greensboro
Mrs. P. R. Rankin, Mount Gilead

District Vice-Presidents
First: Theo Meekins, Manteo
Second: Katherine Pendleton Arrington,
  Warrenton
Third: Minnette Chapman Duffy, New Bern
Fourth: Cora Vaughan Smith, Raleigh
Fifth: Jane Gray, Winston-Salem
Sixth: May Gordon Latham Kellenberger,
  Greensboro
Seventh: Mrs. Henry J. McMillan,
  Wilmington
Eighth: George H. Maurice, Eagle Springs
Ninth: Mrs. Henkel Spillman, Statesville
Tenth: Fay Webb Gardner, Shelby
Eleventh: Ralph Erskine, Tryon
Twelfth: Mrs. Robert T. Cecil, Asheville

November 30, 1950-December 6, 1951

Officers
President: Ruth Coltrane Cannon, Concord
Vice-President: Inglis Fletcher, Edenton
Secretary-Treasurer:
  Mary Emma Parker Branch, Raleigh

Directors
Gertrude S. Carraway, New Bern
Fay Webb Gardner, Shelby
Mrs. James A. Gray, Winston-Salem
Dr. Archibald Henderson, Chapel Hill
Mrs. P. R. Rankin, Mount Gilead

District Vice-Presidents
First: Theo Meekins, Manteo
Second: Katherine Pendleton Arrington,
  Warrenton
Third: Minnette Chapman Duffy, New Bern
Fourth: Cora Vaughan Smith, Raleigh
Fifth: Jane Gray, Winston-Salem
Sixth: May Gordon Latham Kellenberger,
  Greensboro
Seventh: Mrs. Henry J. McMillan,
  Wilmington
Eighth: George H. Maurice, Eagle Springs
Ninth: Mrs. Henkel Spillman, Statesville
Tenth: Mrs. Edward C. Marshall, Charlotte
Eleventh: Ralph Erskine, Tryon
Twelfth: Mrs. Robert T. Cecil, Asheville

December 6, 1951-December 4, 1952

Officers
President: Ruth Coltrane Cannon, Concord
Vice-President: Inglis Fletcher, Edenton
Secretary-Treasurer:
  Mary Emma Parker Branch, Raleigh

Directors
Gertrude S. Carraway, New Bern
Elizabeth Henderson Cotten, Chapel Hill
Fay Webb Gardner, Shelby
Mrs. James A. Gray, Winston-Salem
Dr. Archibald Henderson, Chapel Hill

District Vice-Presidents
First: Aycock Brown, Manteo
Second: Katherine Pendleton Arrington,
  Warrenton
Third: Mrs. Elias Carr, Macclesfield
Fourth: Cora Vaughan Smith, Raleigh
Fifth: Mrs. Edward M. Anderson,
  West Jefferson
Sixth: May Gordon Latham Kellenberger,
  Greensboro
Seventh: Mrs. J. Laurence Sprunt,
  Wilmington
Eighth: George H. Maurice, Eagle Springs
Ninth: Mrs. Henkel Spillman, Statesville
Tenth: Mrs. Edward C. Marshall, Charlotte
Eleventh: Mrs. J. D. Lineberger, Shelby
Twelfth: Mrs. E. Yates Webb, Asheville

December 4, 1952-December 3, 1953

Officers
President: Ruth Coltrane Cannon, Concord
Vice-President: Inglis Fletcher, Edenton
Secretary-Treasurer:
  Mary Emma Parker Branch, Raleigh

Directors
Gertrude S. Carraway, New Bern
Elizabeth Henderson Cotten, Chapel Hill
Fay Webb Gardner, Shelby
Mrs. James A. Gray, Winston-Salem
Dr. Archibald Henderson, Chapel Hill

District Vice-Presidents
First: Aycock Brown, Manteo
Second: Katherine Pendleton Arrington,
  Warrenton
Third: Mrs. Elias Carr, Macclesfield
Fourth: Cora Vaughan Smith, Raleigh
Fifth: Mrs. Edward M. Anderson, West
  Jefferson
Sixth: May Gordon Latham Kellenberger,
  Greensboro
Seventh: Mrs. J. Laurence Sprunt,
  Wilmington
Eighth: George H. Maurice, Eagle Springs
Ninth: Mrs. Henkel Spillman, Statesville
Tenth: Mrs. Edward C. Marshall, Charlotte
Eleventh: Mrs. J. D. Lineberger, Shelby
Twelfth: Mrs. Adrian Shuford, Conover

December 3, 1953-December 2, 1954

Officers
President: Ruth Coltrane Cannon, Concord
Vice-President: Inglis Fletcher, Edenton
Secretary-Treasurer:
  Mary Emma Parker Branch, Raleigh

Directors
Gertrude S. Carraway, New Bern
Elizabeth Henderson Cotten, Chapel Hill
Fay Webb Gardner, Shelby
Mrs. James A. Gray, Winston-Salem
Elizabeth Stevenson Ives
  (Mrs. Ernest L. Ives), Southern Pines

District Vice-Presidents
First: Aycock Brown, Manteo
Second: Katherine Pendleton Arrington,
  Warrenton
Third: Mrs. Elias Carr, Macclesfield
Fourth: Cora Vaughan Smith, Raleigh
Fifth: Mrs. Edward M. Anderson,
  West Jefferson
Sixth: May Gordon Latham Kellenberger,
  Greensboro
Seventh: Mrs. J. Laurence Sprunt,
  Wilmington
Eighth: George H. Maurice, Eagle Springs
Ninth: Mrs. Henkel Spillman, Statesville
Tenth: Mrs. Edward C. Marshall, Charlotte
Eleventh: Mrs. J. D. Lineberger, Shelby
Twelfth: Mrs. Adrian Shuford, Conover

December 2, 1954-December 1, 1955

Officers
President: Ruth Coltrane Cannon, Concord
Vice-President: Inglis Fletcher, Edenton
Secretary-Treasurer:
  Mary Emma Parker Branch, Raleigh

Directors
Gertrude S. Carraway, New Bern
Elizabeth Henderson Cotten, Chapel Hill
Fay Webb Gardner, Shelby
Dr. Archibald Henderson, Chapel Hill
Elizabeth Stevenson Ives, Southern Pines

District Vice-Presidents
First: Aycock Brown, Manteo
Second: Mrs. Edd F. Gardner, North
  Wilkesboro (on letterhead dated June 1,
  1955); Emily Gilliam Gary, Halifax (on
  letterhead dated November 1, 1955)
Third: Mrs. Elias Carr, Macclesfield
Fourth: Cora Vaughan Smith, Raleigh
Fifth: Mrs. Edward M. Anderson, West
  Jefferson
Sixth: May Gordon Latham Kellenberger,
  Greensboro
Seventh: Mrs. J. Laurence Sprunt,
  Wilmington
Eighth: George H. Maurice, Eagle Springs
Ninth: Mrs. Henkel Spillman, Statesville
Tenth: Mrs. Edward C. Marshall, Charlotte
Eleventh: Mrs. J. D. Lineberger, Shelby
Twelfth: Mrs. Adrian Shuford, Conover

December 1, 1955-December 6, 1956

Officers
President: Ruth Coltrane Cannon, Concord
Vice-President: Inglis Fletcher, Edenton
Secretary-Treasurer:
  Mary Emma Parker Branch, Raleigh

Directors
Gertrude S. Carraway, New Bern
Elizabeth Henderson Cotten, Chapel Hill
Fay Webb Gardner, Shelby
Dr. Archibald Henderson, Chapel Hill
Elizabeth Stevenson Ives, Southern Pines

District Vice-Presidents
First: Aycock Brown, Manteo
Second: Mrs. Elias Carr, Macclesfield
Third: Mrs. Claude B. Foy, New Bern
Fourth: Cora Vaughan Smith, Raleigh
Fifth: Elizabeth D. Reynolds, Winston-Salem
Sixth: May Gordon Latham Kellenberger,
  Greensboro
Seventh: Mrs. J. Laurence Sprunt,
  Wilmington
Eighth: George H. Maurice, Eagle Springs
Ninth: Mrs. Henkel Spillman, Statesville
Tenth: Mrs. Edward C. Marshall, Charlotte
Eleventh: Mrs. J. D. Lineberger, Shelby
Twelfth: Mrs. Frank O. Sherrill,
  Hendersonville

December 6, 1956-December 5, 1957

Officers
President: James Alan Stenhouse, Charlotte
Vice-President: Sally Cameron Labouisse (Mrs.
  John W. Labouisse),
  Charlotte and Durham
Secretary-Treasurer:
  Mary Emma Parker Branch, Raleigh

Directors
Gertrude S. Carraway, New Bern
Elizabeth Henderson Cotten, Chapel Hill
Fay Webb Gardner, Shelby
Dr. Archibald Henderson, Chapel Hill
Elizabeth Stevenson Ives, Southern Pines

District Vice-Presidents
First: Aycock Brown, Manteo
Second: Mrs. Elias Carr, Macclesfield
Third: Mrs. Claude B. Foy, New Bern
Fourth: Cora Vaughan Smith, Raleigh
Fifth: Elizabeth D. Reynolds, Winston-Salem
Sixth: May Gordon Latham Kellenberger,
  Greensboro
Seventh: Mrs. J. Laurence Sprunt,
  Wilmington
Eighth: George H. Maurice, Eagle Springs
Ninth: Mrs. Henkel Spillman, Statesville
Tenth: Mrs. Edward C. Marshall, Charlotte
Eleventh: Mrs. J. D. Lineberger, Shelby
Twelfth: Mrs. Frank O. Sherrill,
  Hendersonville

December 5, 1957-December 4, 1958

Officers
President: Elizabeth Stevenson Ives,
  Southern Pines
Vice-President: Edmund H. Harding,
  Washington
Secretary-Treasurer:
  Mary Emma Parker Branch, Raleigh

Directors
Gertrude S. Carraway, New Bern
Elizabeth Henderson Cotten, Chapel Hill
Fay Webb Gardner, Shelby
Dr. Archibald Henderson, Chapel Hill
James Alan Stenhouse, Charlotte

District Vice-Presidents
First: Aycock Brown, Manteo
Second: Mrs. Elias Carr, Macclesfield
Third: Mrs. Claude B. Foy, New Bern
Fourth: Cora Vaughan Smith, Raleigh
Fifth: Elizabeth D. Reynolds, Winston-Salem
Sixth: Robert H. Frazier, Greensboro
Seventh: Mrs. J. Laurence Sprunt,
  Wilmington
Eighth: George H. Maurice, Eagle Springs, and
  Mrs. W. Gaston McBryde, Gibson
Ninth: Marie Long Land
  (Mrs. Edward M. Land), Statesville
Tenth: Mrs. Edward C. Marshall, Charlotte
Eleventh: Mrs. J. D. Lineberger, Shelby
Twelfth: Mrs. Frank O. Sherrill,
  Hendersonville

December 4, 1958-December 3, 1959

Officers

President: Elizabeth Stevenson Ives,
  Southern Pines
Vice-President: Edmund H. Harding,
  Washington
Secretary-Treasurer:
  Mary Emma Parker Branch, Raleigh

Directors

Gertrude S. Carraway, New Bern
Elizabeth Henderson Cotten, Chapel Hill
Fay Webb Gardner, Shelby
Dr. Archibald Henderson, Chapel Hill
James Alan Stenhouse, Charlotte

District Vice-Presidents

First: Aycock Brown, Manteo
Second: Mrs. Elias Carr, Macclesfield
Third: Mrs. Claude B. Foy, New Bern
Fourth: Cora Vaughan Smith, Raleigh
Fifth: Elizabeth D. Reynolds, Winston-Salem
Sixth: Robert H. Frazier, Greensboro
Seventh: Mrs. J. Laurence Sprunt,
  Wilmington
Eighth: George H. Maurice, Eagle Springs, and
  Mrs. W. Gaston McBryde, Gibson
Ninth: Marie Long Land, Statesville
Tenth: Mrs. Edward C. Marshall, Charlotte
Eleventh: Mrs. J. D. Lineberger, Shelby
Twelfth: Mrs. Frank O. Sherrill,
  Hendersonville

December 3, 1959-December 1, 1960

Officers

President: Elizabeth Stevenson Ives,
  Southern Pines
Vice-President: Edmund H. Harding,
  Washington
Secretary-Treasurer:
  Mary Emma Parker Branch, Raleigh

Directors

Gertrude S. Carraway, New Bern
Elizabeth Henderson Cotten, Chapel Hill
Fay Webb Gardner, Shelby
Dr. Archibald Henderson, Chapel Hill
James Alan Stenhouse, Charlotte

District Vice-Presidents

First: Aycock Brown, Manteo
Second: Mrs. Elias Carr, Macclesfield
Third: Mrs. Claude B. Foy, New Bern
Fourth: Cora Vaughan Smith, Raleigh
Fifth: Elizabeth D. Reynolds, Winston-Salem
Sixth: Robert H. Frazier, Greensboro
Seventh: Mrs. J. Laurence Sprunt,
  Wilmington
Eighth: Mrs. W. Gaston McBryde, Gibson
Ninth: Marie Long Land, Statesville
Tenth: Mrs. Edward C. Marshall, Charlotte
Eleventh: Mrs. J. D. Lineberger, Shelby
Twelfth: Mrs. Frank O. Sherrill,
  Hendersonville

December 1, 1960-November 30, 1961

Officers

President: Edmund H. Harding, Washington
Vice-President: Lura Self Tally
  (Mrs. Joseph O. Tally Jr.), Fayetteville
Secretary-Treasurer:
  Mary Emma Parker Branch, Raleigh

Directors

Gertrude S. Carraway, New Bern
Elizabeth Henderson Cotten, Chapel Hill
Fay Webb Gardner, Shelby
Dr. Archibald Henderson, Chapel Hill
Elizabeth Stevenson Ives, Southern Pines
James Alan Stenhouse, Charlotte

District Vice-Presidents

First: Aycock Brown, Manteo
Second: Mrs. Elias Carr, Macclesfield
Third: Mrs. Claude B. Foy, New Bern
Fourth: Cora Vaughan Smith, Raleigh
Fifth: Elizabeth D. Reynolds, Winston-Salem
Sixth: Robert H. Frazier, Greensboro
Seventh: Mrs. J. Laurence Sprunt,
  Wilmington
Eighth: Mrs. W. Gaston McBryde, Gibson
Ninth: Marie Long Land, Statesville
Tenth: Mrs. Edward C. Marshall, Charlotte
Eleventh Mrs. J. D. Lineberger, Shelby
Twelfth: Mrs. Frank O. Sherrill,
  Hendersonville

November 30, 1961-December 6, 1962

Officers

President: Lura Self Tally, Fayetteville
Vice-President: Daniel M. Paul, Raleigh
Secretary-Treasurer:
  Mary Emma Parker Branch, Raleigh

Directors

Gertrude S. Carraway, New Bern
Elizabeth Henderson Cotten, Chapel Hill
Fay Webb Gardner, Shelby
Dr. Archibald Henderson, Chapel Hill
Elizabeth Stevenson Ives, Southern Pines
James Alan Stenhouse, Charlotte

District Vice-Presidents

First: Edmund H. Harding, Washington
Second: Mrs. Elias Carr, Macclesfield
Third: John R. Taylor, New Bern
Fourth: Cora Vaughan Smith, Raleigh
Fifth: Ralph P. Hanes, Winston-Salem
Sixth: Robert H. Frazier, Greensboro
Seventh: Mrs. W. Gaston McBryde, Gibson
Eighth: Elizabeth Stevenson Ives,
  Southern Pines
Ninth: Marie Long Land, Statesville
Tenth: Mrs. J. D. Lineberger, Shelby
Eleventh: Mrs. Newton Duke Angier,
  Flat Rock

December 6, 1962-December 5, 1963

Officers

President: Lura Self Tally, Fayetteville
Vice-President: Daniel M. Paul, Raleigh
Secretary-Treasurer:
  Mary Emma Parker Branch, Raleigh

Directors

Gertrude S. Carraway, New Bern
Elizabeth Henderson Cotten, Chapel Hill
Fay Webb Gardner, Shelby
Dr. Archibald Henderson, Chapel Hill
Elizabeth Stevenson Ives, Southern Pines
James Alan Stenhouse, Charlotte

District Vice-Presidents

First: Edmund H. Harding, Washington
Second: Mrs. Elias Carr, Macclesfield
Third: John R. Taylor, New Bern
Fourth: Cora Vaughan Smith, Raleigh
Fifth: Ralph P. Hanes, Winston-Salem
Sixth: Robert H. Frazier, Greensboro
Seventh: Mrs. W. Gaston McBryde, Gibson
Eighth: Elizabeth Stevenson Ives,
  Southern Pines
Ninth: Marie Long Land, Statesville
Tenth: Mrs. J. D. Lineberger, Shelby
Eleventh: Mrs. Newton Duke Angier,
  Flat Rock

December 5, 1963-December 3, 1964

Officers

President: Daniel M. Paul,
  Raleigh and Atlanta
Vice-President: Lillian Moore Robinson (Mrs.
  Horace P. Robinson), Littleton
Secretary-Treasurer:
  Mary Emma Parker Branch, Raleigh

Directors

Gertrude S. Carraway, New Bern
Elizabeth Henderson Cotten, Chapel Hill
Fay Webb Gardner, Shelby
Dr. Archibald Henderson, Chapel Hill
Elizabeth Stevenson Ives, Southern Pines
James Alan Stenhouse, Charlotte
Lura Self Tally, Fayetteville

District Vice-Presidents

First: Edmund H. Harding, Washington
Second: Mrs. Elias Carr, Macclesfield
Third: John R. Taylor, New Bern
Fourth: Cora Vaughan Smith, Raleigh
Fifth: Ralph P. Hanes, Winston-Salem
Sixth: Robert H. Frazier, Greensboro
Seventh: Mrs. W. Gaston McBryde, Gibson
Eighth: Elizabeth Stevenson Ives,
  Southern Pines
Ninth: Marie Long Land, Statesville
Tenth: Mrs. J. D. Lineberger, Shelby
Eleventh: Mrs. Newton Duke Angier,
  Flat Rock

December 3, 1964-December 2, 1965

Officers
President: Lillian Moore Robinson, Littleton
Vice-President: Henry Jay MacMillan, Wilmington
Secretary-Treasurer: Mary Emma Parker Branch, Raleigh

Directors
Gertrude S. Carraway, New Bern
Elizabeth Henderson Cotten, Chapel Hill
Fay Webb Gardner, Shelby
Elizabeth Stevenson Ives, Southern Pines
James Alan Stenhouse, Charlotte
Lura Self Tally, Fayetteville

District Vice-Presidents
First: Edmund H. Harding, Washington
Second: Mrs. Elias Carr, Macclesfield
Third: John R. Taylor, New Bern
Fourth: Cora Vaughan Smith, Raleigh
Fifth: Ralph P. Hanes, Winston-Salem
Sixth: Robert H. Frazier, Greensboro
Seventh: Chatham Clark, Elizabethtown
Eighth: Elizabeth Stevenson Ives, Southern Pines
Ninth: Marie Long Land, Statesville
Tenth: Mrs. J. D. Lineberger, Shelby
Eleventh: Mrs. Newton Duke Angier, Flat Rock

December 2, 1965-December 1, 1966

Officers
President: Lillian Moore Robinson, Littleton
Vice-President: T. Harry Gatton, Raleigh
Secretary-Treasurer:
    Mary Emma Parker Branch, Raleigh, to early 1966;
    Jane A. Holliday (Mrs. Joseph Q. Holliday), Raleigh, afterward

Directors
Gertrude S. Carraway, New Bern
Elizabeth Henderson Cotten, Chapel Hill
Fay Webb Gardner, Shelby
Alice Slater Guille (Mrs. Gettys Guille), Salisbury
Elizabeth Stevenson Ives, Southern Pines
Sally Cameron Labouisse, Durham

James Alan Stenhouse, Charlotte
Lura Self Tally, Fayetteville

District Vice-Presidents
First: Edmund H. Harding, Washington
Second: Mrs. Elias Carr, Macclesfield
Third: John R. Taylor, New Bern
Fourth: Cora Vaughan Smith, Raleigh
Fifth: Ralph P. Hanes, Winston-Salem
Sixth: Robert H. Frazier, Greensboro
Seventh: Chatham Clark, Elizabethtown
Eighth: Elizabeth Stevenson Ives, Southern Pines
Ninth: Mrs. Andrew F. Sams Jr., Statesville
Tenth: Mrs. J. D. Lineberger, Shelby
Eleventh: Mrs. Newton Duke Angier, Flat Rock

December 1, 1966-November 30, 1967

Officers
President: Lillian Moore Robinson, Littleton
Vice-President: T. Harry Gatton, Raleigh
Secretary-Treasurer: Jane A. Holliday, Raleigh

Directors
Gertrude S. Carraway, New Bern
Fay Webb Gardner, Shelby
Alice Slater Guille, Salisbury
Elizabeth Stevenson Ives, Southern Pines
Sally Cameron Labouisse, Durham
Lura Self Tally, Fayetteville

District Vice-Presidents
First: Edmund H. Harding, Washington

Second: Mrs. Elias Carr, Macclesfield
Third: John G. Newton, Beaufort
Fourth: Cora Vaughan Smith, Raleigh, and
    Elizabeth Stevenson Ives, Southern Pines
Fifth: Ralph P. Hanes, Winston-Salem
Sixth: Robert H. Frazier, Greensboro
Seventh: Chatham Clark, Elizabethtown, and
    Henry Jay MacMillan, Wilmington
Eighth: Irwin Belk, Charlotte
Ninth: Alice Slater Guille, Salisbury, and
    Ernest L. Hardin, Salisbury
Tenth: Mrs. J. D. Lineberger, Shelby, and Mrs.
    Andrew F. Sams Jr., Statesville
Eleventh: Paul A. Rockwell, Asheville

November 30, 1967-December 5, 1968

Officers
President: T. Harry Gatton, Raleigh
Vice-President: Tempie Harris Prince
  (Mrs. S. R. Prince), Reidsville
Secretary-Treasurer: Jane A. Holliday, Raleigh

Directors
Gertrude S. Carraway, New Bern
Fay Webb Gardner, Shelby
Alice Slater Guille, Salisbury
Elizabeth Stevenson Ives, Southern Pines
Sally Cameron Labouisse, Durham
Lillian Moore Robinson, Littleton
Lura Self Tally, Fayetteville

District Vice-Presidents
First: Edmund H. Harding, Washington
Second: Mrs. Elias Carr, Macclesfield
Third: John G. Newton, Beaufort
Fourth: Cora Vaughan Smith, Raleigh
Fifth: Nicholas Bragg, Winston-Salem
Sixth: Robert H. Frazier, Greensboro
Seventh: Henry Jay MacMillan, Wilmington
Eighth: Ernest L. Hardin, Salisbury
Ninth: Irwin Belk, Charlotte
Tenth: Mrs. J. D. Lineberger, Shelby
Eleventh: Paul A. Rockwell, Asheville

December 5, 1968-December 4, 1969

Officers
President: T. Harry Gatton, Raleigh
Vice-President: Tempie Harris Prince, Reidsville
Secretary-Treasurer: Jane A. Holliday, Raleigh,
  to June 1969; Barbara Barnes, acting, June to
  September 1969; Nancy P. Adams (Mrs. Roy D.
  Adams), Raleigh, after September 1969

Directors
Gertrude S. Carraway, New Bern
Fay Webb Gardner, Shelby
Alice Slater Guille, Salisbury
Sally Cameron Labouisse, Durham

Lura Self Tally, Fayetteville

District Vice-Presidents
First: Edmund H. Harding, Washington
Second: Mrs. William H. Fillmore, Tarboro
Third: John G. Newton, Beaufort
Fourth: Cora Vaughan Smith, Raleigh
Fifth: Nicholas Bragg, Winston-Salem
Sixth: Robert H. Frazier, Greensboro
Seventh: Henry Jay MacMillan, Wilmington
Eighth: Ernest L. Hardin, Salisbury
Ninth: Irwin Belk, Charlotte
Tenth: Mrs. Robert C. Huffman, Morganton
Eleventh: Paul A. Rockwell, Asheville

December 4, 1969-December 3, 1970

Officers
President: T. Harry Gatton, Raleigh
Vice-President: Virginia Ford Zenke (Mrs.
  Henry C. Zenke), Greensboro
Secretary-Treasurer: Nancy P. Adams, Raleigh,
  to no later than May 1970;
  Sharon Sandling, Raleigh, from no later than
  May 1970

Directors
Gertrude S. Carraway, New Bern
Alice Slater Guille, Salisbury
Sarah Houser, Charlotte
Sally Cameron Labouisse, Durham
Lura Self Tally, Fayetteville

District Vice-Presidents
First: E. Frank Stephenson Jr., Murfreesboro
Second: Mrs. Jack E. Brinson, Tarboro
Third: John G. Newton, Beaufort
Fourth: Banks C. Talley Jr., Raleigh
Fifth: Nicholas Bragg, Winston-Salem
Sixth: William J. Moore, Greensboro
Seventh: Katherine Howell, Wilmington
Eighth: Mrs. J. H. Winkler, North Wilkesboro
Ninth: M. Mellanay Delhom, Charlotte
Tenth: C. David Blanton, Marion
Eleventh: Harley E. Jolley, Mars Hill

December 3, 1970-December 2, 1971

Officers

President: John Edward Tyler II, Roxobel
Vice-President: Virginia Ford Zenke,
  Greensboro
Secretary-Treasurer: Sharon J. Sandling,
  Raleigh. (Beth M. Boxley served as Sandling's
  assistant after September 1971.)

Directors

Gertrude S. Carraway, New Bern
Sarah Houser, Charlotte
Sally Cameron Labouisse, Durham
William J. Moore, Greensboro
Lura Self Tally, Fayetteville

District Vice-Presidents

First: E. Frank Stephenson Jr., Murfreesboro
Second: Mrs. Jack E. Brinson, Tarboro
Third: John G. Newton, Beaufort
Fourth: Banks C. Talley Jr., Raleigh
Fifth: Nicholas Bragg, Winston-Salem
Sixth: John Harden, Greensboro
Seventh: Katherine Howell, Wilmington
Eighth: Mrs. J. H. Winkler,
  North Wilkesboro
Ninth: M. Mellanay Delhom, Charlotte
Tenth: C. David Blanton, Marion
Eleventh: Harley E. Jolley, Mars Hill

December 2, 1971-November 30, 1972

Officers

President: John Edward Tyler II, Roxobel
Vice-President: Virginia Ford Zenke,
  Greensboro
Secretary-Treasurer: Sharon J. Sandling,
  Raleigh. (Beth M. Boxley served as Sandling's
  assistant after September 1971.)

Directors

Gertrude S. Carraway, New Bern
Sarah Houser, Charlotte
Sally Cameron Labouisse, Durham

District Vice-Presidents

First: E. Frank Stephenson Jr., Murfreesboro
Second: Mrs. Jack E. Brinson, Tarboro
Third: John G. Newton, Beaufort
Fourth: Banks C. Talley Jr., Raleigh
Fifth: Thomas A. Gray, Winston-Salem
Sixth: John Harden, Greensboro
Seventh: Katherine Howell, Wilmington
Eighth: Mrs. J. H. Winkler,
  North Wilkesboro
Ninth: M. Mellanay Delhom, Charlotte
Tenth: C. David Blanton, Marion
Eleventh: Harley E. Jolley, Mars Hill

November 30, 1972-November 17, 1973

Officers

President: Virginia Ford Zenke, Greensboro
Vice-President: William J. Moore,
  Greensboro
Secretary-Treasurer: Beth M. Boxley to no later
  than March 1973; John G. Zehmer Jr. after
  March 1973. (Frances Harmon Whitley [Mrs.
  Robert Whitley] served as Zehmer's assistant
  from March 1973.)

Directors

Gertrude S. Carraway, New Bern
T. Harry Gatton, Raleigh
Sarah Houser, Charlotte
Sally Cameron Labouisse, Durham
Lura Self Tally, Fayetteville

District Vice-Presidents

First: E. Frank Stephenson Jr., Murfreesboro
Second: Mrs. Jack E. Brinson, Tarboro
Third: John G. Newton, Beaufort
Fourth: Banks C. Talley Jr., Raleigh
Fifth: Thomas A. Gray, Winston-Salem
Sixth: John Harden, Greensboro
Seventh: Katherine Howell, Wilmington
Eighth: Mrs. J. H. Winkler, North Wilkesboro
Ninth: M. Mellanay Delhom, Charlotte
Tenth: Frances Moody
  (Mrs. H. Leslie Moody), Hickory
Eleventh: Harley E. Jolley, Mars Hill

November 15, 1973-February 4, 1974

Officers

President: Virginia Ford Zenke, Greensboro
Vice-President: William J. Moore, Greensboro
Secretary-Treasurer: John G. Zehmer Jr. to January 1974; Elizabeth Wall Wilborn after January 1974. (Frances Harmon Whitley [Mrs. Robert Whitley] served as Zehmer's assistant from March 1973 and as Wilborn's assistant from January 1974.)

Directors

Gertrude S. Carraway, New Bern
T. Harry Gatton, Raleigh
Sarah Houser, Charlotte
Sally Cameron Labouisse, Durham
Lura Self Tally, Fayetteville

District Vice-Presidents

First: E. Frank Stephenson Jr., Murfreesboro
Second: Mrs. Jack E. Brinson, Tarboro
Third: Mrs. Copeland Kell, Beaufort
Fourth: Banks C. Talley Jr., Raleigh
Fifth: Thomas A. Gray, Winston-Salem
Sixth: John Harden, Greensboro
Seventh: Mrs. Thomas H. Wright Jr., Wilmington
Eighth: Mrs. J. H. Winkler, North Wilkesboro
Ninth: M. Mellanay Delhom, Charlotte
Tenth: Frances Moody, Hickory
Eleventh: Harley E. Jolley, Mars Hill

Ex Officio Members of the Board of Directors

The number of ex officio members of the board of directors varied through the years. According to the 1939 constitution, ex officio members included: the governor of North Carolina, the director of the North Carolina Department of Conservation and Development, the chairman of the North Carolina Highway and Public Works Commission, the secretary of the North Carolina Historical Commission (renamed in 1943 the Department of Archives and History), and the officers of the Antiquities Society.

Beginning about 1957, the SPA letterhead listed only the governor and the director of the Department of Archives and History as ex officio board members, omitting the other state department heads. By 1966 the constitution had been amended to include as ex officio members only the director of the Department of Archives and History, officers of the SPA, and the immediate past president of the society.

Appendix C

SPA Grants and the Revolving Fund

(Names of projects, people, or properties are generally spelled as they appear in the society's records, with corrections or possible alternate spellings and names shown in brackets.)

SPA Grants: 1940-1973

1940   Tryon Palace, William Foster, and A. T. Dill, part payment, historical research, $200.00
1940   Clerk's Office, Halifax, $100.00
1940   L. A. Shore, survey of Richmond Hill, $5.00
1940-1941   Andrew Johnson House, Raleigh, $200.00
1941   St. Thomas Church, Bath, $25.00
1941-1942   Thomas Waterman, measured drawings of the Michael Braun House, $260.00
1942   Richard [Richmond] Pearson House [Richmond Hill], $300.00
1946   Shaw House, Southern Pines, $200.00
1946   William Gaston Law Office, New Bern, $200.00
1948   State [Carolina] Charter, $1,000.00
1948   Chowan County Courthouse, $200.00
1949   Allen Jay House, High Point, $200.00
1949   James Iredell House, Edenton, $200.00
1949   Hezekiah Alexander House, Charlotte, $200.00
1949   St. Thomas's Church, Bath, $175.00
1949   Wilson Log House, Shelby, $200.00
1949   William Gaston Law Office, New Bern, $200.00
1949   John Locke manuscript of the model drawn up by [Lord] Ashley for the government of North Carolina [document: unsigned 1682 manuscript, possibly by John Locke, summarizing the provisions of the 1669 Fundamental Constitutions of Carolina], $346.50
1950   Thomas Wolfe House, Asheville, $200.00
1950   Chowan College "birthplace" restoration, Murfreesboro, $200.00
1950   Boulder for marker, Halifax, $100.00
1950   Zebulon Vance House, Statesville, $200.00
1950   Alumnae House, Salem College, Winston-Salem, $200.00
1950   Washington [Salem] Tavern "sofa," Old Salem, Winston-Salem, $200.00
1950   Octagon House, Washington, D.C., $25.00
1950   Library preservation, Lincolnton, $200.00
1951   Library preservation, Jackson, $200.00

1951 Washington [Salem] Tavern, Winston-Salem $200.00

1951 John Henry Boner House [Lick-Boner House], Old Salem, Winston-Salem, $200.00

1951 Historic Halifax, $200.00

1951 Wallace restoration [check stub indicates that grant was "refunded"], $200.00

1951 Kings Mountain Little Theatre for drama *Then Conquer We Must* [concerning Battle of Kings Mountain], $200.00

1952 Shrine for Pocahontas, Kent County, England, $200.00

1952 Donation toward Sir Walter Raleigh Cup Award, $200.00

1952 Governor Aycock House, Fremont, $200.00

1952 St. John's Church, Williamsboro, $200.00

1952 Penelope Barker House, Edenton, $200.00

1953 Wright Brothers First Flight Memorial Society, Kill Devil Hills, $200.00

1953 New Bern Historical Society [project not described], $200.00

1953 Randall Church, Stanly County, $200.00

1953 Attmore-Oliver House, New Bern, $200.00

1953 Maxwell Chambers House, Salisbury, $200.00

1953 Old Gaol, Halifax, $200.00

1954 Kensington Gate, Elizabethan Gardens, Manteo, $201.00

1954 St. Thomas Church, Bath, $203.00

1954 House in the Horseshoe, Moore County, $200.00

1954 Woman's Club, "Old House Preservation," Kinston [project not described], $200.00

1954 Richard Gwyn Museum, Elkin, $200.00

1955 Old Temperance Hall, Wagram, $200.00

1955 Halifax Restoration Association, Halifax [project not described], $200.00

1955 "Old Ball Room" [ballroom], Fayetteville, $200.00

1956 Bellamy House [Mansion], Wilmington, $191.00

1956 Purchase of Cutter [Cutten] Silver Collection, $200.00

1956 Carolina Playmakers [project not described], $200.00

1956 Calvin Jones House, Wake Forest, $200.00

1957 Bentonville Battleground, $200.00

1957, 1959 Old tavern [Person's Ordinary], Littleton [grants of $200.00 each year], $400.00

1958 Restoring Log House [check made to Mrs. T. C. Dillinger], Crossnore, $200.00

1959 Michael Braun House, Rowan County, $200.00

1959 Machpelah Presbyterian Church, Lincoln County, $200.00

1959 Historic building inventory [James Stenhouse], $200.00

1960 Edenton Woman's Club, Chowan County Courthouse paint removal, promotional film and spring tour, $50.00

1960 Old Marsh House [Palmer-Marsh House], Bath, $200.00

1961 General Gregory Old Brick House, Elizabeth City, $200.00 [grant returned in 1968]

1961 Blue Masque of Catawba College Organization Program, Salisbury, $200.00

1962 Swansboro Historical Association, local restoration, $200.00

1962 Fayetteville Woman's Club, restoration "of an old Home (1840)," the oval ballroom, and preservation of the "Old Machet [Mallett] House," $50.00

1963 Hillsboro Historical Association [project not described], $200.00

1963 Raleigh Woman's Club [project not described], $50.00

1964 Old Becton House [Joseph Bell House], Beaufort, brochure for fund-raising drive to purchase and restore Becton House and other historic properties, $200.00

1964 Edenton Woman's Club [project not described], $50.00

1964 Old Pantego Academy, Pantego, $200.00

1964 Carson House, Old Fort, $200.00

1964 William Brogden, N.C. State School of Design, measured drawings for National Trust files, $200.00

1965 Cupola House Library and Museum [restoration of portraits], Edenton, $200.00

1965 Hope Plantation, Bertie County, $200.00

1965 North Carolina Federation of Women's Clubs [project not described], $50.00

1965 Allen House, Alamance Battleground, $200.00

1965 Henry Clay Oak, Raleigh Tree Society, $25.00

1966 Ringware House, Swansboro, $200.00

1966 Smithfield Woman's Club, Hastings House, $50.00

1966 Moorefields, Hillsborough, $200.00

1966 Montague Building, Mars Hill College, $200.00

1966 Hastings House, Smithfield, $200.00

1967 Fayetteville Woman's Club [seven preservation projects, including purchase and restoration of an 1803 house adjoining its clubhouse], $50.00

1967 Greensboro Preservation Society, Blandwood, $200.00

1968 Fayetteville Woman's Club [project not described], $50.00

1968 Murfreesboro Historical Association [project not described], $200.00

1969 North Carolina Federation of Women's Clubs [project not described], $50.00

1969 Iredell County Historical Society, Fort Dobbs restoration, $200.00

1970 Rockingham County Historical Society, Wright House, Wentworth, $200.00

1971 Wake Forest Woman's Club [landscaping grounds of the Calvin Jones House and restoring the interior of the house], $50.00

1971 Historic Bath Commission, Van der Veer House, $300.00

1971 Perquimans County Restoration Association, Newbold-White House, $300.00

1972 Moore County Historical Association, Bryant House, $300.00

1972 Old Wilkes, Old Wilkes Jail, $200.00

1972 Beaufort Woman's Club [project not described], $50.00

1973 Dolley Madison Birthplace Memorial, Isley Cabin, Guilford County, $200.00

1973 Lower Cape Fear Historical Society, Latimer House, Wilmington, $200.00

1973 William Gaston House Restoration Association, William Gaston House, New Bern, $200.00

Total Grants: $18,756.50

The Revolving Fund: July 1948-July 1966

(Most information is taken from "Financial Statements" dated July 19, 1966.)

Revolving Fund Loans:

Edenton Tea Party Chapter of the DAR, James Iredell House (loan 1949 paid in full), $2,500.00

Moore County Historical Association, Philip Alston House, "House in the Horseshoe" (due 1955 and paid in full), $2,500.00

New Bern Historical Society Foundation, Attmore-Oliver House (loan 1954 due 1957 and paid in full by 1960), $2,500.00

Beaufort County Historical Society, Palmer-Marsh House (loan made May 1958 and canceled December 1964), $ 2,500.00

Total loans made: $10,000.00

Revolving Fund Grants:

Elizabethan Garden Projects, Manteo (1951), $200.00

Roanoke Island Historical Association, remodeling stage sets (1955 or before), $2,500.00

Elizabethan Garden Projects, Gate House Fund, Manteo (1956), $1,000.00

Bennett Place Memorial Commission, Bennett Place (1958-1959), $8,000.00

Historic Bath Commission [ca. 1957-1960], $3,500.00

Beaufort County Historical Society (includes $2,500 for note cancelled by the society on December 3, 1964). In either the total $3,500 for the Beaufort County Historical Society or in the total for the Historic Bath Commission, the sum included $200 grants each in 1957 for the Bonner House and the Palmer-Marsh House at Bath. $3,500.00

Total Revolving Fund Grants: $18,700.00

Total Revolving Fund Grants and Loans: $28,700.00

Total Financial Assistance from SPA: $47,456.50

Total of all financial assistance from SPA roughly adjusted for inflation (using 1956 halfway point in life of the SPA as base year) in 1990 dollars: $231,500.00

Appendix D

Winners of the Cannon Cup Award, 1948-1974

1948

Mrs. J. E. Latham, Greensboro
Mrs. Inglis Fletcher, Edenton
Miss Gertrude S. Carraway, New Bern
Dr. Adelaide Fries, Winston-Salem
Paul Green, Chapel Hill
Dr. Archibald Henderson, Chapel Hill
Dr. Christopher Crittenden, Raleigh
Dr. Douglas L. Rights, Winston-Salem
Dr. Charles Lee Smith, Raleigh

1949

James Boyd Jr. for the
    late Dr. Joseph Hyde Pratt, Chapel Hill
Mrs. James Gray, Winston-Salem
Mrs. Katherine P. Arrington, Warrenton
Mrs. R. N. Duffy, New Bern
Mrs. Ernest Ives, Southern Pines
Rev. A. C. D. Noe, Bath

1950

Mrs. Burton Craige, Winston-Salem
Mrs. Charles A. Cannon, Concord
Mrs. E. C. Marshall, Charlotte
Mrs. John Meredith Jones, Edenton
Bruce Cotten, Baltimore, Md.
Mrs. Sterling M. Gary, Halifax
Carl Goerch, Raleigh
Mrs. Ernest A. Branch, Raleigh

1951

Gerald W. Johnson, Baltimore, Md.
Ben Dixon MacNeill, Buxton
Alonzo Thomas Dill Jr., Norfolk, Va.
Mrs. W. H. Belk, Charlotte
Mrs. Claudius Fowler Foy, New Bern
Chalmers G. Davidson, Davidson
Aycock Brown, Manteo

1952

Laurence Sprunt, Wilmington
Kermit Hunter, Chapel Hill
Richard Walser, Raleigh
James Stenhouse, Charlotte
Miss Virginia Horne, Wadesboro
Miss Clara Byrd, Greensboro
George Ross, Raleigh

1953

Hon. and Mrs. O. Max Gardner, Shelby
    [posthumously to Governor Gardner,
    who died on February 6, 1947]
John Sprunt Hill, Durham
Dr. Hugh Talmage Lefler, Chapel Hill
LeGette Blythe, Huntersville
Mrs. Marshall De Lancey Haywood
    for her late husband, Raleigh

1954

Mr. and Mrs. George G. Allen,
    New York, N.Y.
Cecil B. deMille, Hollywood, Calif.
Miss Cora A. Harris, Charlotte
Atty. Gen. Harry McMullan, Raleigh
Col. J. F. Stanback, Mount Gilead
Mrs. Walter M. Stearns, Raleigh

1955

Edmund Harding, Washington
Mrs. Frank Smethurst, Raleigh
Bill Sharpe, Raleigh
Robert Frazier, Greensboro
Donald Shoemaker, Nashville, Tenn.

1956

Kay Kyser, Chapel Hill
Mrs. R. L. McMillan, Raleigh

Penelope S. (Mrs. Sidney M.) McMullan,
Edenton
Mrs. Blanche Manor, Raleigh
George H. Maurice, Eagle Springs
Clarence W. Griffin, Forest City

1957

Miss Lucy M. Cobb, Raleigh
Mrs. R. N. Simms, Raleigh
Dr. Clarence Poe, Raleigh
William S. Powell, Chapel Hill
Mrs. Elizabeth D. Reynolds,
Winston-Salem
Grayson H. Harding, Edenton

1958

D. Hiden Ramsey, Asheville
James G. W. MacLamroc, Greensboro
Gov. and Mrs. Luther Hodges, Raleigh
Mr. and Mrs. W. D. Campbell,
Southern Pines
Mr. and Mrs. W. G. Guille, Salisbury

1959

Edward and Blanche Benjamin, Greensboro
Dr. Lawrence Lee, Charleston, S.C.
Fielding Lewis Fry, Greensboro
Frank L. Horton, Winston-Salem
W. S. Tarlton, Raleigh

1960

Mrs. Oscar Smith, Norfolk, Va.
Mrs. Roy Charles, Norfolk, Va.
Edward Draper-Savage, Hillsborough
Dr. David J. Rose, Goldsboro
Louis T. Moore, Wilmington
Literary Society and
Temperance Hall, Wagram

1961

Hon. R. O. Everett, Durham
Mrs. W. C. Tucker, Greensboro
John R. Taylor, New Bern
Smith Richardson, New York, N.Y.

1962

Donald Carrow, Bath
Jack Hudgens Knox, Salisbury
Sam T. Snowden Jr., Louisburg

1963

Dr. Lenox D. Baker, Durham
James A. Gray, Winston-Salem
Tucker A. Littleton, Swansboro
Francis E. Winslow, Rocky Mount

1964

Ernest L. Hardin, Salisbury
Elizabeth D. Horne, Wadesboro

Gordon Gray, Washington, D.C.
P. D. Midgett Jr., Engelhard

1965

John D. Costlow, Beaufort
Mrs. Alfred G. Engstrom, Hillsborough
Mr. and Mrs. Fred Morrison,
Washington, D.C.

1966

Mrs. Barbara B. Lassiter, Winston-Salem
The late David M. Warren, Edenton
Fayetteville Woman's Club

1967

John Edward Tyler II, Roxobel
William Henley Deitrick, Raleigh
Sally Cameron Labouisse, Durham

1968

Historic Edenton, Inc.
Margaret Harper, Lenoir
Mary Lyon Caine, Greensboro
Jeanelle C. Moore, Raleigh

1969

Wilbert M. Kemp, Hertford
North Carolina National Bank, Raleigh
Tempie Harris Prince, Reidsville
Elizabeth W. Wilborn, Raleigh

1970

Ed U. Lewis, Tarboro
Linn D. Garibaldi, Anson County
Earl Weatherly, Greensboro
E. Frank Stephenson Jr., Murfreesboro

1971

Mrs. Samuel C. Kellam, Wilmington
Dr. H. G. Jones, Raleigh
Raleigh Historic Sites Commission, Raleigh

1972

Mrs. Joye E. Jordan, Raleigh
Miss M. Mellanay Delhom, Charlotte
Gov. Robert W. Scott, Raleigh
The Historic Hope Foundation, Inc.,
Windsor

1973

Dr. Robert E. Stipe, Chapel Hill
A. L. Honeycutt Jr., Raleigh
Dr. Henry C. Landon III,
North Wilkesboro

1974

Mr. and Mrs. Henry C. Zenke, Greensboro
R. V. Asbury, Wilmington
Ray Wilkinson, Raleigh

Appendix E

Current Status of North Carolina
Buildings and Sites Mentioned in Text

Compiled by Nan Farley, volunteer, Preservation North Carolina

Research assistance by Michael T. Southern, State Historic Preservation Office

KEY: NR = National Register
F = Funds given by SPA
O = Open to the public

A. C. D. NOE LIBRARY. *See* St. Thomas Episcopal Church

ALAMANCE BATTLEGROUND (Alamance County). Site of 1771 defeat of the Regulators by Gov. William Tryon. The John Allen House, a log house built ca. 1782, was moved to the site from the Snow Camp vicinity in 1967. A state historic site. (NR, F, O)

ALLEN HOUSE. *See* Alamance Battleground

ALLEN JAY HOUSE (High Point, Guilford County). Compact two-story frame house that may date from the eighteenth century. After the Civil War the home of Allen Jay, an important Quaker leader. Restored twice—once through the efforts of Ruth Cannon. Owned by the adjacent Springfield Friends Meeting and used by the American Friends Service Committee. (F)

ALSTON HOUSE. *See* House in the Horseshoe

ALUMNAE HOUSE. *See* Salem College Alumnae House

ANDREW JOHNSON BIRTHPLACE (Raleigh, Wake County). Small building moved several times and presently located in Mordecai Historic Park; owned by city of Raleigh. (F, O)

ANDREW JACKSON LAW OFFICE. *See* Spruce Macay Law Office

ANNE CARTER LEE GRAVE (Warrenton vicinity, Warren County). Daughter of Gen. Robert E. Lee. Died at the Jones White Sulpher Springs Hotel, a Warren County mineral springs resort, during the Civil War and was buried in the Jones family cemetery near the hotel. In 1995 her remains were removed to Lexington, Virginia, to be with those of other members of her family.

ARCHIBALD HENDERSON HOUSE (721 East Franklin Street, Chapel Hill, Orange County). Built in first decade of twentieth century on land owned by Henderson's wife, Barbara Bynum Henderson, North Carolina poet. The two-story frame Colonial Revival house has a spacious wraparound one-story porch. Also called Fordell by the Hendersons. Privately owned

ATTMORE-OLIVER HOUSE (New Bern, Craven County). Built ca. 1790, enlarged ca. 1834. Now a museum with period furniture and a Civil War exhibit. Owned by New Bern Historical Society. (NR, F, O)

AYCOCK BIRTHPLACE (Fremont vicinity, Wayne County). Birthplace of Charles B. Aycock, the "Education Governor." A state historic site. (NR, F, O)

AYR MOUNT (Hillsborough, Orange County). Built 1814. A transitional Georgian/Federal-style brick plantation house of tripartite form. Privately owned. Preservation North Carolina maintains the property. (NR, O)

BANDON PLANTATION (Edenton vicinity, Chowan County). Home of author Inglis Fletcher. Built 1829. Burned 1963. Two outbuildings were later moved to the Iredell House in Edenton.

BANKER'S HOUSE (Shelby, Cleveland County). Built 1875. Second Empire style. G. S. H. Appleget is the attributed architect. Owned by Preservation North Carolina. (NR)

BECTON HOUSE. *See* Joseph Bell House

BELLAMY MANSION (Wilmington, New Hanover County). Built 1859-1860. Imposing antebellum colonnaded frame house. Owned by Preservation North Carolina and operated as a museum of decorative arts. (NR, F, O)

BENNEHAN HOUSE. *See* Stagville

BENNETT PLACE (Durham vicinity, Durham County). Small farm complex that was the site of the April 26, 1865, surrender of the last main army of the Confederacy. Now a state historic site. (NR, F, O)

BENTONVILLE BATTLEGROUND (Johnston County). Scene of largest battle ever fought on North Carolina soil; also last major battle of the Civil War. A state historic site. (NR, F, O). A National Historic Landmark

BLANDWOOD (Greensboro, Guilford County). Alexander Jackson Davis, architect. Italianate villa built 1844 for Gov. John Motley Morehead. Owned by the John Motley Morehead Memorial Commission (NR, F, O). A National Historic Landmark

BONER HOUSE. *See* Lick-Boner House

BONNER HOUSE (Bath, Beaufort County). Built 1835. Side-passage-plan house. Part of Historic Bath State Historic Site. (NR, F, O)

BRAUN HOUSE (Granite Quarry vicinity, Rowan County). Built 1766 by German settler Michael Braun. Also called Old Stone House. Restored 1966. Operated by Rowan Museum. (NR, F, O)

BRUNSWICK TOWN (Brunswick County). Site of an important colonial town on the Cape Fear River. Only the ruins of St. Philip's Church and archaeological displays remain. A state historic site. (NR, F, O)

BRYANT HOUSE (Moore County). Built ca. 1820 by James Bryant. A modest vernacular farmhouse. The Bryant Kitchen, a small structure forty feet from the main house, may date from the eighteenth century and was probably built by Joel McLendon, an earlier owner of the property. Owned by the Moore County Historical Association. (NR, F, O)

BUCK SPRING (Warren County). Modest late eighteenth-century plantation home of influential U.S. congressman and senator Nathaniel Macon. Restored by the WPA in 1939. Site includes a smokehouse, an unusual log corncrib with cantilevered sheds, and Macon's grave site. House suffered a fire in recent years but was again restored. Owned by Warren County. (NR, O)

BUNKER HILL COVERED BRIDGE (Claremont vicinity, Catawba County). Built 1894. One of the last two covered bridges surviving in the state. Owned by Catawba County Historical Association. (NR, O)

BURGWIN-WRIGHT HOUSE (Wilmington, New Hanover County). Built 1770, expanded 1845. Combines regional form, including two-tier engaged porches, with sophisticated Georgian-style finish. Owned by the National Society of the Colonial Dames in North Carolina. (NR, O)

C. S. BROWN SCHOOL (Winton, Hertford County). Established in 1886 by Calvin Scott Brown as Chowan Academy, a private academy for African Americans. The school became part of the public school system after 1923. The oldest building, Brown Hall (1926), has been adapted as a community center and museum, though the surrounding complement of later buildings is still a public school campus. (NR)

CALDWELL LOG COLLEGE (Greensboro, Guilford County). Site of important regional school established in 1767 by Presbyterian leader David Caldwell. Now an archaeological site with no visible remains but maintained as a public park by the city of Greensboro, with a historical marker at the site. (NR, F, O)

CALVIN JONES HOUSE (Wake Forest, Wake County). Built by 1820; became the first home of Wake Forest College in 1830s. Owned by the Wake Forest College Birthplace Society. (NR, F, O)

CAMERON PLANTATION. *See* Stagville

CAPITOL BUILDING (Raleigh, Wake County). Town and Davis, architects. Completed 1840. One of American's greatest Greek Revival buildings. Presently used as the governor's office and a museum. (NR, O). A National Historic Landmark

CARSON HOUSE (Marion vicinity, McDowell County). Began in the 1790s as a two-story log house with dog-trot passage; expanded and embellished into the 1840s. Served as the county courthouse 1843-1845. Owned by Carson House Foundation. (NR, F, O)

CHAMBERS HOUSE (Utzman-Chambers House; Salisbury, Rowan County). Built 1820. Presently serves as the Rowan Museum and is owned by the museum. (NR, F, O)

CHOWAN COLLEGE BIRTHPLACE (Murfreesboro, Hertford County). Probably Hertford Academy (ca. 1810), a two-story brick structure laid in Flemish bond. From 1848 to 1852 it housed the newly formed Chowan Baptist Female Institute, which became Chowan College in 1910. Owned by the Murfreesboro Historical Association. (NR, F, O)

CHOWAN COUNTY COURTHOUSE (Edenton, Chowan County). Built 1767-1774. One of the finest Georgian public buildings in the southern colonies. Owned by the state and under restoration in a state-county partnership as part of Historic Edenton State Historic Site, with some continued use as a local court facility anticipated. (NR, F, O). A National Historic Landmark

CLERK'S OFFICE (Halifax, Halifax County). Built 1833. One-story red-brick building that was used at various times as a printing shop and a residence. Now restored. Part of Historic Halifax State Historic Site. (NR, F, O)

CONSTITUTION HOUSE (Burgess House; Halifax, Halifax County). Small frame building traditionally believed to be site of the drafting of the North Carolina Constitution. First restored by the DAR. Now part of Historic Halifax State Historic Site. (NR, O)

COOLMORE (Tarboro vicinity, Edgecombe County). Built 1860. Italianate design by E. G. Lind. Owned by Preservation North Carolina. (NR). A National Historic Landmark

COOR-GASTON HOUSE. *See* William Gaston House

COOR-GASTON DEPENDENCY. *See* Gaston Law Office

CROSSNORE LOG CABIN (Crossnore, Avery County). Old log building on the grounds of the Crossnore School, owned by the local chapter of the DAR. (F)

CUPOLA HOUSE (Edenton, Chowan County). Built 1758. Wood frame colonial house with an unusual second-story overhang. Original downstairs interior woodwork removed to the Brooklyn Museum of Art in 1918; present first-floor woodwork reproductions created by craftsman Wilbert Kemp. Owned by the Cupola House Association and a part of the Historic Edenton Tour. (NR, F, O). A National Historic Landmark

DANIEL BOONE HOUSE (Davie County). Boone's family moved to North Carolina in 1757, and Daniel lived in the area for the most part until his final move to Kentucky. Part of his family's home is said to have been incorporated into one or two other still-standing houses in the area.

DOLLEY MADISON BIRTHPLACE. *See* Isley Cabin

ELIZABETHAN GARDEN (Manteo, Dare County). Adjacent to Fort Raleigh National Historic Site. Established in 1951 as a memorial to the "Lost Colony" of English settlers. Consists of many individual gardens, each with plantings indigenous to the period. Owned by the North Carolina Federation of Garden Clubs. (F, O)

EXECUTIVE MANSION (200 South Blount Street, Raleigh, Wake County). A Queen Anne-style brick mansion designed by Samuel Sloan of Philadelphia. Completed in 1891 as the official residence of North Carolina's governors and continues to serve in that capacity. (NR, O)

FAIRFIELD (Camden County). In ruins before 1975. Brick home of Revolutionary War general Isaac Gregory. (F [grant returned])

FAIRNTOSH PLANTATION (Durham vicinity, Durham County). Begun in 1810 by planter Duncan Cameron and later the home of his son Paul, North Carolina's wealthiest citizen in the antebellum period. Many of the outbuildings remain. Privately owned. (NR)

FARMVILLE PLANTATION (Elmwood, Iredell County). Built 1818. Includes Federal-style brick house. Privately owned. (NR)

FOR PITY'S SAKE (Kannapolis vicinity, Cabarrus County). Early frame house built by Bolland Stirewalt. Ruth Cannon's country home. Purposely burned by the local fire department in 1975 following the death of her husband, Charles, in 1971.

FORDELL. *See* Archibald Henderson House

FORT DOBBS (Iredell County). Built 1756 for protection of settlers during the French and Indian War; later dismantled. Excavations show features of the fort. A state historic site. (NR, F, O)

FORT FISHER (Wilmington vicinity, New Hanover County). Confederate stronghold to protect the port of Wilmington. Fell 1865. A state historic site. (NR, O). A National Historic Landmark

FORT JOHNSTON (Southport, Brunswick County). Established 1748; oldest building is the Officers Quarters, built 1805-1809. Still serves as a military installation. (NR)

FORT MACON (Atlantic Beach vicinity, Carteret County). Built 1826-1834. The five-sided brick fort is the state's best-preserved nineteenth-century fortification. Now a state park. (NR, O)

FORT RALEIGH (Manteo, Dare County). Reconstruction of the 1585 earthwork at the site of the first attempted English settlement in North America. A National Historic Site. (NR, O)

FOURTH CREEK BURYING GROUND (Statesville, Iredell County). Important cemetery with graves dating from 1756 to 1888, including those of many prominent early citizens of Statesville and Iredell County. It is located in the Mitchell College Historic District in Statesville, adjacent to the First Presbyterian Church, which owns the cemetery. (NR)

FRUTCHEY INDIAN MOUND. *See* Town Creek Indian Mound

GASTON LAW OFFICE (New Bern, Craven County). Built ca. 1800; moved to present location at 307 Craven Street and rebuilt in a much altered state by the New Bern Garden Club in 1949. (F)

GLEBE HOUSE. *See* St. Thomas Episcopal Church

GREAT SMOKY MOUNTAINS NATIONAL PARK (Swain, Graham, and surrounding counties). Historic buildings maintained by the National Park Service include Mingus Mill and a number of buildings at the Pioneer Farmstead. A federal national park.

GREGORY ESTATE. *See* Hill Airy

GREGORY HOUSE. *See* Fairfield

THE GROVE (Halifax County). Built late eighteenthth century by Willie Jones, Revolutionary statesman. Destroyed. Had a racetrack.

GUILFORD BATTLEGROUND (Greensboro, Guilford County). Site of a major Revolutionary War battle between a British force led by Lord Cornwallis and American troops commanded by Gen. Nathanael Greene. A National Military Park. (NR, O)

GWYN MUSEUM (Elkin, Surry County). A 24-by-36-foot building constructed in 1850 by Richard Gwyn, founder of Elkin, for use as a church, school, and community building. Saved from demolition in 1953 by the local chapter of the DAR and moved to its present location to serve as a museum. (F, O)

HARMONY HALL. *See* Peebles House

HASTINGS HOUSE (Smithfield, Johnston County). Greek Revival house built 1853; used by Confederate general Joseph E. Johnston as his headquarters before the Battle of Bentonville. Moved in 1964 to Front Street in Smithfield to be saved from demolition. Owned by the town of Smithfield and used as offices for the Smithfield Parks and Recreation Department and the Smithfield Downtown Development Corporation. (F, O)

HEZEKIAH ALEXANDER HOUSE (Charlotte, Mecklenburg County). Built 1774. A fully restored rock house. Owned by the Alexander House Foundation. (NR, F, O)

HILL AIRY (Oxford vicinity, Granville County). Plantation house and mill built in 1830s. Has remained in the Gregory family for at least five generations Privately owned. (NR)

HOPE PLANTATION (Windsor vicinity, Bertie County). Built 1796-1803. Plantation home of Gov. David Stone. Restored in 1960s. Owned by Historic Hope Foundation. (NR, F, O)

HORTON GROVE. *See* Stagville

HOUSE IN THE HORSESHOE (Carthage vicinity, Moore County). Pre-Revolutionary house, with bullet holes in the weatherboards said to result from attack by tories led by David Fanning on patriot Philip Alston, first owner of the house. Later owned by Gov. Benjamin Williams. A state historic site. (NR, F, O)

IREDELL HOUSE (Edenton, Chowan County). Built 1800; expanded in 1820s. Outbuildings include some original to the site and an office and dairy moved from Bandon Plantation. Formerly the James Iredell House State Historic Site; now part of the Historic Edenton State Historic Site, which also includes the Ziegler House (the visitors center) and the Chowan County Courthouse. (NR, F, O)

ISLEY CABIN (Greensboro, Guilford County). Log house restored as a memorial to Dolley Madison. On the grounds of the Greensboro Historical Museum. (F, O)

JAMES KNOX POLK BIRTHPLACE (Pineville, Mecklenburg County). A reconstruction of the log house in which Polk was born. Presently a state historic site known as James K. Polk Memorial. (O)

JASMINE (Concord, Cabarrus County). Name given by Ruth Cannon to her town home. Built in 1928 from the design of architect Charles Barton Keen. Privately owned. (NR)

JOEL LANE HOUSE (Raleigh, Wake County). Built 1760. Home of planter who sold land to state for the creation of the new state capital in 1792. Moved to present site on Hargett Street, Raleigh, in 1913; owned and operated by the National Society of the Colonial Dames in North Carolina. Also known as Wakefields. (NR, O)

JOHN WRIGHT STANLY HOUSE (New Bern, Craven County). Built 1779-1783. One of the state's finest examples of Georgian architecture. Moved and restored by the Tryon Palace Commission. (NR, O)

JOSEPH BELL HOUSE (Beaufort, Carteret County). Early frame house traditionally dated 1767. Restored and operated by the Beaufort Historical Association. Known in 1964 as the Ruby Becton House. (NR, F, O)

LATIMER HOUSE (Wilmington, New Hanover County). Grand Italianate house of brick and stucco. Built in 1852 by merchant Zebulon Latimer. Headquarters of and museum building for the Lower Cape Fear Historical Society. (NR, F, O)

LEE COUNTY COVERED BRIDGE (Lee County). The bridge no longer exists. The reference is apparently to one of two covered bridges that once spanned the Deep River.

LEWIS-SMITH HOUSE (Raleigh, Wake County). Built 1855. Moved to Blount Street, Raleigh, in 1978 to make way for construction of the state government mall north of the Legislative Building. Now houses the offices of the Restoration Branch and the Survey and Planning Branch of the State Historic Preservation Office. (NR)

LIBRARY (Old Northampton County Clerk's Office; Jackson, Northampton County). Built 1831. One-story red brick building with stepped parapet gables built as county clerk's office. It has served as a library, museum, and offices for various agencies and is now the county manager's office. Owned by the county. (NR, F)

LIBRARY (Pleasant Retreat Academy; Lincolnton, Lincoln County). Built 1817-1820 as Pleasant Retreat Academy, a private school that operated until the 1870s. Leased by the United Daughters of the Confederacy and presently known as Old Memorial Hall; open for special events and by appointment. (NR, F, O)

LICK-BONER HOUSE (Old Salem, Winston-Salem, Forsyth County). Built 1787. Germanic building of log construction, with heavy rock foundation and central chimney. Restored in 1956. Privately owned. (NR, F)

LITTLE MANOR (Littleton, Halifax County). Built 1799 and early nineteenth century. Large Federal-style frame house now in ruins. Had a private racetrack. Also known as Mosby Hall. (NR)

LOMBARDY (Salisbury, Rowan County). Federal-style house built in 1799 for John Steele, first comptroller of the United States, and meticulously restored by private owner in recent years. (NR)

McCONNELL-GRAY-ZENKE HOUSE. *See* Zenke House

MACHPELAH PRESBYTERIAN CHURCH (Machpelah vicinity, Lincoln County). Brick church built 1848. Slave gallery and pews are thought to be original. Now used intermittently. Owned by the church. (F)

MALLETT HOUSE (Fayetteville, Cumberland County). Two-story Federal-style house built ca. 1830; moved in 1986 to present location on the campus of Methodist College, Fayetteville. (F)

MARS HILL COLLEGE (Mars Hill, Madison County). Montague Building was constructed in 1918 of native stone; first served as college library. Enlarged in 1933. Since 1979 it has housed the Rural Life Museum. Owned by the college. (F, O)

MONTAGUE BUILDING. *See* Mars Hill College

MONTMORENCI (Warren County). One of the state's grandest Federal-style houses, built 1820. Destroyed. Montmorenci's curving staircase was removed and reassembled at the Winterthur Museum in Delaware, where it is presently on display.

MOOREFIELDS (Hillsborough vicinity, Orange County). Two-story frame plantation house built ca. 1785. Privately owned. (NR, F)

MOORES CREEK BATTLEGROUND (Pender County). Site of first southern victory of patriots over a loyalist force in the Revolutionary War. Now a National Battlefield. (NR, O)

MOSBY HALL. *See* Little Manor

NASH-KOLLOCK SCHOOL (Hillsborough, Orange County). Early frame house used as a school for young women from 1858 to 1890. The house previously had been the residence of Frederick Nash, chief justice of the North Carolina Supreme Court from 1852 to 1858. Razed in 1947 and replaced with a concrete-block building (Farmer's Exchange). Interior woodwork salvaged.

NEWBOLD-WHITE HOUSE (Hertford vicinity, Perquimans County). Once thought to be the state's oldest house, dating as early as 1685. Recent dendrochronology findings indicate a construction date of 1730, which makes it the second-oldest house, after Sloop Point in Pender County, which dates from 1726. Restored, owned, and operated by the Perquimans County Restoration Association. (NR, O)

OLD GAOL (Old Halifax County Jail; Halifax, Halifax County). The first jail was built 1764 and burned by escaping prisoners. The present two-story brick structure was built in 1838. Now part of Historic Halifax State Historic Site. (NR, F, O)

OLD MEMORIAL HALL *See* Library (Pleasant Retreat Academy; Lincolnton, Lincoln County)

OLD SALEM (Winston Salem, Forsyth County). The SPA made several contributions toward the restoration of Old Salem: two grants for buildings—the Lick-Boner House and Salem Tavern (formerly referred to as the Washington Tavern, by reason of George Washington's having lodged there in 1791)—and one grant for a sofa for the tavern. Owned by Old Salem, Inc., although some properties in the district are privately owned. (NR, F, O). A National Historic Landmark

OLD STONE HOUSE. *See* Braun House

OLD TEMPERANCE HALL (Richmond Temperance and Literary Society Hall; Wagram, Scotland County). Small six-sided brick building erected 1860 (before Scotland County was formed from Richmond County) by the Richmond Temperance and Literary Society. Owned by the Scotland County Historical Commission. (NR, F)

OLD WILKES COUNTY JAIL (Wilkesboro, Wilkes County). Built 1859. Tom Dula of folk song "Tom Dooley" fame was held here briefly after the murder of Laura Foster. Restored and owned by Old Wilkes, Inc. (NR, F, O)

OVAL BALLROOM (Fayetteville, Cumberland County). Elegant Adamesque-style oval room built in 1818 as an addition to the Halliday House. When that house was razed, the ballroom was moved to the grounds of the Fayetteville Woman's Club. (NR, F, O)

PAINT HILL FARM (Southern Pines, Moore County). Home of Elizabeth "Buffie" Stevenson Ives, Moore County preservation leader. Burned; later rebuilt by Mrs. Ives's son. Privately owned.

PALMER-MARSH HOUSE (Bath, Beaufort County). Built 1750. One of the state's major surviving buildings of the colonial era, with a massive double chimney. Part of Historic Bath State Historic Site. (NR, F, O). A National Historic Landmark

PANTEGO ACADEMY (Pantego, Beaufort County). One of the largest surviving frame school buildings in the state. The first section was built in 1874 and was expanded in the early twentieth century to its present form. In 1907 it became part of the public school system. Owned by the Pantego Alumni Association. (NR, F)

PEARSON HOUSE *See* Richmond Hill

PEEBLES HOUSE (Kinston, Lenoir County). Built 1772; expanded through nineteenth and twentieth centuries. Once considered former home of Richard Caswell, first governor of North Carolina after independence. Owned by the Lenoir County Historical Association. Also known as Harmony Hall. (NR, O)

PENELOPE BARKER HOUSE (Barker-Moore House; Edenton, Chowan County). A late eighteenth-century house first owned by the Barker family and enlarged by the Moore family in the early nineteenth century. Mrs. Barker is thought to have helped organize the "Edenton Tea Party." The house was moved to present location on Edenton Bay in 1952 and served until recent years as the Edenton visitors center. Now under development as a site on the Historic Edenton Tour and as a multi-use facility for the community. Owned by the Edenton Historical Commission. (NR, F, O)

PERSON'S ORDINARY (Littleton, Halifax County). Late eighteenth-century tavern. Restored. Owned by town of Littleton and operated by the Littleton Woman's Club. (NR, F, O)

RANDALL METHODIST CHURCH (Stanly County). Frame country church built in 1858. Demolished in 1974 for a new church. (F)

RICHMOND HILL LAW SCHOOL (Rockford vicinity, Yadkin County). Built 1859. Law office and school of Judge Richmond M. Pearson. Many students there rose to state and national prominence in law and politics. Restored by Richmond Hill Law School Commission. (NR, F, O)

RICHMOND TEMPERANCE AND LITERARY SOCIETY HALL. *See* Old Temperance Hall

RINGWARE HOUSE (Swansboro, Onslow County). Late eighteenth-century two-story frame house. Privately owned. (NR, F)

ROSEDALE (Charlotte, Mecklenburg County). Early nineteenth-century Federal-style plantation house. Restored by Historic Rosedale Foundation. (NR, O)

RUBY BECTON HOUSE. *See* Joseph Bell House

RURAL LIFE MUSEUM. *See* Mars Hill College

ST. JOHN'S EPISCOPAL CHURCH (Williamsboro, Vance County). Built 1773. Oldest frame church in North Carolina. Restored, 1946-1956; original box pews remain. Held by the trustees of the Diocese of North Carolina. (NR, F, O)

ST. PAUL'S EPISCOPAL CHURCH (Edenton, Chowan County). Begun 1735 and erected over a period of decades, with spire added in early nineteenth century. Held by the trustees of the Diocese of Eastern North Carolina. (NR, F, O)

ST. THOMAS EPISCOPAL CHURCH (Bath, Beaufort County). Built 1734. The compact brick building is the oldest standing church in North Carolina and is still in use. Two other associated buildings nearby are the Williams or Glebe House (privately occupied) and the A. C. D. Noe Library. Held by the trustees of the Diocese of Eastern North Carolina. (NR, F, O)

SALEM COLLEGE ALUMNAE HOUSE (Winston-Salem, Forsyth County). Built in 1817 as an addition to the 1813-1814 washhouse of the girls' boarding school. The older section was later removed to make way for the Salem College Chapel, leaving the 1817 addition, which now houses the college's alumnae offices. Owned by Moravian Church. Within the boundaries of the Old Salem National Historic Landmark district, (NR, F)

SALEM TAVERN. *See* Old Salem

SHAW HOUSE (Southern Pines, Moore County). Regional vernacular house built ca. 1820, expanded ca. 1842; home of first mayor of town. Owned by Moore County Historical Association and used as a museum and educational and cultural center. (NR, F, O)

SHELL STATION (Winston-Salem, Forsyth County). 1929 service station of concrete and stucco in the form of a shell. Leased by Preservation North Carolina. (NR)

SPACH HOUSE (Davidson County). Stone house built 1774 for early Moravian settler Adam Spach. Destroyed. Archaeological site owned by Wachovia Historical Society.

SPRUCE MACAY LAW OFFICE (Salisbury, Rowan County). Built in the 1780s. The building in which Andrew Jackson read law in 1784 or 1785. Dismantled and shipped to the Centennial Exposition in Philadelphia in 1876, never to be seen again.

STAGVILLE (Durham vicinity, Durham County). Plantation home of the Bennehan and Cameron families. Frame plantation house built in the 1780s and enlarged about 1799. The property includes some of the state's best-preserved slave houses and a magnificent mid-nineteenth-century barn, all of which are located in a section of the plantation known as Horton Grove. The site is operated by the North Carolina Division of Archives and History as a history conference center. (NR, O)

THALIAN HALL (Wilmington, New Hanover County). Built 1855 as a city hall and theater. Still in use. (NR, F, O)

THOMAS WOLFE MEMORIAL (Asheville, Buncombe County). A boardinghouse built ca. 1883; operated as "My Old Kentucky Home" by Julia Wolfe, mother of novelist Thomas Wolfe. A state historic site. (NR, F, O). A National Historic Landmark

TOWN CREEK INDIAN MOUND (Mount Gilead vicinity, Montgomery County). Ca. 1450-1500. Site of village and ceremonial center created by Indians of Mississippian culture related to Creek Indians of the lower South. A state historic site. (NR, O)

TRYON PALACE (New Bern, Craven County). One of the outstanding colonial buildings in British North America. Built 1767 and destroyed by fire in 1798, except for one wing. Reconstructed in the 1950s with the financial assistance of the Latham and Kellenberger families. Owned by the Tryon Palace Commission. Operated by the North Carolina Division of Archives and History. (F, O)

VAN DER VEER HOUSE (Bath, Beaufort County). Late eighteenth-century gambrel-roof house. Moved to Bath from its original location in rural Beaufort County and restored as part of the Historic Bath State Historic Site. (NR, F, O)

VANCE BIRTHPLACE (Buncombe County). Reconstruction of log birthplace of the state's popular Civil War governor and United States senator. A state historic site. (O)

VANCE HOUSE (Statesville, Iredell County). House rented by Mrs. Zebulon Vance at the end of the Civil War; residence of Gov. Zebulon Vance when he was arrested by Federal authorities on May 13, 1865. Moved to West Sharpe Street from Broad Street in the mid-twentieth century. Owned by the city of Statesville and operated by the Statesville Chapter, No. 276, United Daughters of the Confederacy. (NR, F)

VANCE MONUMENT (Asheville, Buncombe County). Monument to popular governor Zebulon B. Vance; designed by Richard Sharp Smith and funded by public subscription and contributions from George W. Pack. On Pack Square in downtown Asheville. Owned by the city of Asheville. (O)

WAKEFIELDS. *See* Joel Lane House

WALLACE RESTORATION. No further information located. (F)

WASHINGTON TAVERN. *See* Old Salem

WILLIAM GASTON HOUSE (Coor-Gaston House; New Bern, Craven County). Built ca. 1770; enlarged ca. 1850. Interior Georgian motifs of exceptional sophistication. Owned by Tryon Palace Council of Friends. (NR, F, O)

WILLIAMS HOUSE. *See* St. Thomas Episcopal Church

WILSON LOG HOUSE (Shelby, Cleveland County). No further information located. (F)

WOLFE HOUSE. *See* Thomas Wolfe Memorial

WRIGHT TAVERN (Wentworth, Rockingham County). Built 1817 and later by the Wright family; one of the state's best examples of public houses once common to small courthouse towns. Restored and owned by the Rockingham County Historical Society. (NR, F, O)

ZENKE HOUSE (McConnell-Gray-Zenke House; Greensboro, Guilford County). The original portion of the two-story frame house was built about 1830, and the front block with paired windows similar to those of Blandwood was added about 1847. It was the home of Emma Morehead Gray, daughter of Governor Morehead, and her husband Julius Gray, banker and railroad president. Moved from its original location and restored in the 1950s by Henry and Virginia Zenke.

Selected Bibliography

Articles

"Annual Meeting December 2." *Antiquities* 2 (November 1971): 1.

"Antiquities Award Presented to Wake Forest Woman's Club." *Antiquities* 2 (August 1971): 4.

Bishir, Catherine W. "Landmarks of Power: Building a Southern Past." *Southern Cultures*, Inaugural Issue (1993): 5-45.

Cheeseman, Bruce S. "The Survival of the Cupola House: 'A Venerable old Mansion.'" *North Carolina Historical Review* 63 (January 1986): 40-73.

"Cupola House Receives 300-year Old Fireback." *Antiquities* 1 (April 1971): 1.

"Directors of the Society Will Consider Several Ideas for Increasing the Service of the Society at Charlotte Meeting." *North Carolina Preservation News* 1 (November 1968): 1.

Gatton, T. Harry. "President's Message." *North Carolina Preservation News* 2 (May 1970): 2.

"Incentive Grants Increased." *Antiquities* 1 (April 1971): 4.

"John Tyler Elected Society President." *Antiquities* 1 (March 1971): 1.

Johnston, Frontis W. "The North Carolina Literary and Historical Association, 1900-1975." *North Carolina Historical Review* 53 (April 1976): 155-167.

Jones, H. G. "Preserving, Promoting Historic Resources." *News and Observer: North Carolina Quadricentennial Commemorative Edition*. Raleigh: *News and Observer*, July 1985.

Leloudis, James L., II. "School Reform in the New South: The Woman's Association for the Betterment of Public School Houses in North Carolina, 1902-1919." *Journal of American History* 69 (March 1983): 886-909.

Moore, Elizabeth Vann. "Edenton's New Community Building: Moving the Barker House." *Southern Architect* (August 1955): 13-15 (photocopy).

"1970 Cannon Cup Awards." *Antiquities* 1 (March 1971): 1-2.

"1971 General Assembly Aids Preservation." *Antiquities* 2 (August 1971): 4.

Obituary of Elizabeth Stevenson Ives. *Carolina Comments* 42 (September 1994): 137.

"Profile: John E. Tyler." *Antiquities* 1 (March 1971): 1.

McMillan, Mary Lee. "President's Message." *North Carolina Gardens* (May 1938): 1.

"Restored Houses: Architectural Century Plan." *Home and Garden Remodeling Guide* (fall and winter 1963-1964): 68-73.

"Richardson Foundation Grants for 1972." *Antiquities* 2 (March 1972): 2.

Stroupe, Henry S. "The North Carolina Department of Archives and History—the First Half Century." *North Carolina Historical Review* 31 (April 1954): 184-200.

Books

Aldridge, John W. *In the Country of the Young*. New York: Harper's Magazine Press, 1969.

Bishir, Catherine W. *North Carolina Architecture*. Chapel Hill: University of North Carolina Press, 1990.

Bishir, Catherine W., and Michael T. Southern. *Guide to the Historic Architecture of Eastern North Carolina*. Chapel Hill: University of North Carolina Press, 1996.

Brawley, James S. *The Rowan Story 1753-1953: A Narrative History of Rowan County, North Carolina*. Salisbury: Rowan Printing Company, 1953.

Cannon, Ruth Coltrane, Elizabeth Henderson Cotten, and Maude Moore Latham, eds. *Old Homes and Gardens of North Carolina*. Chapel Hill: University of North Carolina Press, 1939.

Chafe, William H. *The Unfinished Journey: America Since World War II*, 2d ed. New York: Oxford University Press, 1991.

Coe, Joffre Lanning. *Town Creek Indian Mound: A Native American Legacy*. Chapel Hill: University of North Carolina Press, 1995.

Coffey, Mary Ann, and Murphy Moss. *Deliverance of a Treasure: The Cupola House Association and Its Mission*. Fuquay-Varina: Research Triangle Publishing, 1995.

Crow, Jeffrey J., ed. *Public History in North Carolina, 1903-1978: The Proceedings of the Seventy-Fifth Anniversary Celebration, March 7, 1978*. Raleigh: Division of Archives and History, North Carolina Department of Cultural Resources, 1979.

Davis, Kenneth A. *The Politics of Honor: A Biography of Adlai E. Stevenson*. New York: G. P. Putnam's Sons, 1967.

Edmunds, Mary Lewis Rucker. *Governor Morehead's Blandwood and the Family Who Lived There*. Greensboro: Greensboro Printing Company, 1976.

Fitch, James Marston. *Historic Preservation: Curatorial Management of the Built World*. Charlottesville: University Press of Virginia, 1981.

Fussell, Paul. *Class*. New York: Ballantine Books, 1983.

Glass, James A. *The Beginnings of a New National Historic Preservation Program, 1957 to 1969*. Nashville: American Association for State and Local History, 1990.

Haywood, Marshall De Lancey. *Governor William Tryon, and his Administration in the Province of North Carolina, 1765-1771*. Raleigh: E. M. Uzzell, Printer, 1903; Raleigh: Edwards and Broughton Co. for the North Carolina Society for the Preservation of Antiquities, 1958.

Hosmer, Charles B., Jr. *Presence of the Past: A History of the Preservation Movement in the United States before Williamsburg*. New York: Putnam, 1965.

_____. *Preservation Comes of Age: from Williamsburg to the National Trust, 1926-1949*, 2 vols. Charlottesville: University Press of Virginia, 1981.

Johnston, Frances Benjamin, and Thomas Tileston Waterman. *The Early Architecture of North Carolina: A Pictorial Survey*. Chapel Hill: University of North Carolina Press, 1941.

Kell, Jean B. *Beaufort, North Carolina, in Color*. Beaufort: the author, 1983.

Mackintosh, Barry. *The National Historic Preservation Act and the National Park Service: A History*. Washington, D.C.: National Park Service, 1986.

Morrison, Jacob H. *Historic Preservation Law*. Washington, D. C.: National Trust for Historic Preservation, 1965; reprinted 1974.

Murtagh, William J. *Keeping Time: The History and Theory of Preservation in America*. Pittstown, N. J.: Main Street Press, 1988.

Nash, Ann Strudwick. *Ladies in the Making*. Durham: the author, 1964.

Pleasants, Julian M., and Augustus M. Burns III. *Frank Porter Graham and the 1950 Senate Race in North Carolina*. Chapel Hill: University of North Carolina Press, 1990.

Posner, Ernst. *American State Archives*. Chicago: University of Chicago Press, 1964.

Powell, William S., ed. *Dictionary of North Carolina Biography*, 5 vols. to date. Chapel Hill: University of North Carolina Press, 1978—.

_____. *North Carolina Lives: The Tar Heel Who's Who*. Hopkinsville, Ky.: Historical Record Association, 1962.

_____. *North Carolina through Four Centuries*. Chapel Hill: University of North Carolina Press, 1989.

Preservation North Carolina [Historic Preservation Foundation of North Carolina]. *The Complete Guide to North Carolina Historic Sites*. Raleigh: Preservation/North Carolina, n.d.

Robinson, Blackwell P. *Three Decades of Devotion: The Story of the Tryon Palace Commission and the Tryon Palace Restoration*. New Bern: Tryon Palace Commission, 1978.

Scott, Anne Firor. *Making the Invisible Woman Visible*. Urbana and Chicago: University of Illinois Press, 1984.

Stipe, Robert E., and Antoinette J. Lee, eds. *The American Mosaic: Preserving A Nation's Heritage*. Washington, D.C.: United States Committee, International Council on Monuments and Sites, 1987.

de Tocqueville, Alexis. *Democracy in America*. Ed. Richard D. Heffner. New York: Penguin Books, 1984.

Wallace, Michael. "Reflections on the History of Historic Preservation," in *Presenting the Past: Essays on History and the Public*, ed. Susan Porter Benson, Stephen Brier, and Roy Rosenzweig. Philadelphia: Temple University Press, 1986.

Wilder, Lee, ed. *A Lonesome Place against the Sky*. Raleigh: North Carolina Department of Archives and History, 1971.

Winks, Robin W., ed. *The Historian as Detective*. New York, Hagerstown, San Francisco, London: Harper and Row, 1969.

Interviews

John Acker, executive director, Preservation Greensboro, Inc., Greensboro, telephone conversation with author, July 16, 1996.

Catherine W. Bisher, architectural historian and survey coordinator, State Historic Preservation Office, North Carolina Division of Archives and History, interview with author, Raleigh, August 22, 1994.

Joseph B. Cheshire Jr., attorney, conversation with author, Raleigh, May 5, 1994.

T. (Thomas) Harry Gatton, former president (1967-1970) of the North Carolina Society for the Preservation of Antiquities, interview with author, Raleigh, February 12, 1993; telephone conversation with author, October 6, 1994.

Joanne Gwaltney, executive director, New Bern Historical Society Foundation, telephone conversation with author, October 17, 1994.

Ava (Al) L. Honeycutt Jr., head, Restoration Branch, Archaeology and Historic Preservation Section, North Carolina Division of Archives and History, interviews with author, Raleigh, February 4, 1993, January 3, 31, April 7, December 15, 1994.

John E. Hunter Jr., Wilmington, Delaware, former neighbor of Janie Fetner Gosney, telephone conversation with author August 23, 1994.

H. G. (Houston Gwynne) Jones, former director (1968-1974), North Carolina Department of Archives and History, telephone conversation with author, July 29, 1991; interviews with author, Raleigh, November 8, 1991, Chapel Hill, April 6, 1994.

Joye Elizabeth Esch Jordan, former secretary-treasurer (1946), North Carolina Society for the Preservation of Antiquities; administrator (1945-1969), Division of Museums; administrator (1969-1972), Division of Museums and Historic Sites; and assistant administrator (1972-1974), Office (now Division) of Archives and History, interview with author, Raleigh, September 17, 1993; telephone conversation with author, August 3, 1994.

William J., Moore, former vice-president (1972-1974), North Carolina Society for the Preservation of Antiquities, interview with author, Greensboro, April 26, 1994.

William S. Price Jr., director (1981-1995), North Carolina Division of Archives and History, and state historic preservation officer, interview with author, Raleigh, September 28, 1994.

E. Frank Stephenson Jr., former vice-president (1969-1974), First Congressional District, North Carolina Society for the Preservation of Antiquities, interview with author, Murfreesboro, April 19, 1994.

Robert E. Stipe, former professor of public law and government (1969-1974), University of North Carolina at Chapel Hill; director (1974-1975), North Carolina Division of Archives and History, and state historic preservation officer, interview with author, Chapel Hill, April 22, 1994.

Jim Sumner, curator of sports, recreation, and leisure, North Carolina Museum of History, interview with author, Raleigh, October 6, 1994.

Lura Cowles Self Tally, former president (1961-1963), North Carolina Society for the Preservation of Antiquities, interview with author, Raleigh, April 7, 1994, Raleigh.

John Edward Tyler II, former president (1970-1972), North Carolina Society for the Preservation of Antiquities, interview with author, Hope Plantation, Bertie County, April 19, 1994.

R. Beverly R. Webb, conversation with author, Greensboro, October 14, 1994, Greensboro.

Frances Harmon Whitley, former assistant secretary-treasurer (1973-1974), North Carolina Society for the Preservation of Antiquities, interviews with author, Raleigh, August 26, 1991, and April 7, 1994.

Virginia Ford Zenke, former vice-president (1972-1974), North Carolina Society for the Preservation of Antiquities, interview with author, Greensboro, April 26, 1994.

Letters

John D. Costlow, letter by facsimile to author, August 22, 1996.

Lee A. Craig, Department of Economics, North Carolina State University, letter to author, December 30, 1994, including table showing consumer price index (CPI) for the United States from 1789 through 1990.

Linda Jordan Eure, Historic Sites Section, Division of Archives and History, letters to author, January 16, June 19, 1996, including information on historic buildings and historical organizations in Edenton.

James A. Stenhouse, letter to author, April 13, 1994, enclosing *Charlotte Observer* editorial on Stenhouse.

Robert E. Stipe, letter by facsimile to author, August 18, 1996, including information on plans and discussions of revolving fund by Antiquities Society in early 1970s.

Minutes, Papers, and Records

Clipping File, North Carolina Collection, University of North Carolina Library, Chapel Hill.

Elizabeth Henderson Cotten Papers, Southern Historical Collection, University of North Carolina Library, Chapel Hill.

Death certificate for Janie Fetner Gosney dated October 3, 1988, North Carolina Department of Human Resources, Division of Health Services, Vital Records Branch, Raleigh.

Joseph Hyde Pratt Papers, Southern Historical Collection.

McDaniel Lewis Papers, Private Collections, Archives, Division of Archives and History, Raleigh.

"Meeting on Historic Sites [among the North Carolina Department of Conservation and Development, the North Carolina Society for the Preservation of Antiquities, the North Carolina Historical Commission, the National Park Service, and others], January 21, 1941" [minutes of the Raleigh meeting signed by C. C. Crittenden, "Acting Secretary"), McDaniel Lewis Papers, State Archives.

Minutes of the Executive Board of the North Carolina Department of Archives and History, Archives, Division of Archives and History.

Minutes of the Historic Preservation Society of North Carolina, Historic Preservation Foundation of North Carolina, Raleigh.

Minutes of the North Carolina Society for the Preservation of Antiquities, Historic Preservation Foundation of North Carolina.

Minutes of the North Carolina Society for the Preservation of Antiquities, State Archives.

National Register of Historic Places Inventory—Nomination Forms [completed for North Carolina], State Historic Preservation Office, Division of Archives and History.

Records of the North Carolina Society for the Preservation of Antiquities, Historic Preservation Foundation of North Carolina.

Records of the North Carolina Society for the Preservation of Antiquities, State Archives.

Miscellaneous

Hickerson, T. F. "Joseph Hyde Pratt, M. Am. Soc. C.E.: Died June 2, 1942." *Memoirs: American Society of Civil Engineers* (No. 1231) (pamphlet). No date or place of publication indicated.

Hill's Raleigh City Directory (for years 1939 through 1967). Richmond: Hill Directory Company.

"Organizational Information" [information sheet]. Raleigh: Historic Preservation Foundation of North Carolina, summer 1994.

Polk's Raleigh City Directory: 1986. Richmond: R. L. Polk and Co., 1986.

Research questionnaire by author dated March 4, 1994. Respondents included James A. Gray Jr., Winston-Salem; Thomas Gray, Winston-Salem; A. L. Honeycutt Jr., Raleigh; William J. Moore, Greensboro; Mary Virginia Camp Smith, Raleigh; E. Frank Stephenson Jr., Murfreesboro; William Samuel Tarlton, Raleigh; Banks C. Talley Jr., Raleigh; and Virginia Ford Zenke, Greensboro.

Newspaper Articles

Bradbury, Tom. "A Life of History: With architecture, politics, and a sharp pen, James Stenhouse pioneered historic preservation here." *Charlotte Observer*, November 23, 1991.

"Buffie Ives Dies At 96; Rites Held." *Pilot* (Southern Pines), undated newspaper clipping.

Engstrom, Mrs. Alfred. "School Lives in Memory of Hillsboro Residents. *Durham Morning Herald*, February 16, 1964.

Jones, H. G. "Christopher Crittenden: Spokesman for History." *High Point Enterprise*, November 1, 1979.

"Stevenson Party in Moore Tonight." *News & Observer* (Raleigh), March 26, 1954.

Workman, Bill. "For Pity's Sake: 18th Century Home Destroyed." *Daily Independent* (Kannapolis), November 6, 1975.

Reports

Cross, Jerry L. "A Profile of State Historic Sites Administered by the Division of Archives and History." Unpublished report, Research Branch, Division of Archives and History, Raleigh, 1987.

North Carolina Commission on Reorganization of State Government. *Sixth Report*. Excerpt on "Historic Sites," for period 1961-1963. Remainder of document missing.

North Carolina Department of Archives and History. *Biennial Report 1954-1956*. Raleigh: North Carolina Department of Archives and History, 1956.

_____. *Biennial Report 1968-1970*. Raleigh: North Carolina Department of Archives and History, 1970.

_____. *Biennial Report 1970-1972*. Raleigh: North Carolina Department of Archives and History, 1972.

_____. *Biennial Report 1972-1974*. Raleigh: North Carolina Department of Archives and History, 1974.

North Carolina Department of Archives and History and the Institute of Government of the University of North Carolina at Chapel Hill. *An Interim North Carolina State Plan for Historic Preservation*. Raleigh: North Carolina Department of Archives and History, 1970.

North Carolina Historical Commission. *Biennial Report 1936-1938*. Raleigh: North Carolina Historical Commission, 1938.

_____. *Biennial Report 1938-1940*. Raleigh: North Carolina Historical Commission, 1940.

_____. *North Carolina Manual*, edited by R. D. W. Connor. Raleigh: North Carolina Historical Commission, 1921.

Pratt, Joseph Hyde, and Christopher Crittenden. "A Proposed Program for the Development of National Historical Areas in North Carolina." Unpublished report, February 1941. Records of the North Carolina Society for the Preservation of Antiquities, State Archives.

Stevens, S. K. *Advisory Council on Historic Preservation: A Report to the President and to the Congress, June 1971*. Washington, D.C.: Advisory Council on Historic Preservation, 1971.

Speeches

Carraway, Gertrude. "Tryon's Palace." Manuscript of speech presented at the annual meeting of the North Carolina Society for the Preservation of Antiquities, Raleigh, December 7, 1939. Records of the North Carolina Society for the Preservation of Antiquities, State Archives.

Chorley, Kenneth. "The Significance of the Preservation of Historic Sites, with Especial Reference to Tryon's Palace." Manuscript of speech presented at the annual meeting of the North Carolina Society for the Preservation of Antiquities, Raleigh, December 4, 1941. McDaniel Lewis Papers, State Archives.

Gatton, T. Harry. "Minding Our Own Business." Manuscript of speech presented to the Greensboro Kiwanis Club, Greensboro, March 14, 1968. Copy in possession of the author.

Henderson, Archibald. "In Memoriam: Joseph Hyde Pratt: Builder." Manuscript of speech presented at the annual meeting of the North Carolina Society for the Preservation of Antiquities, Raleigh, December 2, 1942. Records of the North Carolina Society for the Preservation of Antiquities, State Archives.

Latham, Maude Moore. "Address Before the Society for the Preservation of Antiquities." Manuscript of speech presented at the annual meeting of the North Carolina Society for the Preservation of Antiquities, Raleigh, December 6, 1944. Records of the North Carolina Society for the Preservation of Antiquities, State Archives.

Lewis, McDaniel. "A New History Museum for North Carolina." Manuscript of speech presented at a meeting of the North Carolina State Literary and Historical Association, Raleigh, December 7, 1962. McDaniel Lewis Papers, State Archives.

Whitehill, Walter Muir. "The Responsibilities of Historic Preservation." Manuscript of speech presented at the annual meeting of the North Carolina Society for the Preservation of Antiquities, Winston-Salem, December 1, 1966. Records of the North Carolina Society for the Preservation of Antiquities, State Archives.

Statutes

Historic Districts and Landmarks. N.C. Gen. Stat. sec. 160A-400.1-400.14. 1989, as amended.

North Carolina Archives and History Act. N.C. Gen. Stat. secs. 121-1 to 121-42. 1973, as amended.

Historic Sites Act. U.S. Code. Vol. 16, sec. 461 (1935).

National Historic Preservation Act. Vol. 16, sec. 470 et seq. (1966).

Index

Prepared by Nan Farley